ARIS & PHILLIPS CLASSICAL TEXTS

PLATO
Republic
1–2.368c4

with
Introduction, Translation and Commentary by

Chris Emlyn-Jones

Aris & Phillips Classical Texts
are published by
Oxbow Books, Oxford

Printed and bound by CPI Group (UK) Ltd, Croydon, CR0 4YY

ISBN 978-0-85668-762-4 cloth
ISBN 978-085668-757-0 paper

A CIP record for this book is available from the British Library.

CONTENTS

PREFACE

A full commentary in English on the introductory sections of *Republic,* Plato's best known and most frequently read dialogue, has not been attempted for more than fifty years. In that period scholarship has moved on, and this edition aims to take into account recent developments in the study of Plato's literary style and dramatic technique as well as of his ideas. The arguments have always been of great interest to philosophers, especially the sophist Thrasymachus' clash with Socrates in defending injustice as the most profitable life-choice. But there is a great deal more to this introduction than abstract ideas; Plato chooses to begin his great work by staging a dramatic debate, arising out of a social meeting between Socrates and friends in the Athenian port of the Piraeus during a religious festival. The case for and against justice as a state of affairs leading to *eudaimonia* ('happiness') is put with great force and humour, not to mention bad temper, and in the cut-and-thrust of argument and the clash of personalities, Plato brings vividly to life the cultural and social world of his times and the crucial issues at stake for his contemporaries. He also puts as effectively as possible the adversarial case which Socrates has to answer in the rest of *Republic.* Alongside Book 1, I have deliberately included the first part of Book 2, since the restatement of the case against Socrates by Glaucon and Adeimantus belongs, thematically and dramatically, to what precedes it, and sharply redefines the problem, as well as greatly expanding the cultural context.

In this edition I have tried to keep in mind the needs of as wide a spectrum of readers as possible. The commentary, following the main purpose of the Series, is based principally on the translation and is aimed chiefly at readers without advanced Greek; I have been particularly concerned that this group should, as far as possible, find the language no barrier to appreciation of the subtleties of Plato's dramatic style and ideas. At the same time, for those who read the Greek, I have frequently included discussion of significant literary, linguistic and textual issues.

In the preparation of this edition I have been the fortunate recipient of much expert advice for which I give grateful thanks: to William Preddy for refining the translation, and to the late Malcolm Willcock and Chris Wilson who read the whole manuscript and made many useful suggestions for improvement. I must also thank Clare Litt and Tara Evans of Oxbow Books for their helpful and efficient mediation.

November 2006   Chris Emlyn-Jones
                                                     The Open University

INTRODUCTION

1. Preliminaries

The early sections of *Republic,* the most widely-known dialogue of Plato, are important and interesting in presenting the parameters of the arguments for and against the desirability of a state of justice in the community and the individual which Plato's Socrates has to address in the rest of the dialogue. The radical alternative put forward by the sophist Thrasymachus in Book 1, and elaborated by Socrates' young friends Glaucon and Adeimantus in the first half of Book 2, that any rational individual will pursue a life of injustice as the more profitable option, resonates in many later political theories, bearing witness that the political, social and moral issues generated in this dialogue were not decisively settled by Plato in *Republic* – indeed they still resonate today.[1] Plato's choice of justice as his key concept also reflects its problematic nature in Greek society and culture up to his time.

Radically different from the remainder of this long work in style and content, Book 1, in attempting to define justice, sets out arguments which, on Socrates' side, reflect the debating style of the aporetic dialogues (dialogues without positive conclusion, from the Greek *aporia* 'difficulty of finding a way through'). This type of ending is typical of the dialogues of Plato's early period, such as *Charmides, Euthyphro, Hippias Minor, Laches* and *Lysis.* Moreover the vivid presentation of the characters of Socrates and his fellow-debaters, typical of the style of the 'early period' dialogues, allows the full exploration of the cultural milieu of the late fifth and fourth century in Athens, to the extent that this part of the dialogue has fairly been characterised as Plato's critical philosophical and cultural commentary on his times.[2]

Yet Book 1 is not a typical aporetic dialogue. Following Socrates' confession of personal failure at the end (1.354a–c), the argument is unexpectedly resumed at the beginning of Book 2 by Glaucon and Adeimantus, who are dissatisfied with what they see as Socrates' merely formal victory over his opponent Thrasymachus in the latter part of Book 1. Abandoning the questioning method of Book 1, again typical of Socrates in the early dialogues (the *elenchus*: 'examination of another's views for

---

[1] An issue recently taken up in Rosen.
[2] See *e.g.* Lycos 2.

purposes of refutation'), they each make lengthy speeches in an attempt to restate in a more coherent and convincing manner Thrasymachus' position that the life of the unjust person is better than that of the just. Although personally unconvinced by Thrasymachus, they wish to hear this position more effectively refuted by Socrates. It is after this (2.368c) that two things happen:

1. Socrates, after congratulating Glaucon and Adeimantus on their perspicacity, begins the positive outline of his ideal state – an answer, but in a very different style and at much greater length, to the arguments thrown up by the dialogue up to this point;
2. S's contribution settles into an exposition of the elements of his ideal state, interspersed with short and largely positive interventions from his hitherto articulate and argumentative respondents.

Books 1–2.368c can be regarded, therefore, as comprising two related introductions to the whole of *Republic,* bound together by a common theme, and subject to certain over-arching questions and long-standing interpretative problems of form and content. As such, they merit close attention.[3]

On the central concept with which *Republic* is concerned: the term 'justice' translates *dikē, dikaiosunē, to dikaion* (δίκη, δικαιοσύνη, τὸ δίκαιον). The title of the dialogue is usually rendered *Πολιτεία ἢ περὶ δικαίου· Republic, or on Justice.* The Greek word has a much wider semantic range than the English equivalent, which has led some translators to render *dikē* and its cognates (sometimes consistently, sometimes not) as 'morality' or 'right' as well as 'justice' (*e.g.* Lee, Waterfield (1993)). The implied anachronism in such renderings (there is, notoriously, no Greek equivalent for 'moral') makes a consistent use of the literal rendering the most satisfactory (as in *e.g.* Reeve (2004) and in the translation presented here), provided the specifics of its semantic range in Greek are kept in mind.[4] As will become

---

[3] The middle of Book 2 (368c4) as a terminus for this edition, far from being arbitrary, is dictated by the content and dramatic structure of the work, which indicates a clear break at this point and a transition to a new aspect of the subject. In making this division, while attention would have been given to the natural breaks in the subject-matter, an important factor also would have been how much text would fit onto a papyrus roll (see Reynolds and Wilson 2). The division of *Republic* into the current ten 'Books' was made almost certainly not by Plato himself, but at some point later in the history of transmission.

[4] Distinctions in meaning between *dikē* and its cognates are often hard to establish in translation. In particular *dikaiosunē* (δικαιοσύνη) and *to dikaion* (τὸ δίκαιον = literally 'the just thing') are often used almost interchangeably, *e.g.* 336a9–10 – where, however, Socrates,

apparent 'justice', (*dikē*) and its contrary, 'injustice' (*adikia, ἀδικία*) and their cognates range widely: they both indicate external relationships, *e.g.* between individuals and communities, and also describe the inner state of the individual: justice as a kind of inner, or psychological harmony. Plato's Socrates is also concerned with how both these relationships lead, or fail to lead, to *eudaimonia* (*εὐδαιμονία*) ' 'happiness', 'prosperity' as an end in life – another concept not easily rendered into English.[5] This relationship between internal and external justice, while underlying the dialogue as a whole, is particularly relevant to the sections of *Republic* we are concerned with here.

2. Composition of Republic

Despite the absence of absolute dating criteria for this or any other Platonic dialogue, there is general agreement that *Republic* was composed (or reached its final form) in the mid-370's, before Plato's second visit to Sicily. There is also a consensus that the dialogue is to be placed in Plato's late 'middle period' (after *Symposium* and before *Theaetetus*: see Chronology of Plato's Life and Works). More controversial than relative chronology is how *Republic* relates in compositional terms to the dialogues which precede it, an issue which raises fundamental questions of perspective on Plato's work taken as a whole. While most would agree that *Republic* in some way reflects or sums up many issues and doctrines in earlier Platonic thought, exactly how the relationship works is disputed. One approach sees *Republic* as an important staging-post in Plato's philosophical development up to that point, away from a Socratic or Platonic-Socratic base (a 'developmentalist' view);[6] alternatively, a 'unitarian' view sees pre-*Republic* dialogues as contributing to a unified 'project', implicitly present from early on, of which *Republic* represents a culmination.[7] An argument in favour of a modified version of the former position seems to be suggested by the tripartite psychology of Book 4, the separation of intellect, emotion and appetite in the individual, which represents a radical break from the Socratic intellectualism and 'no-

---

in using *dikaiosunē* and *to dikaion* in close proximity, may be making a distinction between a more abstract concept and a practical application ('justice' and 'doing what is just').

[5] *Eudaimōn* has a more objective connotation than English 'happy'; it means rather, 'fortunate', 'prosperous', literally = 'having a good destiny (*eu-daimōn*)'.

[6] See *e.g.* Vlastos (1991) 45–106.

[7] See *e.g.* Kahn (1996). For a brief and judicious review of the strengths and weaknesses of both positions, see Rutherford 23–5.

one does wrong intentionally' of the early dialogues, *e.g. Protagoras* 358c. On the other hand a doctrine like the theory of separable Forms, or Ideas, also central to *Republic* (Books 6–7 and 10), has its anticipation in middle period, but pre-*Republic*, dialogues, *e.g. Meno, Phaedo* and *Symposium*.

A work as massive as *Republic* was doubtless a long time in gestation; it has been suggested that the roots of *Republic* 2–5, including theories of the extended role of women in the state and the disappearance of the family (Book 5), may go back as far as a possible 'Proto-*Republic*', an outline of an 'Ideal State', from the 390's (the earliest period of Platonic composition), since these particular issues appear to be the subject of parody by Aristophanes in his *Ecclesiazousae* (*Women in the Assembly*), c. 392; Plato's reference in this connection to the 'jests of the wits' which would greet Socrates' proposals concerning the role of women in the state (5.452b7) has plausibly been seen as a reaction to Aristophanes' play.[8] An independent existence for the outline of society contained in these Books may also be suggested by the introductory sections of *Timaeus*, in which, in a report of a discussion purporting to have taken place 'yesterday', Socrates outlines the basic subject matter of Books 2–5 (17c–19a).[9] There is also suggestive evidence from the Roman writer Aulus Gellius (2nd century A.D.) who, in a discussion of the rivalry of famous authors, reports that Xenophon wrote his *Education of Cyrus* as an answer to the first two, separately published, 'books' of *Republic*.[10]

Of much greater significance in the present context, however, is the possible genesis of Book 1. The radical difference in content and style from the rest of the *Republic* (noted above, p.1) has long suggested to some scholars that Book 1 may be a revival of an early dialogue, perhaps called *Thrasymachus* (after the major interlocutor with Socrates in Book 1), which Plato re-used as an Introduction to the *Republic* as a whole, with minimal alterations to fit the new context.[11] Plato then engineered dramatically a new transition to join the original dialogue to the rest of *Republic*; Socrates discovers that, contrary to his assumption that, following failure, they

---

[8] For details of possible cross-references, see Thesleff 103–4.

[9] This conjecture is not affected by doubt over the position of *Timaeus* in Platonic chronology; it could be a reference back to *Republic* or, if *Timaeus* precedes *Republic*, to an earlier version of Books 2–5 (see above).

[10] *Attic Nights* 14. 32. 'Papyrus scrolls' (*libri*), containing more than two books (plausibly 2–5), are meant.

[11] See Vlastos (1991) 248–50, with earlier bibliography.

would agree to abandon the discussion (as in other aporetic dialogues), two of his interlocutors (Glaucon and Adeimantus) regard Book 1 merely as a 'prelude' (*prooimion* 357a2), and that they expect Socrates to give answers to their reformulation of the Book 1 issues between him and Thrasymachus. Then follows Plato's 'new' introduction – the speeches of Glaucon and Adeimantus. Socrates' 'answer' to the challenge posed by the argument of these speeches then constitutes the rest of *Republic* (from 368c5).

   Whether there ever existed a dialogue which Plato reused and later turned into *Republic* 1 is an issue which cannot be settled either way, for lack of evidence. More significant is why, for the introduction to this seminal work, he apparently reverted to a style of argument (whether newly-composed or re-used) which has the appearance of a throwback to the dramatic aporetic form, which had been partly abandoned in works written around the time of the *Republic* (*Phaedo, Symposium, Phaedrus)*, and which contrasts so strikingly with the remainder of *Republic*. The view that Plato writes like this in order to remind us of the Socratic dialogues[12] begs the question of why he actually wished to compose like this at all at this particular point in his career. This is an issue to which it will be appropriate to return when we have explored the context in more detail.

3. Dramatic context, characters and structure

The dramatic date imagined for the setting of *Republic* appears to be determined partly by the participation of the elderly Cephalus, the paterfamilias of the *metic* (non-citizen resident) family in the Athenian port of the Piraeus where the dialogue takes place. His son, Lysias, in his forensic speech *Against Eratosthenes,* tells us that his father had been persuaded by Pericles to emigrate to Athens in the late 450's and that he established a flourishing shield-factory in the Piraeus (Lysias 12.4), living for a further 30 years. This suggests the late 420's for the dramatic setting of the dialogue. On the other hand, there is a reference at *Republic* 368a3 to Glaucon and Adeimantus having distinguished themselves in a battle at Megara. Two dates for the battle are possible candidates here, 424 and 409; the latter seems preferable, since Glaucon and Adeimantus as brothers (younger or older) of Plato (born c. 429) would have been far too young for the earlier engagement.[13] The reference to the gathering involving the

---

[12] See Giannantoni 143f.

[13] On the birth dates of Glaucon and Adeimantus and the battle(s) of Megara, see Nails 2–3,

festival of Bendis (327a1ff., 354a10–11) does not help with dating, since we do not know exactly when the cult was introduced to Athens, nor whether Plato's description ('...this was the first time they were holding it' 327a3–4) refers to such an introduction or perhaps some new aspect of the festivities.[14] The participation of Thrasymachus may give additional support to the later dramatic date if his presence in Athens is indicated by the fragment of a speech attributed to him (*The First Philosophers* 272–4) representing the sophist's advocacy in 407 for his native city of Chalcedon, which had mounted an unsuccessful revolt against Athens.[15] The later date (after c. 411) also fits the incidental reference to the Thessalian pancratiast Polydamas (338c7–9), who won his first Olympic victory in 408. But there are also obvious irreconcilable anachronisms, such as the reference to the incident involving Ismenias of Thebes (336a5), which probably took place c. 395, after Socrates' death (see Comm. *ad loc.*). In his dialogues Plato frequently brings together historically inconsistent characters, allusions and details for his own dramatic purposes and Nails' conclusion on *Republic* that we are dealing with a 'prosopographically scrambled dialogue' can be seen to have significance in the case of Books 1 and 2.[16]

Republic is, like many dialogues, set in a narrative frame by Socrates himself, relating the content of the dialogue the day after it took place to unknown auditor(s), from whom we never hear. Socrates is presented, therefore, as controlling the progress of the dialogue. We view the preliminary social intercourse through his eyes, and in the course of the argument he offers us a privileged perception of his thoughts and feelings (cf. *Charmides, Lysis, Protagoras*), and provides a vivid commentary from his point of view on the temperament and behaviour of his chief opponent Thrasymachus, his surprise at the resumption of the discussion at the beginning of Book 2, and his pleasure at the prowess of Glaucon and Adeimantus. It is notable, however, that, though the narrative element is maintained formally throughout by means of the standard 'I said', 'he said' etc., 2.368c onwards is effectively direct dialogue (and much of it monologue by Socrates); the 'first person'

154–5.
[14] On the dating of the cult of Bendis, see Parker 170ff., Vegetti (Vol.1) 117ff.
[15] For the detailed case, see White 324–7.
[16] Nails 325. See also N. under the names of the various characters for full discussion of all prosopographical issues connected with *Republic*. Taking a radically 'separatist' view of the composition of the various parts of the dialogue, N. conjectures different dramatic dates for Book 1 and 'most of *Republic* 2–5'.

commentary mostly disappears, along with the oppositional relationships between Socrates and the other characters.[17] This alteration of dramatic style reflects the radical change in philosophical approach, engineered by Socrates, after 368c, which we have already mentioned (above p.1).

Whatever the date at which we are supposed to see the dialogue as taking place (see above, pp. 5–6), Socrates comes across as a middle-aged man. The social context is of his journey of 9 km. to the Piraeus, accompanied by Glaucon, to attend a religious festival, still however within the extended walls of Athens, which he is presented as being always notoriously unwilling to venture outside (for an exception, see *Phaedrus* 230c–d). He also receives a warm welcome from the aged Cephalus and his family, which suggests a picture of a respectable citizen, with no surface hint of the intellectual and social antagonism from Athenians suggested by his trial and condemnation (cf. *e.g. Laches*, where there is a similar amicable encounter with an elderly friend; for detailed language similarities with *Republic* 1, see Comm. on 328c6). In other respects his *persona* of ignorant enquirer, laced with urbane irony, conforms very closely to that of the early Socratic dialogues, with the notable addition that exposure of his argumentative manoeuvres is much more frank and detailed, both by his opponent Thrasymachus (*e.g.* 337a) and even by Socrates himself (354a–b).

With regard to Socrates' hosts, present in *Republic* (and named at 328b) we are unusually well-informed, since Lysias, a silent presence in *Republic*, in his speech *Against Eratosthenes,* mentioned above in connection with Cephalus, dwells on the subsequent fate of his *metic* family in the violent oligarchic coup of 404/3 which followed the end of the Peloponnesian War. Wealthy non-citizens may have been regarded as fair game by the new regime. At all events, Lysias and his brother Polemarchus (a major respondent in Book 1 of the dialogue) were arrested and their business (the shield-factory founded by Cephalus) seized by the authorities. Polemarchus was executed, forced to drink hemlock, while his brother managed to escape and sail to nearby Megara (Lysias 12.8–20).

The picture painted by Plato, in contrast, is of a contented, socially well-integrated and prosperous family, with time to enter into philosophical discussion; as Lysias says in his speech, looking back to the past before his family misfortunes: '…thus we lived in the democracy, committing no

---

[17] Not entirely; see *e.g.* Adeimantus and Glaucon at 449bff., 471cff. and 487bff. But these interventions are not sustained, and appear to serve less as challenges and more as structural markers in the on-going dialogue.

fault against others, nor being wronged by them' (Lysias 12.4). Their former wealth is perhaps indicated by the liturgies Lysias claims they undertook (Lysias 12.20: liturgies were prestigious activities undertaken by wealthy individuals, financing particular state activities, *e.g.* the fitting out of warships or providing choruses for the drama).

In the dialogues, in presenting his characters, Plato frequently exploits the tension between the dramatic situation in which they are placed and the known historical facts. In presenting Cephalus' family as he does, but with the knowledge of what dreadful fate awaited them, Plato may be bringing a retrospective, almost dramatic, irony to bear, not only in Cephalus' air, in his conversation with Socrates, of social well-being and contentment (329a–331b), but perhaps also in Glaucon's discussion of the hypothetical case of the falsely accused just person (361c) – far from hypothetical in reality, but exactly the fate which later befell the *metic* brothers (see Comm. note on 361e1). Such a fate, of course, also famously befell Socrates himself, prosecuted for impiety in 399 under the democratic regime which followed the downfall of the oligarchic junta.[18]

Plato's choice of a *metic* residence for the dialogue may also have another motive altogether; together with a geographical setting removed from the city of Athens, it may be a deliberate attempt to provide for Socrates' radically new vision of the state – a venue suitably distanced from the established values of the Athenian citizen democracy.[19]

Within the dialogue Socrates' interlocutors are vividly drawn: the elderly Cephalus acts in many respects as the 'warm-up man', whose conversation with Socrates on how best to live one's life and avoid fear of death turns on the relationship between personal circumstances (wealth would be a sensitive subject for a commercially-oriented *metic*) and personal disposition. His style is leisurely and discursive, with copious reference to traditional wisdom in the form of poetic citations. The degree to which Cephalus' contribution should be taken seriously is a matter of dispute (for an assessment of the cogency of his arguments, see section 5). There is no doubt, however, that he is presented, from Socrates' point of view, as a man with intellectual limitations, and his abrupt exit from the argument as soon as it takes a 'Socratic' turn (331d) clearly indicates Plato's intention that Cephalus' views on life and conduct are to be superseded in the argument.

---

[18]   For a detailed discussion of dramatic irony in its relation to subsequent historical events in the Cephalus episode, see Gifford 54ff.

[19]   See Lycos 24.

Polemarchus, Cephalus' son and Lysias' elder brother, abruptly takes over the argument from his father at 331d4–5, as 'heir' to his discussion with Socrates as well as heir to his property.[20] His assertive personality has already been established early in his semi-joking coercion of Socrates into changing his plans for a return to Athens at 327c4–5, and in his emphatic and perceptive intervention in the Thrasymachus debate at 340a1 (see Comm. note *ad loc.*). He is not sharp enough, though, to present a serious challenge to Socrates when his turn comes to debate (see below, section 5 (b)).

The discussion is equally abruptly interrupted by the third and most formidable of Socrates' interlocutors, the visiting sophist Thrasymachus. Despite (or perhaps because of) being the most able opponent Plato's Socrates ever encountered, this character is the object of a uniquely negative portrait by Plato of an aggressive, rude and over-confident debater.[21] As narrator, Socrates has the whip-hand in presenting all the characters in the dialogue, and Plato uses this device to prejudice us particularly against Thrasymachus (see detailed notes in Comm., *e.g.* on 336b1). It is therefore important, especially in the case of Thrasymachus, to try to distinguish Socrates' (Plato's) highly pejorative presentation of Thrasymachus' character from the quality of the argument he is given and its significance in the overall structure of the dialogue (see below, section 5 (c)).[22] In the Platonic dialogues the nearest match to Thrasymachus is Callicles, Socrates' last and most formidable opponent in the earlier dialogue *Gorgias*; Callicles' argumentative position is not dissimilar to that of Thrasymachus, and, like Thrasymachus, he ends up by ultimately withdrawing emotionally from the argument. However, Thrasymachus is more formidable a debater than Callicles, and, as we shall see (below, section 5 (c)), it is by no means agreed among commentators that Socrates ultimately comes off best in this encounter.

Republic continues beyond the *aporia* of Book 1 and Thrasymachus' ambivalent acquiescence in Socrates' position. Two new characters enter the debate, who are destined to be Socrates' interlocutors for the rest of

---

[20] At 328b4 the venue is described as 'Polemarchus' house', and it seems likely that Cephalus can be seen as having retired and having handed over control of his property to his son and heir. (For this practice see MacDowell 91).

[21] For a detailed attempt to relate Thrasymachus' *Republic* personality to the external evidence, see Quincy.

[22] It is significant that after Book 1, Thrasymachus effectively 'disappears' from the debate. (For his later single, pointed and quite perceptive intervention, see *Republic* 450b4–5).

Republic, Plato's brothers, Glaucon and Adeimantus.[23] Socrates' brief ironic comments on their 'display speeches' (361d4–6, 362d6–9, 367e5ff.), as well as the language of the speeches themselves (see eg. Comm., notes on 358e5ff., 361c4–5), suggest that Plato intends here a parody of sophistic rhetoric (the boys have learned their lessons well and are trying so hard to impress their elders!); but nevertheless, the substance of their arguments forms the basis of the case Socrates has to answer in the remainder of the dialogue.

4. The cultural background

Republic is typical of Plato's dialogues in the prominence of references to the Greek cultural background of his time. This takes the form of copious quotations from the 'wisdom' of poets, such as Homer, Hesiod, Pindar, Simonides and Aeschylus, and traditional religious teachings concerning the fate of individuals in the afterlife attributed to such legendary figures as Musaeus and Orpheus, as well as apposite, often witty, proverbial sayings, all of which fall naturally from the lips of Plato's characters in their dramatic setting, including Socrates himself. We also encounter the expression of radical political ideas concerning government and power which were clearly derived from the intellectual ferment of the late fifth century associated with the sophists, with historians such as Thucydides and dramatists such as Euripides.[24]

Plato strongly disapproved of the Athenian democratic constitution of his day on the grounds that it gave political power to all citizens, irrespective of their fitness to rule. In his *Republic* he wished to create an entirely new society with philosophers in charge. As he tells us in the arguably autobiographical *Seventh Letter* '...the troubles of mankind will never cease until either true and genuine philosophers attain political power or the rulers of states by some dispensation of providence become genuine philosophers'.[25] The attitude of the *Republic* Socrates to the cultural heritage of the poets representing the established order of society is, predictably,

---

[23] In introducing his siblings, Plato, as usual, avoids all explicit authorial self-reference (for a possible covert allusion, see Comm., note on 368a1).

[24] On this background, see in general, Guthrie (1969). Detailed discussion of individual quotations and references will be found in the Commentary.

[25] *Letter VII,* 325dff. The authenticity of the *Letters* has long been disputed; the Seventh, if not by Plato, may well have been written in his lifetime, and reflect his views on politics and society. (On the question of authenticity, see Edelstein).

highly critical. This is most clearly demonstrated in the latter part of Book 2 and Book 3, where he argues that most of the poetic and religious writings from the past, and the most prestigious, need to be eliminated from his ideal state as morally harmful in various ways for the education of the young.[26] In Book 1 Socrates is presented as treating poets ostensibly with respect often thinly covering an ironically critical attitude. The seriousness of the criticism depends on the dramatic situation: Cephalus is allowed to get away with his reference to Pindar on the consolations of a virtuous life (331a); in the case of Polemarchus, however, when he produces Simonides' (alleged) saying that justice is to give back to every person what he is owed (331e3–4), Socrates turns the saying inside out, making the transparently ironic observation that Simonides must have been '...defining the just in riddles, like a poet' (332b9–c1). Socrates also makes short work of the popular Greek value of 'doing good to friends and harm to enemies' (see below, section 5 (b)).

Socrates reserves his most serious attack, however, for Thrasymachus' definition of justice as 'what is advantageous to the stronger' (338c2–3). This idea, refined by Glaucon and Adeimantus in Book 2, owes much to the sophistic idea of the primacy of nature (*physis*) over law/convention (*nomos*), found in *e.g.* Antiphon and Thucydides,[27] and apparently validated in such myths as that of Gyges the Lydian in Book 2.359c7ff. (a story similar to one also found in the historian Herodotus, Book 1.6ff.). The idea of *pleonexia* (excess, outdoing your neighbour) as a natural excellence (*aretē*) leading to *eudaimonia* (happiness), ultimately desired by all and curbed only by conventional restraint and individual weakness, gains a great deal of its cogency from the basic competitive values which underlay ordinary Athenian social relations in the democracy.[28] It is argued for at some length by Glaucon and Adeimantus (see below section 5 (d)), who also introduce a version of the 'social compact' theory of society and its origins which relates closely to ideas found in Protagoras and other fifth/ early fourth century sources.[29] The reformulation of these ideas by Glaucon and Adeimantus represents the key position Socrates has to oppose in the remainder of *Republic*.

In making their speeches, Glaucon, and especially Adeimantus, in Book 2 cast their net widely, surveying a wide cross-section of Greek social

---

[26] On Plato's attitude to poetry in general and in *Republic* in particular, see Murray.
[27] See Guthrie (1969) 84–8, 285–92.
[28] See in general, Cartledge 11–16.
[29] See Guthrie (1969) 135–147.

activities, including business transactions, politics, the law, marriage and the family. They bring to bear in support of their assumed position, the advantage to be enjoyed by the doers of injustice, all the traditional wisdom associated with attitudes of the gods and authoritative poets towards transgressive human behaviour. These attitudes, they claim, universally commend such behaviour. Revelations about the fate of human souls in the afterlife, the 'babble of books' toted around Greek cities by prophets with dubious credentials (364e3ff.), assure people that wrongdoing can be expiated simply by due sacrifice and other rituals. As for those who have lived a just life, the tone of Adeimantus' exposition makes fun of the traditional eschatology: '...for the story goes that when [the gods] have conducted them down to Hades, they sit them down to a wine-party of the pious that they have laid on, and have them pass the whole time in drinking with garlands on their heads, in the belief that the finest reward of virtue is to be drunk for all eternity' (363c5–d3). 'Advanced' thinking even suggests, declares Adeimantus, that the gods may not exist, or even if they do exist, they cannot possibly have any interest in human activities (365d).[30]

Young men, potential leaders of the state, will have to have exceptional innate qualities, Adeimantus argues, to resist the weight and authority of this tradition and sort out its inherent contradictions (366cff.).

5. The arguments

The early stages of the dialogue exhibit, as stated above (p.1), an argumentative structure totally distinct from the rest of *Republic*. Book 1 more resembles the earlier *Gorgias* not only in its subject-matter, but in its clear tripartite division, marked by the clear succession of three Socratic interlocutors, Cephalus, Polemarchus and Thrasymachus, involved in discussions of increasing philosophical significance. The Book also reflects *Gorgias* in the abrupt, dramatically subtle transitions from speaker to speaker (Gorgias/Cephalus – Polus/Polemarchus – Callicles/Thrasymachus) and the increasing space given to each, reflecting their relative importance in the argument. However the differences between the two dialogues are more significant than the similarities. Whereas until near the end *Gorgias* sticks mainly to the *elenchus,* for each speaker in *Republic* 1 Plato devises a different mode of

---

[30] Disbelief in the traditional view of the gods, including atheism and scepticism about their concern for humans, can be found in sophistic texts and drama (*e.g.* Aristophanes, Euripides) of the 5th century; see Guthrie (1969) 226–47.

discourse appropriate to the personality: for the elderly Cephalus a gentle, discursive chat, for the younger and intellectually aspiring Polemarchus, a series of more demanding *elenchus* arguments. It is with the third speaker, Thrasymachus, that Plato presents his most radical departure from previous practice: Thrasymachus' dialogue with Socrates is in effect a tussle over the form of discourse they are to adopt – whether Socrates is to be allowed to get away with his traditional *elenchus* mode of argument, which Thrasymachus believes to be methodologically suspect (*e.g.* 336b7ff), or whether Socrates will be drawn into Thrasymachus' expository mode (where the latter's most telling arguments are deployed). In the end, Socrates' *elenchus* arguments, to which Thrasymachus submits, formally win the day (as they almost always do); but the latter's expository style contains a speech (343b1–344c9) which, despite being ridiculed by Socrates (344d1ff.), produces the nub of his argument – the advantage to the stronger person of pursuing the unjust life. This is the thesis which in Book 2 Glaucon and Adeimantus consider that Socrates still has to counter. They set out the revised Thrasymachus case in yet another form of discourse, which Plato has not used in earlier dialogues in precisely this form: paired, complementary display speeches (*epideixeis*) of some length, formally 'speaking in praise of the unjust life' (Glaucon at 358d5f.).[31]

(a) Socrates and Cephalus
The beginning of *Republic* is a particularly elaborate example (fitting the dialogue's great length) of a common Platonic literary device: allowing the argument to emerge from chit-chat accompanying the hospitality appropriate to a social visit. Deflected from his initial plan of returning to Athens following the festival, and going with his friends to Polemarchus' house, Socrates out of natural courtesy first addresses the elderly head of the family and enquires how he copes with old age. Socrates probes Cephalus' somewhat complacent answer by suggesting that some might say that his wealth (likely to be a touchy subject for a *metic*) rather than any innate personal quality might be responsible for the ease with which Cephalus bears old age. This takes them on to the role wealth might play in attitudes to approaching death, and how these might relate to the just life. There is

---

[31] For the *Republic* 2 speeches in the genre of 'praise' discourse, see Nightingale 132. For Plato's previous use of the extended speech mode, cf. *Protagoras* 320c–28d (Protagoras' 'Great Speech') and by Socrates himself, in the guise of the Laws of Athens, in *Crito* 50a–54d.

considerable dramatic skill in how Socrates (Plato) contrives to move the discussion from Cephalus' personality to his wealth and from there to the more sensitive subject of the advantages wealth has brought. At this point, however (331c1), Socrates abruptly ups the tempo of the discussion and fixes on Cephalus' concern with how wealth might enable its possessor to avoid the injustices which generate the fear of approaching death, by asking for a definition of justice (implied rather than stated in the conversation), thereby sowing the first stages of an *elenchus*. This somewhat contrived transition to a typically Socratic search for a definition nevertheless has the result of Cephalus being abruptly dismissed (actually dismissing himself) from the scene.[32]

Strictly philosophical commentaries on *Republic* have tended to regard this introductory section of the dialogue as superficial moralising and not worthy of much attention.[33] Those who, more recently, have valued the scene artistically and dramatically differ over how far Plato intends us to take Cephalus seriously; Annas, for example, believes '...that we are being presented with a limited and complacent man', but others disagree.[34] There is no doubt that Cephalus is presented, in Socratic terms, as a man with intellectual limitations. What he anticipates in his desire for and pleasure in 'conversation' (*logoi* 328d4) is a little gentle sententious moralising (perhaps *e.g.* on the lines of Xenophon's Socratic *logoi*). But Plato makes it clear that he would not stand a chance in argument against (or perhaps even be capable of understanding) anyone who questioned the basis of his morality, *e.g.* Thrasymachus. Plato may be implying that Cephalus' rules of conduct, rooted as they are in a stable social morality and the conventional wisdom of the poets, do not offer a deeper analysis of values of the sort which might survive the destruction of that stable base (see above section 3, on the historical reality of this scenario – the subsequent tragic fate of Cephalus' family).

Yet Cephalus' position does have some strengths. Against the objection

---

[32] For an analysis of Plato's artistry in this initial scene, with a rather more favourable assessment of the plausibility of Socrates' dramatic move towards the introduction of the *elenchus* at 331c1 than that advanced here, see Harrison 27–8.

[33] E.g. Cross and Woozley 2, who begin their philosophical analysis with the Polemarchus episode.

[34] Annas 19; see in clear contrast, Reeve (1988) 6 and further, on either side of the argument, Lycos 21–31, Irwin (1995) 170, Beversluis 185–202, Gifford; for further detail, see Comm., note on 328b8.

that his morality depends entirely on favourable external circumstances (made explicitly by Socrates: see 329e3–4 and Comm. *ad loc.*), Cephalus counterattacks quite effectively: without denying the importance of his wealth, he emphasises the significance of *tropos* ('disposition'), which is expressed in terms of 'decency', 'order' and 'contentment' – qualities which reveal the kind of person you are, and without which wealth will not suffice for happiness. The idea of human disposition as central to the good life was developed, albeit in more sophisticated form, in the ethical writings of Aristotle (who lived 384–322), as well as in the psychological studies of his pupil Theophrastus (370–285) in his *Characters,* and in the comedies of *his* pupil, Menander (342–290). In his development of the *elenchus* following Cephalus' exit, Socrates moves the argument away from justice as an internal order in the individual towards viewing it as a characteristic rather of *relationships* between individuals – a definition in terms of society rather than of individual psychology.[35] However, the idea that the good life is rooted in internal qualities and not, as the dialogues with Polemarchus and Thrasymachus tend to emphasise, simply revealed in social relationships, is an idea which, more sharply developed, becomes important for the argument of *Republic* as a whole.

Yet the very vagueness of these concepts in Cephalus' discourse – how they are to be defined and acquired – would, of course, have made him a sitting duck for Socrates, had he chosen to pursue him along those lines, since Socrates' much more sharply-defined values were, as we shall see, grounded in knowledge and existed in a necessary rather than a contingent relation to the good life. But all the same, Cephalus argues quite convincingly, in his own discursive way (see 329e6ff.), that, for him, the values by which he lives are not simply a matter of 'rules to follow and duties to perform',[36] but depend upon something internal to his character (however imprecisely defined), and it is this, rather than purely prudential considerations, which motivates his attitude to life.

(b) Socrates and Polemarchus
Polemarchus, as a younger man (assuming a late 420's dramatic date for *Republic*, he would be about 30 years old[37]), is more combative than his father, and much more prepared to engage in the *elenchus*. In *Phaedrus* 257b

---

[35] See Lycos 33–5.
[36] Annas 20.
[37] See Nails 251.

Socrates describes him as having been turned (from rhetoric) to philosophy (a reference which Kahn takes to be '…a discreet allusion to the conversation in *Republic* 1'.[38]). The abrupt change of participant at 331d signals also a movement in the style and topic of discussion: from a leisurely exchange of observations on life to concentrated argument, and from a consideration of right living (latterly 'justice') as a function of individual temperament to the role of justice as it should function in relation to others.

At the same time the focus of the discussion narrows and sharpens; instead of a casual and approving citation of a range of quotations conveying popular Greek wisdom (see above (a)), there is close and critical concentration on one saying of a single figure, the sixth-early fifth century lyric poet Simonides: 'that it is just to give back to every man what is owed'. This position is advanced on Simonides' behalf by Polemarchus (331e3–4),[39] modifying Socrates' initial 'knock-down' suggestion to Cephalus that justice is 'truthfulness and giving back whatever we may have taken from someone' (331c1–3). Polemarchus' modification meets Socrates' own objection that it would not be just to tell the truth, or return a weapon, to a madman (in such a situation, the original donor would, by implication, not be receiving back what was 'owed' to him).

Socrates attacks the 'Simonides' saying, utilising a typically 'Socratic' method of argument, eliciting from his interlocutor an 'interpretation' of Simonides' saying, to which he lodges a series of objections:

1. On an analogy with skills such as medicine and cookery, which have precisely-defined due and appropriate activities and objects, what activity and object would justify classifying justice as a skill? To Polemarchus' answer 'doing good to friends and bad to enemies' (a popular moral position), Socrates argues that professional skills such as medicine and navigation and others having specific procedures and areas of operation are much more effective in realising the desired good or bad ends than justice.
2. The aforementioned skills, and others like them, render their practitioners equally effective at doing good and harm to their objects. So, by analogy, the just person will also be skilled at being unjust.

---

[38] Kahn (1996) 373. The validity of this allusion depends, of course, on the assumption that the composition of *Phaedrus* followed *Republic,* or at least some form of Book 1. On the composition of *Republic* see above, section 2.

[39] There is no independent citation of this saying extant (see Comm., note on 331d5).

3. In harming enemies, you may be mistaken as to who are your friends and enemies, which means that justice may involve harming friends.
4. Harming means making worse; but the just person cannot by his skill make anyone less just, any more than *e.g.* a musician, by exercise of his professional skill, can make anyone less musical.

For detailed analysis of these arguments (331e1–336a10), see Comm. There is general agreement that these four arguments are unsatisfactory, chiefly because behind them all lies the assumption that justice is an art, craft or skill (*techne*) like other crafts and professions which Socrates habitually, as here, cites. A *techne* is an activity characterised by *episteme* (knowledge), which has a clearly-defined area of expertise and a product or outcome.[40] On this assumption, Socrates can construct a series of mutually incompatible positions: justice can *either* be shown not to have any area (or no significant area) of expertise which is not covered by skills like medicine or navigation (argument 1. above), *or,* if it does share the characteristics of these other skills, it is capable, like them, of effecting either good or evil on its objects (argument 2.). Alternatively, it is argued that justice is only capable of effecting good outcomes (argument 4, directly contradictory to argument 2.). There is also another implied contradiction, this time with argument 3., since possession of a *techne* would rule out ignorance as to the nature of its object – you could never be mistaken as to who were your friends and who were your enemies. There is a further difficulty with argument 4., apparently unnoticed by either Socrates or Polemarchus: *blapto* ('harm') is ambiguous in Greek, meaning either to make worse or to inflict damage/ hurt; the latter sense is obviously the one Polemarchus has in mind, but this does not obviously lead to the conclusion that the sufferer is being made more unjust (for details, see Comm., note on 335c1).

Some of these arguments are also reminiscent of those found in much earlier dialogues: argument 1, narrowing (or eliminating) the possible area of operation of the expertise of a claimed skill, can be found in *e.g. Ion* 537a–41c, *Gorgias* 447d–452e; argument 2, demonstrating that expertise renders the possessor equally effective at doing good or bad can be found

---

[40] 'Art', 'craft' or 'skill' are common alternative English equivalents for *techne*, although none is entirely satisfactory. The latter two convey more of the idea of rational procedure which Plato wishes to give to the word; however, the common modern associations of 'skill' or 'craft' tend to be narrower than the Greek word implies, while 'art' has other obvious anachronistic associations.

in *e.g. Hippias Minor* 375e–76c. *Republic* is notable in throwing these arguments all together, with the result that conclusions are reached which are unacceptable to both interlocutors and the discussion is doomed to *aporia* (failure to reach a positive conclusion). Polemarchus, despite expressing some misgivings about the direction of the argument (*e.g.* 332d4–5, 333d2, 334a9, d6), is unable to counter Socrates at any point.

The key question here is: what did Plato intend to be the purpose of the arguments? And this question is still relevant even if the arguments are dredged up from some earlier *Republic,* which might make them contemporary with *Ion, Hippias Minor* etc.; if this is the case, why did Plato deploy them here, and in this unsatisfactory way?

A typical older view is that either Plato was incapable of seeing the flaws or that we misunderstand the arguments (the latter alternative is more popular).[41] More recent discussions, *e.g.* Annas, have suggested that Plato was having Socrates consciously and deliberately use less than satisfactory arguments to tie Polemarchus up in knots and reveal how little he had really thought about the issues involved – exposing his 'moral complacency'.[42] Another approach, related to the previous one, is to see the arguments as looking forward to the main thrust of *Republic,* in that Plato is anxious to clear the ground by discarding erroneous 'popular' ideas, while retaining in his exploration of justice some aspects of his long-standing 'craft-analogy', namely the emphasis on specialist knowledge – the knowledge of justice which will enable the rulers of his state to exhibit the requisite expertise. The conclusion of the fourth and final argument (4. above), that it is never just to do harm (335e3), points in this direction: towards an ideal 'justice' which can never be 'sometimes just and sometimes unjust' (331c1) – a possible reference to the theory of Forms at 479a5–8. Moreover, if we put together Cephalus' emphasis on 'disposition' with the Polemarchus-section emphasis on justice as social regulation, there we have the crude basis of the remainder of the *Republic.*

This emphasis on the 'proleptic' elements in the speech (elements which look forward to later aspects of the dialogue[43] – of which there are undoubtedly many in Book 1) needs to be balanced by consideration of the actual dramatic structure and form in which Socrates casts the arguments. There is a strong 'eristic' element, i.e. arguing to win rather than to reach

---

[41]   *E.g.* Joseph 1–2.
[42]   Annas 30.
[43]   See *e.g.* Kahn (1993).

the truth, coupled with rhetorical language typical of the discourse of the sophists, (see *e.g.* Comm. on 333d12). Socrates also, in a rather obvious manner, suppresses and steers away from conclusions which might lead in a more positive direction (see Comm. on 332e5). The most notable example of this technique is at the end (see Comm. on 335e5–6), where the acceptable Platonic conclusion that it is never just to harm anyone is presented negatively as a contradiction of Simonides' saying.

Furthermore, the 'craft-analogy' is deployed simplistically, ignoring reservations expressed by Socrates in earlier dialogues, *e.g. Laches,* or *Euthydemus* 288bff., where the idea is introduced of a 'superordinate' branch of knowledge governing the conventional *technai,* for example, knowledge of when (as opposed to how) it is appropriate to apply skills, a role which might well fit justice. An argument along these lines, if competently handled, could have stopped Socrates in his tracks.

All this might suggest that an important element in the Polemarchus episode might be the staging by Plato of a deliberate breakdown of the 'Socratic method', including even the *elenchus* itself (see later critical comments on this method by Socrates' young friend Adeimantus at *Republic* 487bff.). And as we shall see Socrates is later presented as being only too aware of how unconvincing his performance has been in Book 1. It is Socrates, perhaps more than Polemarchus, who is here under negative scrutiny.

Finally, does Plato intend what seems to be the cause of all the trouble, the unreconstructed craft-analogy, to go the way of the *elenchus*?[44] Or does Socrates, in the remainder of the *Republic,* keep a grip on the idea of justice as a *technē,* but of a very different sort, and with a very different product or outcome, namely 'happiness', 'well-being' (*eudaimonia*)?[45]

(c) Socrates and Thrasymachus
So far the partners in the discussion have been essentially reactive to Socrates. Cephalus simply answers his enquiries as best he can, and Polemarchus, despite his assertive entry into the discussion at 331d4, accepts without question his role as subordinate partner in the *elenchus,* the characteristic form in which Socrates casts the conversation. With Thrasymachus, it is another matter. Before they even manage to get on to the substance of the

---

44 See Reeve (1985) 263.
45 See *e.g.* Irwin (1995) 69, Kahn (1996) 118.

discussion there is an argument between him and Socrates about method and procedure. If we separate the content of what Thrasymachus says from the highly pejorative portrait of his character and behaviour painted by Socrates (using his narrator's advantage), we can see that in the initial stages of his dialogue with Socrates (336b1–338c1) Thrasymachus, underneath the bluster and coarse abuse, delivers a significant criticism of Socrates' procedure; he makes it clear that he wishes to question the whole value of the *elenchus* method, depending as it does on Socrates asking 'leading' questions (which admit certain avenues of speculation and close off others) and luring the unsuspecting answerer in the direction of refutation, without ever venturing an answer himself (336c1ff.). Thrasymachus also confronts directly the central justification of Socrates' method – his assumed ignorance of the answers to the questions he asks. This ignorance is essentially a sham, says Thrasymachus, an 'ironic evasion' (337a4) of the responsibility to make a positive contribution to the discussion – a pose of deference which conceals Socrates' strong control over the direction of the argument.

We need to be aware, therefore, that here, unlike the previous conversations in *Republic* 1, there are two important and distinct perspectives on the discussion from the outset, that of Socrates and that of Thrasymachus.

First, Socrates: in immediate response to Thrasymachus' first positive assertion – that 'justice is nothing other than what is advantageous to the stronger' (we are calling this *T1*, 338c2–3), under guise of 'clarification' Socrates first resorts to a facetious attempt at comparison with the pancratiast Polydamas (a manoeuvre reminiscent of an initial response to Callicles in *Gorgias* 490d, see Comm. on 338c7–9.). This draws from Thrasymachus what looks like a modification, or an explanation of *T1*, namely that, since rulers pass laws to their own advantage, justice is what is to the advantage of the established rule in any state and it is just for the ruled to obey such a rule (we are calling this *T2*, 338e1ff.). Socrates' response is this time a serious request for clarification, which has far-reaching consequences for his argument: is Thrasymachus talking about rulers who are in error, who mistake what is to their advantage, or rulers in the strict sense – those who infallibly choose what is to their advantage? When Thrasymachus firmly chooses the latter – that the ruler in the strict sense is what he means (341b8–9, in effect abandoning *T2*), Socrates makes a familiar analogy with other skilled professionals (doctors and ship's captains) and argues that they only seek the advantage of the object of their skill; so Thrasymachus' ruler (the strictly infallible skilled professional, as he has agreed) will seek the advantage not of himself but of the object of his skill, his subjects (341c5–342e10, reminiscent of argument 4. of the Polemarchus episode, see above, p.12: skills properly understood must benefit those on whom they are practised). At this point, Thrasymachus, in a long speech, comes back at Socrates with another argument – that in fact Socrates is mistaken; the shepherd is not concerned with the welfare of his sheep but with preserving them for the good of their owners; skilled people, contrary to what Socrates maintains, do not actually consider the good of their subjects but of themselves. Justice is in reality someone else's good (that of the ruler – what he really meant by *T1*) and 'injustice is profitable and advantageous to oneself' (we are calling this *T3, 344c7–9*).

In answer to this Socrates produces a series of arguments designed further to counter Thrasymachus:

1. Rulers (*qua* skilled professionals practising a *technē*) consider not their own interest but those of their subjects. The wages they receive (*via* the 'skill of wage earning') are incidental to the exercise of their professional skill. That rulers do require payment testifies to the fact that no intrinsic advantage accrues to them from their skill (345e5–347b5).
2. In response to Thrasymachus' statement that injustice is not only profitable but good and wise, Socrates argues further that, like other skilled professionals (musicians, doctors), the individual skilled in justice (having wisdom) will not want to outdo another just person; so it is the just person who is 'good and wise, the unjust ignorant and bad' (350c10).
3. Justice is more powerful than injustice since, to achieve anything, individuals and groups must cooperate, i.e. have a minimal component of justice within them (351c7–352d1).
4. Everything, animal, part of the body or activity, has a function (*ergon*), by means of which it can do what it is designed to do better than anything else (*e.g.* eyes have sight, a pruning-knife is designed to cut a vine-shoot); everything which has a particular function can also be said to have an excellence (*aretē*): in the case of our examples, to function well. The function of the human soul is living, and the *aretē* is to do it well, i.e. with justice (352e1–354a9).

These arguments all receive Thrasymachus' formal but reluctant assent.

Against 1. and 2. he puts up something of a fight, but for 3. and 4. he has more or less disengaged himself, and turned into a token presence; by the end of the Book, despite his generally positive answers, we cannot assume that he has been convinced by anything Socrates has said. As in the arguments with Polemarchus, the first two of the arguments above again rely heavily on the 'craft-analogy' (see above, pp.16–17) and are vulnerable to any approach which does not accept the assumptions behind this analogy. In argument 1. above, the odd concept of the 'skill of wage earning' is open to several objections (for details, see Comm. on 346b1). More seriously, argument 2. is open to the objection (which Thrasymachus does not actually advance, but it is implied in his position) that rather than 'outdoing' someone else in the sense of better practising their *technē*, skilled individuals (*e.g.* rulers) might 'outdo' others in the sense of 'getting the better' of them.

Argument 3. takes the discussion in a new direction, but is still vulnerable to the objection that the power of the individual (ruler or tyrant) might well make cooperation between individuals (i.e. justice) unnecessary for effective action. Argument 4. is perhaps the most convincing, and, as we shall see, has significance for the argument of the later *Republic*, but in the immediate context also depends too heavily on the unspoken assumption that the soul behaves like *e.g.* the senses or pruning-knives; Thrasymachus' argument implies, on the contrary, that the *aretē* of the function of living might equally plausibly be injustice, in the sense that the wholly unjust person can most effectively attain his version of 'living well' i.e. prosperous wickedness.[46]

While Socrates might well be criticised for continually rerunning versions of the same argument, involving the 'craft-analogy', Thrasymachus has often been accused of the contrary fault, inconsistency – of producing, at different stages of his discussion with Socrates, arguments which do not cohere with each other. At first sight this certainly seems to be the case: *T1* (*justice* is the advantage of the stronger) appears to be inconsistent with *T3* (*injustice* is the advantage of oneself, i.e. of the stronger over the weaker). And both of these seem inconsistent with *T2* (justice is what is to the advantage of the established rulers, of whatever political complexion, and however successful: 338e1ff.).

A consistent thread discernibly running through Thrasymachus' arguments is his belief that justice is not a desirable thing to have because

---

[46] On all these arguments, see *e.g.* Irwin (1995) 69, Kahn (1996) 118.

it puts its practitioner in the disadvantageous position of having less of everything, power, riches, etc., than the person who does not follow justice, in fact, as the weaker to the stronger. Problems have arisen over how he actually expresses this at various points in the dialogue. In particular, the opening argument, *T1*, in making *justice* the advantage of the stronger, seems at first sight directly contrary to Thrasymachus' basic idea. The most convincing solution to this problem was propounded more than fifty years ago by G. Kerferd who argued that in defining justice at this point, Thrasymachus was doing so from the point of view of the weaker: what for them is 'justice', is to obey the dictates of the stronger, i.e. the rulers.[47] This can then be seen to be consistent with *T3*, expounded later on, and at that point taken from the viewpoint of the stronger, that injustice is 'the advantage of oneself'. The two statements describe the same situation from opposite points of view, from that of the weaker or ruled and, on the other hand, from that of the stronger or ruler. Why, therefore, does Thrasymachus begin in such a confusing way? An obvious solution to this is to see that Thrasymachus is simply trying to give an answer to the question in the form it has been put by Socrates at 336a10 (when he and Polemarchus have failed): 'what else can anyone suggest [justice] is?' The clearest statement of Thrasymachus' position is contained in *T3* , but he is forced to produce his argument back to front, as it were, by the form in which Socrates casts the discussion.[48] *T3* is Thrasymachus' real position (as Glaucon and Adeimantus make clear when they reformulate it, see below, pp. 25–27).

This does not entirely dispose of the problems of consistency. *T2* suggests a 'legalist' definition of justice: it states that rulers make laws in their own interest (hence these laws reflect the complexion of the government: democracy, tyranny etc. (338e1–339a4)), with Thrasymachus agreeing that justice is obeying whatever laws are laid down by the rulers (a 'conventionalist' definition: the yardstick of what is just is simply what the law or convention says it is). This appears to be inconsistent with *T1*; Socrates points out that if *T2* is true, rulers may pass laws which are not in their own interest, so that it turns out to be just to do what is both to their advantage and to their disadvantage (339d1–3). Thrasymachus is therefore

---

[47] Kerferd (1947). There has been a substantial discussion over whether at 338c2–3 Thrasymachus is defining or simply describing or characterising justice, and whether such a distinction has relevance in the context of his argument; see *e.g.* Nicholson, Johnson, Chappell, Everson.

[48] See Johnson.

compelled to extricate himself from this dilemma by repudiating *T2* and
taking back his statement that rulers, conventionally understood, always pass
laws in their own interest. He manages to do this by refining his definition of
ruler: the ruler, strictly conceived, is never in error about his own advantage
(contrary to the situation in *T2,* where it is just for the ruled to obey any law
whether promulgated for the ruler's advantage or not). All the same, taking
T1–3 together, despite Thrasymachus' *volte face*, it may still seem unclear
whether or not he is supporting an 'immoralist' or a 'conventionalist' position
vis à vis justice or (at different times) both.[49]

It is true that Thrasymachus is presented as a forceful rather than a tidy
thinker. He does, however, have a 'big idea' about justice which is radically
opposed to that of Socrates. It is surely highly significant that inconsistency
between Thrasymachus' *T1* and *T3* is not a fault which Socrates picks upon
in the course of his confrontation with him; this suggests that Thrasymachus'
incoherence is not something which Plato wished to emphasise. I would
argue (along with Kerferd and Reeve, and against *e.g.* Everson) that the
incoherence detected in his exposition is actually more apparent than real;
it is better seen as an opening of different perspectives on this single big
idea; he believes that the ability to exercise power, to get more than one's
fellows, is the key to the good life; this applies, whether the context is a
political one (with the unjust person as a monarch, a tyrant, or a member
of any political group, acting through law or extra-legally) or just a private
situation involving a successful criminal. So injustice, rather than justice, is
to one's advantage and this is what the rational person ought to pursue.

In holding this position Thrasymachus, although formally in debate
with Socrates, really bypasses him, in the sense that there is no common
basis on which they can conduct the debate (something which Socrates
comes close to recognising at 348e5ff.). True, they both agree that ruling
is a craft and the true ruler is an expert, and that, as such, he must do what
is to his advantage. For Socrates, this is justice, but for Thrasymachus it is
injustice. Thrasymachus therefore produces something approximating to a
'mirror image' of the Socratic skilled professional; his expert is an 'inverted
Socratic',[50] his wisdom and skill being devoted to excess – taking more than
his fair share. For him injustice rather than justice is the virtue which leads
to the good life. In the face of this position, Socrates' *elenchus* arguments,

---

[49] For a closely argued case for the essential incoherence of Thrasymachus' position, see
Everson.
[50] Reeve (1988) 13.

while formally effective, in the sense that Thrasymachus is presented as paying lip-service to them, are really beside the point, as Socrates himself seems to realise by the end of the Book.

d) Glaucon and Adeimantus

In the first major turning point in the *Republic,* Glaucon, the young friend of Socrates, who has only briefly intervened up to this point, unexpectedly prolongs what seemed at the conclusion of Book 1 to be the end of the affair: at the beginning of Book 2 he challenges Socrates' conclusions of the previous discussion; the victory over Thrasymachus was too easily won, in his opinion. In reality he sides with Socrates in believing that justice, not injustice, is the key to the good life, but he does not believe that Socrates has made a good enough case. He therefore challenges Socrates by reintroducing, as a kind of devil's advocate, Thrasymachus' argument in a novel way which gives it more coherence.

Glaucon makes a division of things which are good into three categories: 1. things good in themselves, such as pleasant and harmless emotions; 2. things good both in themselves and for their consequences, *e.g.* sight and health; 3. things burdensome in themselves but necessarily experienced or undertaken for the ultimate benefits they bring, *e.g.* taking exercise, making money in various ways. Justice, according to Socrates would fit into category 2., but Glaucon would place it in 3., along with the majority of people, as something burdensome which one only practises for its consequences, principally financial rewards and social esteem (357e4–358a6). If one could obtain these consequences without needing to be just in the first place, this would be the obvious choice, which, in practice, most people would make if they could.

Glaucon develops this thesis by means of a version of a 'social compact': individuals consider that it is in their interest to make an agreement with each other not to practise injustice, so as to avoid the consequences of suffering it. Therefore justice is not good in itself (which is what Socrates is committed to demonstrating) but a compromise between the good of being able to commit injustice with impunity and the evil of being forced to suffer it. If you possessed the ring of Gyges the Lydian, and were able to make yourself invisible, you would, as Gyges allegedly did, naturally pursue injustice so as to attain happiness (*eudaimonia*: 359c7–360c5). Glaucon elaborates this thesis by means of a 'thought experiment': take the perfectly just and perfectly unjust person and give them diametrically opposite reputations: the just person is thought to be perfectly unjust and the unjust person perfectly just; the consequences for each would be such that no rational person could possibly choose the former.

Adeimantus, in a speech of similar length, supplements Glaucon by bringing in the inherited Greek cultural wisdom found in poetry and religion (see above, section 4), all of which supports their thesis: any suggestion that injustice in this world might be punished in the next is refuted by the actual behaviour of the gods and traditional teachings with regard to the fate of individuals after death.

This reformulation of Thrasymachus' argument brings to the fore two ideas which the original formulation did not emphasise: 1. the idea of justice as a good both in itself and for its consequences, as opposed to justice as a good merely *because of* its consequences; 2. the dichotomy, which runs through both speeches, of appearance and reality (*doxa/alētheia)*. These two aspects of Glaucon's position are closely related: in his 'thought experiment' (see above) the truly unjust person who could appear to be just was able to profit from all the artificial consequences of seeming justice (artificial, in the sense that they are not intrinsically connected to the person's character and actions, but only with what people mistakenly believed to be his character and actions). Conversely, the truly just person who seems unjust suffers all the bad consequences of his seeming injustice.

The four-square symmetry of the Glaucon/Adeimantus thesis comes over as itself somewhat artificial, depending as it does on improbably extreme circumstances; you don't often in real life get these kinds of absolutes, and Socrates' somewhat ironic interjection at 361d4–6 suggests that Plato wants us to be aware of this artificiality. There is also a problem with Glaucon's tripartite division at the beginning of the Book: the subsequent speeches seem to concentrate on categories 2. and 3. (see above), i.e. essentially a two- (not three-) fold division; and in category two, Glaucon (and subsequently, Socrates) seems to concentrate on the idea of justice as good in itself, only very summarily talking about actual consequences in Socrates' theological excursus, the 'Myth of Er', at the end of the whole dialogue (see further, Comm. on 357b4ff.).

But despite all this, it is a tough thesis which Socrates has to tackle, tougher than that originally presented by Thrasymachus in Book 1. Plato clearly wants Socrates to show that justice, shorn of all its positive social consequences of approval, good reputation, etc. is intrinsically better for the individual (i.e. more profitable) than injustice, conversely shorn of all its corresponding negative associations (punishment, bad reputation etc.). In these circumstances, say Glaucon and Adeimantus, can justice really be a rational choice? This sets the stage for the remainder of the *Republic*: Socrates has to show that justice has intrinsic, and not just consequential, value.

6. Conclusion

Seeing Book 1 and the first part of Book 2 as setting the stage for the remainder of the *Republic* leaves us with the question we raised at the end of section 2 above (p. 5): we need to ask what kind of stage-set we are presented with, and what its purpose is. Even if we accept Book 1 as an integral, specially-composed part of the dialogue (see above, pp. 4–5) we still need to pose the question of why Plato wished to hark back, as it were, to a form of argument which had been largely abandoned, the *elenchus,* and rely on a basic assumption, the craft-analogy, which, he clearly found, was inadequate to counter the kind of arguments deployed by Thrasymachus, especially when refined by Glaucon and Adeimantus. To quote Reeve: '...far from being a straight Socratic dialogue, Book 1 contains the anti-Socratic arguments which led Plato to see the need for the new departure in moral theory ...which occupies the remaining nine books of his *Republic*.'[51] This seems to imply that for Plato the composition of *Republic* was in itself an ongoing, almost dialectical, process, in which the composer himself came to realise, in the course of his writing, the inadequacy of the traditional Socratic arguments. But there is also a tension in Socrates' Book 1 arguments, especially the later ones, between their immediate, unsatisfactory, presentation, and their significance in what would turn out to be an entirely new context, foreshadowing the direction of the main body of the dialogue.

'Setting the stage' is, where Plato is concerned, never simply metaphor. We need to remember the all-pervasive nature of Plato's inherent dramatic sense. Whatever his philosophical journey may have been in reality (and how can we ever know this?), he is perhaps here deliberately dramatising this journey in Book 1 (and to a lesser extent in Book 2) as a breakdown of much of the old Socratic edifice through the dramatic failure of his main character, Socrates, to convince his main opponent, Thrasymachus, of the truth of what he asserts. The latter is not an independent arguer (as many

---

[51] Reeve (1985) 263.

philosophical assessments almost seem to imply); Plato is pulling all the strings, so that a successful or even partially successful Thrasymachus (not to mention Glaucon and Adeimantus) implies that Plato wishes to present himself ultimately as not really having convinced himself of the truth of the Socratic position, and as needing to move on. And the breakdown is not just in the arguments. As will be demonstrated in detail in the Commentary, Plato is concerned, through Socrates' interlocutors, to parade the evidence of popular culture as part of the world he needs to sweep away before he can successfully build his own Utopia.

So, true to Plato's dramatic instincts, the decisive movement from the persona of '*elenchus* Socrates' to 'dialectical Socrates', which occurs right at the end of the part of *Republic* with which we are here concerned, is dramatically presented as originating from a spontaneous and unexpected prolongation arising out of the failure of the discussion (357a1), just as *Republic* taken as a whole imperceptibly outgrows by far the framework of the social event within which the dialogue is placed, the Bendis festival in the Piraeus. A relatively swift discussion followed by dinner and a post-prandial walk-about to converse further with young men and view the festival is what Polemarchus has promised at 328a7–9, and what, presumably, the habitués of Socrates' usual conversations are expecting; but this is all forgotten in the broad development of Plato's larger structure. We may suppose that Socrates never does get his dinner or promenade, and, in any case, Plato's grand design far outgrows such a plan.

7. The text of this edition

The text reproduced here is S. Slings' Oxford text of 2003. Slings' very full critical apparatus is not included; my own brief apparatus, in the preparation of which I have consulted Slings and a number of other editions, in particular the earlier Oxford text of Burnet (1902), is confined only to occasions where a divergence in textual reading affects the meaning or interpretation of the Greek, or where I consider that Slings' choice of reading requires comment. On the very few occasions where a significant issue of interpretation is at stake I have included an explanatory note in the Commentary.

The following MSS of *Republic* will be found in the apparatus: A (Parisinus Graecus 1807, 9th century A.D.), with marginal additions; D (Marcianus Graecus 185, coll. 576, c.12th century A.D.); F (Vindobonensis, suppl. gr. 39, late 13th–14th centuries A.D.). In addition there are testimonia from ancient authors of the early centuries A.D. who quote from and comment on *Republic*: Justinus (2nd century), Eusebius (3rd–4th centuries), Proclus (5th century), Stobaeus (5th century), and Cyrillus (5th century). I have also included, where appropriate, modern editorial conjectures. For fuller details, see the *Praefatio* of Slings (2003) pp. vii–xxiii, and for the definitive modern discussion of the textual tradition of *Republic,* see Boter (1989).

BIBLIOGRAPHY

Texts, commentaries and translations of Republic

Adam, J., (1963) *The Republic of Plato*, (2 vols.) 2nd ed. revised with introduction by D.A. Rees, (1st ed. 1902), Cambridge, Cambridge University Press.

Allan, D.J., (1977) *Plato: Republic Book I*, 2nd ed. (1st ed. 1940), London, Methuen.

Bloom, A., (1968) *The Republic of Plato*: translated with notes and interpretative essay, New York, Basic Books.

Burnet, J., (1902) *Platonis Respublica*, Oxford, Oxford University Press (Oxford Classical Text).

Chambry, E., (1947) *Platon, La République I–III* edited with French translation, and Introduction by A. Diès (Platon: Oeuvres Complètes, vol. 6), Paris, Budé, Les Belles Lettres.

Cornford, F.M., (1941) *The Republic of Plato*, translated with introduction and notes, Oxford, Oxford University Press.

Grube, G.M.A., (1992) *Plato, Republic*, translation, revised by C.D.C. Reeve, Indianapolis, Hackett.

Hermann, C.F., (1893) *Plato. Politeia*, Leipzig, Teubner (Plato Series Vol. IV).

Jowett, B. and Campbell, L., (1894) *Plato, Republic*, edited with notes and essays (3 vols.), Oxford, Oxford University Press.

Lee, D., (1987) *Plato: The Republic*, translated with introduction and notes, 2nd rev. ed. Harmondsworth, Penguin Books.

Moors, K.F., (1981) *Glaucon and Adeimantus on Justice. The Structure of Argument in Book 2 of Plato's Republic*, Washington, University Press of America (a philosophical commentary on Book 2 up to 368c).

Reeve, C.D.C., (2004) *Plato: Republic*, translated from the new standard Greek text, with introduction, Indianapolis, Hackett.

Shorey, P., (1937) *Plato, The Republic*, (2 vols., Loeb edition) Cambridge MA/ London, Harvard University Press.

Slings, S. (2003) *Platonis Respublica*, Oxford, Oxford University Press (new Oxford Classical Text).

Vegetti, M., (1994–5) *La Repubblica: Libri I & II–III* (2 vols.), traduzione e commento, a cura di M.V. (Elenchos: Collana di testi e studi sul pensiero antico, diretta da Gabriele Giannantoni, XXVIII–1&2) Pavia, Bibliopolis.

Waterfield, R., (1993) *Plato, Republic*, (including *Cleitophon*) translated with introduction and notes, Oxford, Oxford University Press (Oxford World's Classics).

Texts, translations and collections of other ancient sources (confined to those given more than a passing mention in the Commentary)

Aeschylus (1956) *Tragedies* (2 vols.) ed. D. Grene and R. Lattimore, Chicago/ London, University of Chicago Press.

Aristotle (1984) *The Complete Works of Aristotle: the Revised Oxford Translation* (2 vols.) ed. J. Barnes, Princeton, New Jersey, Princeton University Press.

Aristophanes (1993) *Plays: Two; (Wasps, Clouds, Birds, Festival Time, Frogs),* translated by K. McLeish, London, Methuen.

Cicero (1999) *Letters to his Friends,* (3 vols., Loeb edition), edited and translated by D.R. Shackleton Bailey, Cambridge MA/London, Harvard University Press.

Die Fragmente der Vorsokratiker (1961) edited and translated by H. Diels and W. Kranz (3 vols.) 7th ed., Berlin, Weidmannsche Verlagsbuchhandlung.

Diogenes Laertius (1925) *Lives of Eminent Philosophers,* (2 vols., Loeb edition) edited and translated by R.D. Hicks, Cambridge MA/London, Harvard University Press.

Greek Elegiac Poetry: 7th–5th Centuries (1999) (Loeb edition) edited and translated by D.E. Gerber, Cambridge MA/London, Harvard University Press.

Greek Iambic Poetry: 7th–5th Centuries (1999) (Loeb edition) edited and translated by D.E.Gerber, Cambridge MA/London, Harvard University Press.

Greek Lyric Poetry (1991) (Loeb edition, 5 vols.), edited and translated by D.A. Campbell, Cambridge MA/London, Harvard University Press.

Herodotus (1954) *The Histories,* translated by A de Sélincourt, revised with introduction and notes (2003) by J. Marincola, Harmondsworth, Penguin Books.

Hesiod (1973) *Works and Days,* translated by D.S. Wender, in *Hesiod and Theognis,*. Harmondsworth, Penguin Books, pp. 59–86

Homer (1951) *The Iliad,* translated with an introduction by R. Lattimore, Chicago/ London, Chicago University Press.

Homer (1965) *The Odyssey,* translated with an introduction by R. Lattimore, New York, Harper Collins.

Lysias (2000) *Against Eratosthenes,* translated by S.C. Todd, in *Oratory of Classical Greece,* edited by M. Gagarin, Austin, Texas, University of Texas Press, pp. 113–136.

Pindar (1947) *Pindari Carmina cum Fragmentis,* 2nd ed., edited by C.M. Bowra, Oxford, Oxford University Press (Oxford Classical Text).

Plato (1961) *The Complete Dialogues of Plato,* edited by E. Hamilton and H. Cairns, New Jersey, Princeton University Press.

Plato (2004) *Gorgias,* translated by W. Hamilton, revised with introduction, commentary and notes by C. Emlyn-Jones, Harmondsworth, Penguin Books.

Plato (1973) *Seventh Letter,* translated by W. Hamilton in *Phaedrus and Letters VII & VIII,* Harmondsworth, Penguin Books.

Plato (1987) *Theaetetus,* translated with an essay, by R. Waterfield, Harmondsworth, Penguin Books.

Scholia Platonica (1938) edited by W.C. Greene (Philological Monographs, 8), Haverford, Pennsylvania, American Philological Society.

The First Philosophers: the Presocratics and the Sophists (2000) translated with commentary by R. Waterfield, Oxford, Oxford University Press (Oxford World's Classics).

Theognis (1973) *Elegies,* translated by D.S. Wender, in *Hesiod and Theognis,* Harmondsworth, Penguin Books, pp. 97–147.

Thucydides (1972) *History of the Peloponnesian War,* translated by R. Warner, with an introduction and notes, by M.I. Finley, Harmondsworth, Penguin Books.

Xenophon (1923) *Memorabilia,* translated by O.J. Todd (in *Xenophon,* 7 vols. Loeb Edition), Cambridge MA/London, Harvard University Press, vol. 4, pp. 1–359.

Pseudo-Xenophon (2004) *Constitution of the Athenians (The 'Old Oligarch')* introduction, translation and commentary by R. Osborne, Lactor 2, 2nd ed. London, London Association of Classical Teachers.

Modern scholarship

Adkins, A.W.H., (1960) *Merit and Responsibility: a Study in Greek Values,* Oxford, Oxford University Press.

Algra, K.A., (1996) 'Observations on Plato's Thrasymachus: the case for *pleonexia*', in *Polyhistor: Studies in the History and Historiography of Ancient Philosophy,* eds. K.A. Algra, P.W. van der Horst, and D.T. Runia, Leiden, Brill, 41–60.

Allen, R.E., (1987) 'The speech of Glaucon in Plato's Republic', *Journal of the History of Philosophy* 25, 3–11.

Allen, R.E., (1987) 'The speech of Glaucon: on contract and the common good' in *Justice, Law and Method in Plato and Aristotle,* ed. S. Panagiotou, Edmonton, Academic Print Publications, 51–62.

Annas, J., (1981) *An Introduction to Plato's Republic,* Oxford, Oxford University Press.

Aune, B., (1997) 'The unity of Plato's *Republic*', *Ancient Philosophy* 17, 291–308.

Ausland, H.W., (2003) 'Socrates' argumentative burden in the *Republic*', in *Plato as author: the Rhetoric of Philosophy,* ed. A.N. Michelini, Leiden, Brill, 123–43.

Barnes, J., (1991) 'The Hellenistic Plato', *Apeiron* 23, 115–128.

Beatty, J., (1979) 'Justice as dialectic in *Republic* 1', *Southern Journal of Philosophy* 17, 3–17.

Beversluis, J., (2000) *Cross-examining Socrates: a Defense of the Interlocutors in Plato's Early Dialogues,* Cambridge, Cambridge University Press.

Blondell, R., (2003) *The Play of Character in Plato's Dialogues,* Cambridge, Cambridge University Press.

Boter, G.J., (1986) 'Thrasymachus and *pleonexia*', *Mnemosyne* 39, 261–81.

Boter, G.J., (1989) *The Textual Tradition of Plato's Republic* (*Mnemosyne* Suppl. 107) Leiden, Brill.

Brandwood, L., (1990) *The Chronology of Plato's Dialogues,* Cambridge, Cambridge University Press.

Burnyeat, M., (1997) 'First words: a valedictory lecture', *Proceedings of the Cambridge Philological Society,* 43, 1–19.

Buxton, R.G.A., (1982) *Persuasion in Greek Tragedy: a Study of Peitho,* Cambridge, Cambridge University Press.

Cartledge, P., (1997) '"Deep plays": theatre as process in Greek civic life', in *The Cambridge Companion to Greek Tragedy,* ed. P.E. Easterling, Cambridge, Cambridge University Press, 3–35.

Chappell, T.D.J., (1993) 'The virtues of Thrasymachus', *Phronesis* 38, 1–17.

Cross, R.C. and Woozley, A.D., (1964) *Plato's Republic: a Philosophical Commentary,* London, Macmillan.

Davies, J.K., (1971) *Athenian Propertied Families, 600–300 B.C.,* Oxford, Oxford University Press.

Denniston, J.D., (1950) *The Greek Particles,* 2nd ed., Oxford, Oxford University Press.

Dover, K.J., (1978) *Greek Homosexuality,* Cambridge MA, Harvard University Press.

Dover, K.J., (1994) *Greek Popular Morality in the Time of Plato and Aristotle,* 2nd ed., Indianapolis, Hackett.

Edelstein, L., (1966) *Plato's Seventh Letter,* (Philosophia Antiqua vol. 4) Leiden, Brill.

Everson, S., (1998) 'The incoherence of Thrasymachus', *Oxford Studies in Ancient Philosophy* 16, 99–131.

Finley, M.I., (1985) 'Athenian Demagogues', in *Democracy Ancient and Modern,* 2nd ed., London, Hogarth Press, 38–75.

Geach, P.T., (1966) 'Plato's *Euthyphro:* an analysis and commentary', *Monist* 50, 369–82.

Giannantoni, G., (1959) 'Il primo libro della "Repubblica" di Platone', *Rivista Critica di Storia della Filosofia* 12, 123–45.

Gifford, M., (2001) 'Dramatic dialectic in *Republic* Book 1', *Oxford Studies in Ancient Philosophy* 19, 35–106.

Guthrie, W.K.C., (1969) *A History of Greek Philosophy,* Vol. III (*The Fifth Century Enlightenment*), Cambridge, Cambridge University Press.

Guthrie, W.K.C., (1975) *A History of Greek Philosophy,* Vol. IV (*Plato, the Man and his Dialogues: Earlier Period*). Cambridge, Cambridge University Press.

Harrison, E.L., (1967) 'Plato's manipulation of Thrasymachus', *Phoenix* 21, 27–39.

Henderson, T.Y., (1970) 'In defense of Thrasymachus', *American Philosophical Quarterly* 7, 218–28.

Hollander, R., (1983) 'The golden ring of Gyges', *Eos* 71, 211–13.

Hourani, G., (1962) 'Thrasymachus' definition of justice in Plato's *Republic*', *Phronesis* 7, 110–20.

Hyland, D.A., (1988) '*Republic* 2 and the origins of political philosophy', *Interpretation* 16, 247–61.

Inwood, B., (1987) 'Professor Stokes on Adeimantus in the *Republic*' (for details see below under 'Stokes') 97–103.

Irwin, T., (1995) *Plato's Ethics,* Oxford/New York, Oxford University Press.

Irwin, T., (1999) '*Republic* 2: Questions about justice', in *Plato 2: Ethics, Politics, Religion and the Soul (Oxford Readings in Philosophy),* ed. G. Fine, Oxford, Oxford University Press, 164–85.

Jeffery, A., (1979) 'Polemarchus and Socrates on justice and harm', *Phronesis* 24, 54–69.

Johnson, C., (1985) 'Thrasymachean justice: the advantage of the stronger', *Durham University Journal* N.S. 21, 37–49.

Joseph, H.W.B., (1935) *Essays in Ancient and Modern Philosophy,* Oxford, Oxford University Press.

Kahn, C.H., (1993) 'Proleptic composition in the *Republic,* or why Book I was never a separate dialogue', *Classical Quarterly* 43, 131–142.

Kahn, C.H., (1996) *Plato and the Socratic Dialogue: the Philosophical Use of a Literary Form,* Cambridge, Cambridge University Press.

Kerferd, G., (1947) 'The doctrine of Thrasymachus in Plato's *Republic*', *Durham University Journal* 40, 19–27.

Kerferd, G., (1964) 'Thrasymachus and justice: a reply to G. Hourani', *Phronesis* 9, 12–16.

Kerferd, G., (1981) *The Sophistic Movement,* Cambridge, Cambridge University Press.

Kirwan, C., (1965) 'Glaucon's Challenge', *Phronesis* 10, 162–73.

Kraut, R., (1992) 'The defense of justice in Plato's *Republic*', in *The Cambridge Companion to Plato,* ed. R. Kraut, Cambridge, Cambridge University Press, 311–37.

Laird, A., (2001) 'Ringing the changes on Gyges: philosophy and the formation of fiction in Plato's *Republic*' *Journal of Hellenic Studies* 121, 12–29.

Lycos, K., (1987) *Plato on Justice and Power; Reading Book I of Plato's Republic,* London, Macmillan.

MacDowell, D.M., (1978) *The Law in Classical Athens,* London, Thames and Hudson.

March, J.R., (1998) *Dictionary of Classical Mythology,* London, Cassell.

Michelini, A.N., (2003) 'Plato's Socratic mask', in *Plato as Author: the Rhetoric of Philosophy,* ed. A.N. Michelini, Leiden, Brill, 45–65.

Murray, P., (1996) *Plato on Poetry,* Cambridge, Cambridge University Press (Cambridge Greek and Latin Classics).

Nails, D., (2002) *The People of Plato: a Prosopography of Plato and other Socratics,* Indianapolis/Cambridge, Hackett.

Nicholson, P.P., (1974) 'Unravelling Thrasymachus' arguments in the *Republic*', *Phronesis* 19, 210–32.

Nightingale, A.W., (1995) *Genres in Dialogue: Plato and the Construct of Philosophy,* Cambridge, Cambridge University Press.

Ober, J., (1998) *Political Dissent in Democratic Athens: Intellectual Critics of Popular Rule,* Princeton, New Jersey, Princeton University Press.

Osborne, R., (1988) 'Death revisited; death revised. The death of the artist in archaic and classical Greece', *Art History* 11, 1–16.

Osborne, R., (1990) 'Vexatious litigation in Classical Athens: sykophancy and the sykophant', in *Nomos: Essays in Athenian Law, Politics and Society,* eds. P. Cartledge, P. Millet, and S.C. Todd, Cambridge, Cambridge University Press, 83–102.

Parker, R., (1996) *Athenian Religion,* Oxford, Oxford University Press.

Quincy, J.H., (1981) 'Another purpose for Plato *Republic* 1', *Hermes* 109, 300–15.

Reeve, C.D.C., (1985) 'Socrates meets Thrasymachus', *Archiv der Geschichte der Philosophie* 67, 246–65.

Reeve, C.D.C., (1988) *Philosopher Kings: the Argument of Plato's* Republic, Princeton, New Jersey, Princeton University Press.

Reynolds, L.D. and Wilson, N.G., (1968) *Scribes and Scholars: a Guide to the Transmission of Greek and Latin Literature,* Oxford, Oxford University Press.

Rosen, S., (2005) *Plato's* Republic: *a Study,* New Haven, Yale University Press.

Rowe, C.J. and Schofield, M., (2000) *Greek and Roman Political Thought,* Cambridge, Cambridge University Press.

Rutherford, R., (1995) *The Art of Plato,* London, Duckworth.

Sayers, S., (1999) *Plato's Republic,* Edinburgh, Edinburgh University Press.

Schleiermacher, F.E.D., (1973) *Introduction to the Dialogues of Plato,* translated by W. Dobson (1st ed. 1804), New York, Arno Press.

Slings, S.R., (1988) 'Critical notes on Plato's *Politeia:* I.' *Mnemosyne* 41, 276–98.

Slings, S.R., (1989) 'Critical notes on Plato's *Politeia:* II' *Mnemosyne* 42, 380–97.

Slings, S.R., (1990) 'Critical notes on Plato's *Politeia:* III' *Mnemosyne* 43, 341–63.

Slings, S.R., (1999) *Plato Cleitophon: edited. with introduction, translation and commentary,* Cambridge, Cambridge University Press.

Smith, K.F., (1902) 'The tale of Gyges and the king of Lydia.' *American Journal of Philology* 23, 361–87.

Stokes, M.C., (1987) 'Adeimantus in the *Republic*', in *Justice, Law and Method in Plato and Aristotle,* ed. S. Panagiotou, Edmonton, Academic Print Publications, 67–96.

Thesleff, H., (1982) *Studies in Platonic Chronology,* Helsinki, Commentationes Humanarum Litterarum 70, Societas Scientarum Fennica.

Vlastos, G., (1983) 'The Socratic elenchus', *Oxford Studies in Ancient Philosophy* 1, 27–58.

Vlastos, G., (1991) *Socrates: Ironist and Moral Philosopher,* Cambridge, Cambridge University Press.

White, S.A., (1995) 'Thrasymachus the diplomat', *Classical Philology* 90, 307–27.

Williams, B., (1999) 'The analogy of city and soul in Plato's *Republic*', in *Plato 2: Ethics, Politics, Religion and the Soul (Oxford Readings in Philosophy),* ed. G. Fine, Oxford, Oxford University Press.

Wilson, J.R.S., (1995) 'Thrasymachus and the *thumos*: a further case of prolepsis in *Republic* 1', *Classical Quarterly* 45, 58–67.

Young, C.M., (1980) 'Polemarchus' and Thrasymachus' definition of justice', *Philosophical Enquiry* 2, 404–419.

CHRONOLOGY OF PLATO'S LIFE AND WORKS

The chronology, and many of the events of Plato's life, as well as the dates and order of composition of his dialogues, cannot be established with any certainty and are still a matter of lively debate; the following represents a general, but not universal, consensus. (For differing approaches to questions of the chronology of Plato's dialogues, see *e.g.* Vlastos (1991), Brandwood, Thesleff.) Works of disputed authorship have not been included.

*c.***429**   Birth of Plato, from an old and wealthy Athenian family.

404   Defeat of Athens in the war with Sparta (the Peloponnesian War).

403   The rule of a right-wing junta in Athens (the 'Thirty Tyrants'), involving Plato's relatives, followed by the restoration of democracy.

399   The trial, condemnation and execution of Socrates on a charge of 'not acknowledging the gods which the city acknowledges, but introducing new divinities and corrupting the youth'.

390's–early 80's   Following the death of Socrates, Plato and other followers of Socrates withdraw from Athens to the nearby city of Megara. Plato travels extensively.
Composition of the short Early Period dialogues: *Apology, Crito, Charmides, Euthyphro, Hippias Minor, Ion, Laches, Lysis.*

389/8   Plato visits Italy and Sicily, probably in order to make contact with Pythagorean philosophers.

*c.***387**   Plato founds the Academy on the site of the shrine of the hero Academus in the north-west district of Athens.

380s   The later Early Period dialogues ('transitional'): *Gorgias, Menexenus, Protagoras*

late 380s   The Middle Period dialogues: *Cratylus, Euthydemus, Meno, Phaedo.*

370s   The later Middle period dialogues: *Parmenides, Phaedrus, Symposium, Republic, Theaetetus.*

367   Plato visits Sicily for a second time at the invitation of Dion, uncle of the young Dionysius, ruler of Syracuse, possibly in the hope of influencing the government of the city. The attempt is unsuccessful. Aristotle joins the Academy.

360s–50s   The Late Period dialogues: *Critias, Philebus, Sophist, Statesman, Timaeus.*

361   Final visit to Sicily, ending again in failure to influence Dionysius.

late 350s Final dialogue: *Laws.*

347   Death of Plato.

PLATO

REPUBLIC
1–2.368c4

ΣΩΚΡΑΤΗΣ

p. 327

a Κατέβην χθὲς εἰς Πειραιᾶ μετὰ Γλαύκωνος τοῦ Ἀρίστωνος προσευξόμενός τε τῇ θεῷ καὶ ἅμα τὴν ἑορτὴν
βουλόμενος θεάσασθαι τίνα τρόπον ποιήσουσιν ἅτε νῦν
πρῶτον ἄγοντες. καλὴ μὲν οὖν μοι καὶ ἡ τῶν ἐπιχωρίων
5 πομπὴ ἔδοξεν εἶναι, οὐ μέντοι ἧττον ἐφαίνετο πρέπειν ἣν οἱ
b Θρᾷκες ἔπεμπον. προσευξάμενοι δὲ καὶ θεωρήσαντες ἀπῇμεν
πρὸς τὸ ἄστυ. κατιδὼν οὖν πόρρωθεν ἡμᾶς οἴκαδε ὡρμημέ-
νους Πολέμαρχος ὁ Κεφάλου ἐκέλευσε δραμόντα τὸν παῖδα
περιμεῖναί ἑ κελεῦσαι. καί μου ὄπισθεν ὁ παῖς λαβόμενος τοῦ
5 ἱματίου, Κελεύει ὑμᾶς, ἔφη, Πολέμαρχος περιμεῖναι. καὶ ἐγὼ
μετεστράφην τε καὶ ἠρόμην ὅπου αὐτὸς εἴη. Οὗτος, ἔφη,
ὄπισθεν προσέρχεται· ἀλλὰ περιμένετε. Ἀλλὰ περιμενοῦμεν,
ἦ δ᾽ ὃς ὁ Γλαύκων.

c Καὶ ὀλίγῳ ὕστερον ὅ τε Πολέμαρχος ἧκε καὶ Ἀδείμαντος ὁ
τοῦ Γλαύκωνος ἀδελφὸς καὶ Νικήρατος ὁ Νικίου καὶ ἄλλοι
τινὲς ὡς ἀπὸ τῆς πομπῆς.
Ὁ οὖν Πολέμαρχος ἔφη· Ὦ Σώκρατες, δοκεῖτέ μοι πρὸς
5 ἄστυ ὡρμῆσθαι ὡς ἀπιόντες.
Οὐ γὰρ κακῶς δοξάζεις, ἦν δ᾽ ἐγώ.
Ὁρᾷς οὖν ἡμᾶς, ἔφη, ὅσοι ἐσμέν;
Πῶς γὰρ οὔ;
Ἢ τοίνυν τούτων, ἔφη, κρείττους γένεσθε ἢ μένετ᾽ αὐτοῦ.
10 Οὐκοῦν, ἦν δ᾽ ἐγώ, ἔτι ἐλλείπεται τὸ ἢν πείσωμεν ὑμᾶς ὡς
χρὴ ἡμᾶς ἀφεῖναι;
Ἦ καὶ δύναισθ᾽ ἄν, ἦ δ᾽ ὅς, πεῖσαι μὴ ἀκούοντας;
Οὐδαμῶς, ἔφη ὁ Γλαύκων.
Ὡς τοίνυν μὴ ἀκουσομένων, οὕτω διανοεῖσθε.
328 Καὶ ὁ Ἀδείμαντος, Ἆρά γε, ἦ δ᾽ ὅς, οὐδ᾽ ἴστε ὅτι λαμπὰς
ἔσται πρὸς ἑσπέραν ἀφ᾽ ἵππων τῇ θεῷ;
Ἀφ᾽ ἵππων; ἦν δ᾽ ἐγώ· καινόν γε τοῦτο. λαμπάδια ἔχοντες

327c10 ἐλλείπεται ADF: ἐν λείπεται A in margine

BOOK 1

SOCRATES

327

Yesterday I went down to the Piraeus with Glaucon the son of Ariston, to offer my prayers to the goddess and also because I wanted to view the festival and see how they would conduct it, seeing that this was the first time they were holding it. I must say that I thought that the local procession was fine, [a5] but the show put on by the Thracian contingent seemed in no way inferior. When we had said our prayers and viewed the spectacle we started back to town. [b1] Now, as we were heading homeward, Polemarchus the son of Cephalus caught sight of us from a distance and ordered his slave to run on and tell us to wait for him. And the slave caught hold of my cloak from behind and said 'Polemarchus tells you to wait'. [b5] So I turned round and asked where he was. 'There he is', he said, 'behind you, coming this way; do wait'. 'All right, we will' said Glaucon.

[c1] And shortly afterwards Polemarchus came up, and Adeimantus, Glaucon's brother, and Niceratus, the son of Nicias, and some others apparently from the procession.

Then Polemarchus said: 'Socrates, you appear to me to be leaving us and heading back to town.' [c5]

'Yes, that's not a bad guess', I said.

'Do you see how many of us there are?' he asked.

'Of course.'

'Well then', he said 'either prove yourselves stronger than these people, or remain here'.

[c10] 'Yes, but isn't there still the alternative', I said, 'for us to persuade you that you ought to let us go'.

'Would you really have any success', he said, 'in persuading those who refuse to listen?'

'No', said Glaucon, 'we certainly wouldn't'.

'Well then, you'd better face the fact that we won't listen'.

328 'Are you telling us that you don't know' added Adeimantus, 'that there is to be a torch race on horseback this evening in honour of the goddess?'

'On horseback?' I said; 'that really is something new. Will they carry the

διαδώσουσιν ἀλλήλοις ἁμιλλώμενοι τοῖς ἵπποις; ἢ πῶς
5 λέγεις;

Οὕτως, ἔφη ὁ Πολέμαρχος. καὶ πρός γε παννυχίδα
ποιήσουσιν, ἣν ἄξιον θεάσασθαι· ἐξαναστησόμεθα γὰρ μετὰ
τὸ δεῖπνον καὶ τὴν παννυχίδα θεασόμεθα. καὶ συνεσόμεθά τε
πολλοῖς τῶν νέων αὐτόθι καὶ διαλεξόμεθα. ἀλλὰ μένετε καὶ
b μὴ ἄλλως ποιεῖτε.

Καὶ ὁ Γλαύκων, Ἔοικεν, ἔφη, μενετέον εἶναι.

Ἀλλ' εἰ δοκεῖ, ἦν δ' ἐγώ, οὕτω χρὴ ποιεῖν.

Ἦμεν οὖν οἴκαδε εἰς τοῦ Πολεμάρχου, καὶ Λυσίαν τε
5 αὐτόθι κατελάβομεν καὶ Εὐθύδημον, τοὺς τοῦ Πολεμάρχου
ἀδελφούς, καὶ δὴ καὶ Θρασύμαχον τὸν Καλχηδόνιον καὶ
Χαρμαντίδην τὸν Παιανιᾶ καὶ Κλειτοφῶντα τὸν Ἀριστωνύ-
μου. ἦν δ' ἔνδον καὶ ὁ πατὴρ ὁ τοῦ Πολεμάρχου Κέφαλος καὶ
c μάλα πρεσβύτης μοι ἔδοξεν εἶναι· διὰ χρόνου γὰρ καὶ ἑωράκη
αὐτόν. καθῆστο δὲ ἐστεφανωμένος ἐπί τινος προσκεφαλαίου
τε καὶ δίφρου· τεθυκὼς γὰρ ἐτύγχανεν ἐν τῇ αὐλῇ. ἐκαθεζό-
μεθα οὖν παρ' αὐτόν· ἔκειντο γὰρ δίφροι τινὲς αὐτόθι κύκλῳ.

5 Εὐθὺς οὖν με ἰδὼν ὁ Κέφαλος ἠσπάζετό τε καὶ εἶπεν· Ὦ
Σώκρατες, οὐδὲ θαμίζεις ἡμῖν καταβαίνων εἰς τὸν Πειραιᾶ.
χρῆν μέντοι. εἰ μὲν γὰρ ἐγὼ ἔτι ἐν δυνάμει ἦ τοῦ ῥᾳδίως
d πορεύεσθαι πρὸς τὸ ἄστυ, οὐδὲν ἂν σὲ ἔδει δεῦρο ἰέναι, ἀλλ'
ἡμεῖς ἂν παρὰ σὲ ἦμεν· νῦν δέ σε χρὴ πυκνότερον δεῦρο ἰέναι.
ὡς εὖ ἴσθι ὅτι ἔμοιγε ὅσον αἱ ἄλλαι αἱ κατὰ τὸ σῶμα ἡδοναὶ
ἀπομαραίνονται, τοσοῦτον αὔξονται αἱ περὶ τοὺς λόγους
5 ἐπιθυμίαι τε καὶ ἡδοναί. μὴ οὖν ἄλλως ποίει, ἀλλὰ τοῖσδέ
τε τοῖς νεανίσκοις σύνισθι καὶ δεῦρο παρ' ἡμᾶς φοίτα ὡς παρὰ
φίλους τε καὶ πάνυ οἰκείους.

Καὶ μήν, ἦν δ' ἐγώ, ὦ Κέφαλε, χαίρω γε διαλεγόμενος τοῖς
e σφόδρα πρεσβύταις· δοκεῖ γάρ μοι χρῆναι παρ' αὐτῶν
πυνθάνεσθαι, ὥσπερ τινὰ ὁδὸν προεληλυθότων ἣν καὶ ἡμᾶς
ἴσως δεήσει πορεύεσθαι, ποία τίς ἐστιν, τραχεῖα καὶ χαλεπή,
ἢ ῥᾳδία καὶ εὔπορος. καὶ δὴ καὶ σοῦ ἡδέως ἂν πυθοίμην ὅτι
5 σοι φαίνεται τοῦτο, ἐπειδὴ ἐνταῦθα ἤδη εἶ τῆς ἡλικίας ὃ δὴ
ἐπὶ γήραος οὐδῷ φασιν εἶναι οἱ ποιηταί, πότερον
χαλεπὸν τοῦ βίου, ἢ πῶς σὺ αὐτὸ ἐξαγγέλλεις.

329 Ἐγώ σοι, ἔφη, νὴ τὸν Δία ἐρῶ, ὦ Σώκρατες, οἷόν γέ μοι

328c6   οὐδὲ ADF: οὐ δὲ Jowett-Campbell: οὔτι Ast

328d8   γε D Stobaeus: τε F: om. A

328a4

torches as they race on horseback and hand them on to each other? Or how do you mean?' [a5]

'Exactly that', said Polemarchus, 'and, besides, they are going to hold an all-night festival, which will be worth watching. After dinner we will get up and go out and view the festival; we shall meet a lot of young men there and converse. Do stay and don't refuse us.' [b1]

'It looks as if we shall have to stay', replied Glaucon.

'Well, if that's what you decide', I said, 'that's what we must do'.

So we went to Polemarchus' house, and there we found Lysias and Euthydemus, the brothers of Polemarchus, [b5] and besides them Thrasymachus of Chalcedon, Charmantides of the deme Paeania and Cleitophon, son of Aristonymus. Polemarchus' father, Cephalus, was there too – and quite an old man he looked to me, for, you see, it was a long time since I had last seen him. [c1] He was sitting on a sort of chair with a cushion, his head crowned with a wreath, for he had been offering a sacrifice in the courtyard. So we sat down beside him, for there were some seats there placed in a circle.

[c5] Immediately he saw me Cephalus welcomed me and said: 'You don't often come down to see us in the Piraeus, Socrates. Yet you ought to. For if I were still strong enough to make the journey up to town easily, you would have no need to come here, but we would come to you. [d1] But as it is, you should make your visits more frequent; for I would have you know that, for my part, the more the pleasures of the body wither away, the more my desire for conversation and my pleasure in it increase. [d5] So don't refuse, but come and mix with these lads here and make yourself at home here with us as you would with very close and dear friends.'

'Yes indeed, Cephalus', I said, 'I do enjoy talking to very old men; [e1] for I think we ought to learn from them, as it were from travellers who have gone before us on a road which we too will perhaps have to tread – what it is like, rough and difficult or easy and accommodating. I would gladly learn from you in particular how you find it, since you are now at that point in your life [e5] which the poets say is "on the threshold of old age": is it a difficult time of life, or what report do you give of it?'

329 'By Zeus', he said, 'I'll tell you how I feel about it, Socrates. For some of

φαίνεται. πολλάκις γὰρ συνερχόμεθά τινες εἰς ταὐτὸν παρα-
πλησίαν ἡλικίαν ἔχοντες, διασῴζοντες τὴν παλαιὰν παροι-
μίαν. οἱ οὖν πλεῖστοι ἡμῶν ὀλοφύρονται συνιόντες, τὰς ἐν τῇ
5 νεότητι ἡδονὰς ποθοῦντες καὶ ἀναμιμνῃσκόμενοι περί τε
τἀφροδίσια καὶ περὶ πότους τε καὶ εὐωχίας καὶ ἄλλ' ἄττα ἃ
τῶν τοιούτων ἔχεται, καὶ ἀγανακτοῦσιν ὡς μεγάλων τινῶν
ἀπεστερημένοι καὶ τότε μὲν εὖ ζῶντες, νῦν δὲ οὐδὲ ζῶντες.
b ἔνιοι δὲ καὶ τὰς τῶν οἰκείων προπηλακίσεις τοῦ γήρως
ὀδύρονται, καὶ ἐπὶ τούτῳ δὴ τὸ γῆρας ὑμνοῦσιν ὅσων
κακῶν σφίσιν αἴτιον. ἐμοὶ δὲ δοκοῦσιν, ὦ Σώκρατες, οὗτοι
οὐ τὸ αἴτιον αἰτιᾶσθαι. εἰ γὰρ ἦν τοῦτο αἴτιον, κἂν ἐγὼ τὰ
5 αὐτὰ ταῦτα ἐπεπόνθη, ἕνεκά γε γήρως, καὶ οἱ ἄλλοι πάντες
ὅσοι ἐνταῦθα ἦλθον ἡλικίας. νῦν δ' ἔγωγε ἤδη ἐντετύχηκα οὐχ
οὕτως ἔχουσιν καὶ ἄλλοις, καὶ δὴ καὶ Σοφοκλεῖ ποτε τῷ
ποιητῇ παρεγενόμην ἐρωτωμένῳ ὑπό τινος· "Πῶς," ἔφη, "ὦ
c Σοφόκλεις, ἔχεις πρὸς τἀφροδίσια; ἔτι οἷός τε εἶ γυναικὶ
συγγίγνεσθαι"; καὶ ὅς, "Εὐφήμει," ἔφη, "ὦ ἄνθρωπε· ἀσμε-
νέστατα μέντοι αὐτὸ ἀπέφυγον, ὥσπερ λυττῶντά τινα καὶ
ἄγριον δεσπότην ἀποφυγών." εὖ οὖν μοι καὶ τότε ἔδοξεν
5 ἐκεῖνος εἰπεῖν, καὶ νῦν οὐχ ἧττον. παντάπασι γὰρ τῶν γε
τοιούτων ἐν τῷ γήρᾳ πολλὴ εἰρήνη γίγνεται καὶ ἐλευθερία·
ἐπειδὰν αἱ ἐπιθυμίαι παύσωνται κατατείνουσαι καὶ χαλάσω-
d σιν, παντάπασιν τὸ τοῦ Σοφοκλέους γίγνεται, δεσποτῶν πάνυ
πολλῶν ἐστι καὶ μαινομένων ἀπηλλάχθαι. ἀλλὰ καὶ τούτων
πέρι καὶ τῶν γε πρὸς τοὺς οἰκείους μία τις αἰτία ἐστίν, οὐ τὸ
γῆρας, ὦ Σώκρατες, ἀλλ' ὁ τρόπος τῶν ἀνθρώπων. ἂν μὲν
5 γὰρ κόσμιοι καὶ εὔκολοι ὦσιν, καὶ τὸ γῆρας μετρίως ἐστὶν
ἐπίπονον· εἰ δὲ μή, καὶ γῆρας, ὦ Σώκρατες, καὶ νεότης
χαλεπὴ τῷ τοιούτῳ συμβαίνει.

Καὶ ἐγὼ ἀγασθεὶς αὐτοῦ εἰπόντος ταῦτα, βουλόμενος ἔτι
e λέγειν αὐτὸν ἐκίνουν καὶ εἶπον· Ὦ Κέφαλε, οἶμαί σου τοὺς
πολλούς, ὅταν ταῦτα λέγῃς, οὐκ ἀποδέχεσθαι ἀλλ' ἡγεῖσθαί
σε ῥᾳδίως τὸ γῆρας φέρειν οὐ διὰ τὸν τρόπον ἀλλὰ διὰ τὸ
πολλὴν οὐσίαν κεκτῆσθαι· τοῖς γὰρ πλουσίοις πολλά φασι
5 παραμύθια εἶναι.

Ἀληθῆ, ἔφη, λέγεις· οὐ γὰρ ἀποδέχονται. καὶ λέγουσι μέν
τι, οὐ μέντοι γε ὅσον οἴονται. ἀλλὰ τὸ τοῦ Θεμιστοκλέους εὖ

us of about the same age often come together, bearing out the old proverb. Now at these meetings most of us lament, longing for the pleasures of youth, [a5] and recalling making love, drinking, feasts and other things of that sort, and are angry as if deprived of great advantages, imagining we had a good life then, but now no life at all. Some also moan on about the abuse shown to their advanced years by their families, [b1] and it is especially for this reason that they harp on about the great miseries old age causes them. But in my opinion, Socrates, these people are not putting the blame where it belongs. For if old age were the cause, I too would have had just the same experience, at least as far as old age is concerned, [b5] and so would all the others who have reached this time of life. As it is, I have long encountered others who don't feel like this, and in particular I was once present when someone asked the poet Sophocles: "How do you feel about sexual desire, Sophocles? Can you still make love to a woman?" [c1] And he replied: "Hush, man; you know, I am so glad to have escaped from that; it was like getting away from a raging, savage master." I thought he had a good answer then, and I still do now.c5 For undoubtedly in old age one becomes very peaceful and free from feelings of that sort; when the fierce tensions of desire relax, what Sophocles said is undoubtedly true – [d1] it's a release from a great many raging masters. But for all this, and their relationship with their families, there is just one thing to blame: not old age, Socrates, but human character; for if individuals are orderly and contented, even old age is only a moderate burden. [d5] But if not, this makes both old age and youth, Socrates, hard to bear.'

And I was full of admiration for what he said, and, wanting him to say more, [e1] I attempted to draw him out by saying: 'I fancy, Cephalus, that most people hearing you speak like this don't accept it, but reckon that you bear old age lightly not because of your character, but because of the great wealth you have acquired; for the rich, they say, have many consolations'. [e5]

'You're right', he said, 'they don't accept it. And there is something in what they say, though not actually as much as they imagine. But Themistocles' retort is particularly

ἔχει, ὃς τῷ Σεριφίῳ λοιδορουμένῳ καὶ λέγοντι ὅτι οὐ δι᾽
330 αὑτὸν ἀλλὰ διὰ τὴν πόλιν εὐδοκιμοῖ, ἀπεκρίνατο ὅτι οὔτ᾽ ἂν
αὐτὸς Σερίφιος ὢν ὀνομαστὸς ἐγένετο οὔτ᾽ ἐκεῖνος Ἀθηναῖος.
καὶ τοῖς δὴ μὴ πλουσίοις, χαλεπῶς δὲ τὸ γῆρας φέρουσιν, εὖ
ἔχει ὁ αὐτὸς λόγος, ὅτι οὔτ᾽ ἂν ὁ ἐπιεικὴς πάνυ τι ῥᾳδίως
5 γῆρας μετὰ πενίας ἐνέγκοι οὔθ᾽ ὁ μὴ ἐπιεικὴς πλουτήσας
εὔκολός ποτ᾽ ἂν ἑαυτῷ γένοιτο.
   Πότερον δέ, ἦν δ᾽ ἐγώ, ὦ Κέφαλε, ὧν κέκτησαι τὰ πλείω
παρέλαβες ἢ ἐπεκτήσω;
b   Ποῖ᾽ ἐπεκτησάμην, ἔφη, ὦ Σώκρατες; μέσος τις γέγονα
χρηματιστὴς τοῦ τε πάππου καὶ τοῦ πατρός. ὁ μὲν γὰρ
πάππος τε καὶ ὁμώνυμος ἐμοὶ σχεδόν τι ὅσην ἐγὼ νῦν οὐσίαν
κέκτημαι παραλαβὼν πολλάκις τοσαύτην ἐποίησεν, Λυσανίας
5 δὲ ὁ πατὴρ ἔτι ἐλάττω αὐτὴν ἐποίησε τῆς νῦν οὔσης. ἐγὼ δὲ
ἀγαπῶ ἐὰν μὴ ἐλάττω καταλίπω τούτοισιν, ἀλλὰ βραχεῖ γέ
τινι πλείω ἢ παρέλαβον.
   Οὔ τοι ἕνεκα ἠρόμην, ἦν δ᾽ ἐγώ, ὅτι μοι ἔδοξας οὐ σφόδρα
c   ἀγαπᾶν τὰ χρήματα, τοῦτο δὲ ποιοῦσιν ὡς τὸ πολὺ οἳ ἂν μὴ
αὐτοὶ κτήσωνται· οἱ δὲ κτησάμενοι διπλῇ ἢ οἱ ἄλλοι
ἀσπάζονται αὐτά. ὥσπερ γὰρ οἱ ποιηταὶ τὰ αὑτῶν ποιήματα
καὶ οἱ πατέρες τοὺς παῖδας ἀγαπῶσιν, ταύτῃ τε δὴ καὶ οἱ
5 χρηματισάμενοι τὰ χρήματα σπουδάζουσιν ὡς ἔργον ἑαυτῶν,
καὶ κατὰ τὴν χρείαν ᾗπερ οἱ ἄλλοι. χαλεποὶ οὖν καὶ
συγγενέσθαι εἰσίν, οὐδὲν ἐθέλοντες ἐπαινεῖν ἀλλ᾽ ἢ τὸν
πλοῦτον.
   Ἀληθῆ, ἔφη, λέγεις.
d   Πάνυ μὲν οὖν, ἦν δ᾽ ἐγώ. ἀλλά μοι ἔτι τοσόνδε εἰπέ· τί
μέγιστον οἴει ἀγαθὸν ἀπολελαυκέναι τοῦ πολλὴν οὐσίαν
κεκτῆσθαι;
   Ὅ, ἦ δ᾽ ὅς, ἴσως οὐκ ἂν πολλοὺς πείσαιμι λέγων. εὖ γὰρ
5 ἴσθι, ἔφη, ὦ Σώκρατες, ὅτι, ἐπειδάν τις ἐγγὺς ᾖ τοῦ οἴεσθαι
τελευτήσειν, εἰσέρχεται αὐτῷ δέος καὶ φροντὶς περὶ ὧν
ἔμπροσθεν οὐκ εἰσῄει. οἵ τε γὰρ λεγόμενοι μῦθοι περὶ τῶν
ἐν Ἅιδου, ὡς τὸν ἐνθάδε ἀδικήσαντα δεῖ ἐκεῖ διδόναι δίκην,
e   καταγελώμενοι τέως, τότε δὴ στρέφουσιν αὐτοῦ τὴν ψυχὴν
μὴ ἀληθεῖς ὦσιν· καὶ αὐτός, ἤτοι ὑπὸ τῆς τοῦ γήρως
ἀσθενείας ἢ καὶ ὥσπερ ἤδη ἐγγυτέρω ὢν τῶν ἐκεῖ μᾶλλόν

330c5   τὰ F Stobaeus: περὶ τὰ AD

329e8

apt here: in reply to the man from Seriphos who became abusive and told him that he owed his fame not to himself but to his city, **330** Themistocles said that he would not himself have become famous if he had been a Seriphian, and nor would the other if he had been an Athenian. And indeed the same reply nicely fits those who are not rich and find old age hard; an estimable man might not find old age entirely easy to bear if he was poor, [a5] but nor would an unworthy person ever find peace with himself even if he had acquired riches.'

'May I ask, Cephalus, whether you inherited most of your wealth, or made it yourself?'

[b1] 'You want to know how much I made, Socrates?' he said. As a businessman, I come somewhere between my grandfather and my father. For my grandfather and namesake inherited about as much as I now have and multiplied it many times, whereas my father Lysanias reduced it to less than it is now; [b5] for myself, I am well pleased if I pass on to these boys not less, but a little more than I inherited.'

'The reason I asked', I said, 'is that you do not strike me as having an excessive love of money, [c1] and that is generally the case with those who have not made it themselves, while those who have are twice as attached to it as anyone else. For just as poets love their own poems, and fathers their own children, so too, those who have made money take it seriously as their own creation, [c5] as well as valuing its use, as other people do. So they are difficult even to be with, since they are unwilling to praise anything except wealth.'

'You're right', he said.

[d1] 'I certainly am', I said. 'But tell me this too; what do you believe is the greatest benefit you have enjoyed from the acquisition of all your wealth?'

'Something', he said, 'which perhaps would not convince many, if I told them. [d5] For let me tell you, Socrates', he said, 'that whenever someone gets close to thinking he will die, there comes upon him fear and worry about things which didn't occur to him before. The stories told about what goes on in Hades, how the wrong-doer here must suffer punishment there, hitherto laughable,e1 now torment his soul with the possibility that they may be true. And the person himself, either through the weakness of old age or because he is now nearer to the beyond as it

τι καθορᾷ αὐτά, ὑποψίας δ᾽ οὖν καὶ δείματος μεστὸς γίγνεται
5 καὶ ἀναλογίζεται ἤδη καὶ σκοπεῖ εἴ τινά τι ἠδίκηκεν. ὁ μὲν
οὖν εὑρίσκων ἑαυτοῦ ἐν τῷ βίῳ πολλὰ ἀδικήματα καὶ ἐκ τῶν
ὕπνων, ὥσπερ οἱ παῖδες, θαμὰ ἐγειρόμενος δειμαίνει καὶ ζῇ
331 μετὰ κακῆς ἐλπίδος· τῷ δὲ μηδὲν ἑαυτῷ ἄδικον συνειδότι
ἡδεῖα ἐλπὶς ἀεὶ πάρεστι καὶ ἀγαθὴ γ η ρ ο τ ρ ό φ ο ς, ὡς καὶ
Πίνδαρος λέγει. χαριέντως γάρ τοι, ὦ Σώκρατες, τοῦτ᾽
ἐκεῖνος εἶπεν, ὅτι ὃς ἂν δικαίως καὶ ὁσίως τὸν βίον διαγάγῃ,

5   γλυκεῖά οἱ καρδίαν
       ἀτάλλοισα γηροτρόφος συναορεῖ
       ἐλπίς, ἃ μάλιστα θνατῶν
       πολύστροφον γνώμαν κυβερνᾷ.

εὖ οὖν λέγει θαυμαστῶς ὡς σφόδρα. πρὸς δὴ τοῦτ᾽ ἔγωγε
10 τίθημι τὴν τῶν χρημάτων κτῆσιν πλείστου ἀξίαν εἶναι, οὔ τι
b παντὶ ἀνδρὶ ἀλλὰ τῷ ἐπιεικεῖ. τὸ γὰρ μηδὲ ἄκοντά τινα
ἐξαπατῆσαι ἢ ψεύσασθαι, μηδ᾽ αὖ ὀφείλοντα ἢ θεῷ θυσίας
τινὰς ἢ ἀνθρώπῳ χρήματα ἔπειτα ἐκεῖσε ἀπιέναι δεδιότα,
μέγα μέρος εἰς τοῦτο ἡ τῶν χρημάτων κτῆσις συμβάλλεται.
5 ἔχει δὲ καὶ ἄλλας χρείας πολλάς, ἀλλά γε ἓν ἀνθ᾽ ἑνὸς οὐκ
ἐλάχιστον ἔγωγε θείην ἂν εἰς τοῦτο ἀνδρὶ νοῦν ἔχοντι, ὦ
Σώκρατες, πλοῦτον χρησιμώτατον εἶναι.
c   Παγκάλως, ἦν δ᾽ ἐγώ, λέγεις, ὦ Κέφαλε. τοῦτο δ᾽ αὐτό,
τὴν δικαιοσύνην, πότερα τὴν ἀλήθειαν αὐτὸ φήσομεν εἶναι
ἁπλῶς οὕτως καὶ τὸ ἀποδιδόναι ἄν τίς τι παρά του λάβῃ, ἢ
καὶ αὐτὰ ταῦτα ἔστιν ἐνίοτε μὲν δικαίως, ἐνίοτε δὲ ἀδίκως
5 ποιεῖν; οἷον τοιόνδε λέγω· πᾶς ἄν που εἴποι, εἴ τις λάβοι παρὰ
φίλου ἀνδρὸς σωφρονοῦντος ὅπλα, εἰ μανεὶς ἀπαιτοῖ, ὅτι οὔτε
χρὴ τὰ τοιαῦτα ἀποδιδόναι, οὔτε δίκαιος ἂν εἴη ὁ ἀποδιδούς,
οὐδ᾽ αὖ πρὸς τὸν οὕτως ἔχοντα πάντα ἐθέλων τἀληθῆ λέγειν.
d   Ὀρθῶς, ἔφη, λέγεις.
       Οὐκ ἄρα οὗτος ὅρος ἐστὶν δικαιοσύνης, ἀληθῆ τε λέγειν καὶ
ἃ ἂν λάβῃ τις ἀποδιδόναι.
       Πάνυ μὲν οὖν, ἔφη, ὦ Σώκρατες, ὑπολαβὼν ὁ Πολέ-
5 μαρχος, εἴπερ γέ τι χρὴ Σιμωνίδῃ πείθεσθαι.
       Καὶ μέντοι, ἔφη ὁ Κέφαλος, καὶ παραδίδωμι ὑμῖν τὸν
λόγον· δεῖ γάρ με ἤδη τῶν ἱερῶν ἐπιμεληθῆναι.

330e5 ἠδίκηκεν AF Stobaeus: ἠδίκησεν A (lectio supra versum addita) D Justinus
331b1 ἐπιεικεῖ ADF: ἐπιεικεῖ καὶ κοσμίῳ Stobaeus

330e4

were, and so perceives it somewhat more clearly, becomes filled with suspicion and fear and now begins to reckon up [e5] and consider if there is anyone he has wronged in any way. So the person who finds he has committed many injustices in his life continually even wakes up from his dreams in fear, as children do, and lives with a foreboding of evil; **331** but if a person is conscious of having done no wrong, sweet hope is ever present to cheer him and to be the good "nourisher of old age" as Pindar too has it. Yes, this is a beautiful saying of his, Socrates, about the man who lives his life in justice and piety, [a5] that "sweet hope, which most strongly governs the wandering purpose of mortals, walks at his side, gladdening his heart and nourishing his old age." He puts that so wonderfully well! It is indeed for this that I take the acquisition of wealth to be of the most value, [a10] certainly not for everyone, but for the person of an estimable life.

[b1] For when it comes to cheating anyone even unintentionally or telling lies, or again owing anything – any sacrifices to a god, or money to a person, and so departing for the other world in fear, the possession of money goes a long way towards avoiding such a misfortune. [b5] And wealth has many other uses also; but taking one thing with another I would claim that for a man of sense, Socrates, that is not the least important thing for which wealth is particularly useful.'

[c1] 'Bravo, Cephalus', I said. But let's take this very thing, justice: are we to say that it is simply truthfulness without qualification and giving back whatever one may have taken from someone? Or are these actions themselves sometimes just and sometimes unjust? [c5] To take an example of what I mean: everyone would agree, I imagine, that if one were to take weapons from a friend when he was sane, and he were to demand them back when mad, one ought not to return them, nor would the restorer be just to do so, nor again should one be willing to tell the whole truth to somebody in that state.'

'You are right', he replied. [d1]

'Then this is not a definition of justice: telling the truth and giving back what one has taken.'

'Oh, but it is, Socrates,' said Polemarchus interrupting, 'at any rate if we should give any credence to Simonides.' [d5]

'Well now', said Cephalus, 'I hand over the discussion to you both; for it is time for me to see to the sacrifice.'

Οὐκοῦν, ἔφη, ἐγώ, ὁ Πολέμαρχος, τῶν γε σῶν κληρονόμος;
10 Πάνυ γε, ἦ δ' ὃς γελάσας, καὶ ἅμα ᾔει πρὸς τὰ ἱερά.
e Λέγε δή, εἶπον ἐγώ, σὺ ὁ τοῦ λόγου κληρονόμος, τί φὴς τὸν
Σιμωνίδην λέγοντα ὀρθῶς λέγειν περὶ δικαιοσύνης;
Ὅτι, ἦ δ' ὅς, τὸ τὰ ὀφειλόμενα ἑκάστῳ ἀποδιδόναι δίκαιόν
ἐστι· τοῦτο λέγων δοκεῖ ἔμοιγε καλῶς λέγειν.
5 Ἀλλὰ μέντοι, ἦν δ' ἐγώ, Σιμωνίδῃ γε οὐ ῥᾴδιον ἀπιστεῖν,
σοφὸς γὰρ καὶ θεῖος ἀνήρ· τοῦτο μέντοι ὅτι ποτὲ λέγει, σὺ
μέν, ὦ Πολέμαρχε, ἴσως γιγνώσκεις, ἐγὼ δὲ ἀγνοῶ. δῆλον
γὰρ ὅτι οὐ τοῦτο λέγει, ὅπερ ἄρτι ἐλέγομεν, τό τινος
παρακαταθεμένου τι ὁτῳοῦν μὴ σωφρόνως ἀπαιτοῦντι ἀπο-
332 διδόναι. καίτοι γε ὀφειλόμενόν πού ἐστιν τοῦτο ὃ παρακα-
τέθετο. ἦ γάρ;
Ναί.
Ἀποδοτέον δέ γε οὐδ' ὁπωστιοῦν τότε ὁπότε τις μὴ
5 σωφρόνως ἀπαιτοῖ;
Ἀληθῆ, ἦ δ' ὅς.
Ἄλλο δή τι ἢ τὸ τοιοῦτον, ὡς ἔοικεν, λέγει Σιμωνίδης τὸ
τὰ ὀφειλόμενα δίκαιον εἶναι ἀποδιδόναι.
Ἄλλο μέντοι νὴ Δί', ἔφη· τοῖς γὰρ φίλοις οἴεται ὀφείλειν
10 τοὺς φίλους ἀγαθὸν μέν τι δρᾶν, κακὸν δὲ μηδέν.
Μανθάνω, ἦν δ' ἐγώ, ὅτι οὐ τὰ ὀφειλόμενα ἀποδίδωσιν ὃς
b ἄν τῳ χρυσίον ἀποδῷ παρακαταθεμένῳ, ἐάνπερ ἡ ἀπόδοσις
καὶ ἡ λῆψις βλαβερὰ γίγνηται, φίλοι δὲ ὦσιν ὅ τε ἀπολαμ-
βάνων καὶ ὁ ἀποδιδούς· οὐχ οὕτω λέγειν φὴς τὸν Σιμωνίδην;
Πάνυ μὲν οὖν.
5 Τί δέ; τοῖς ἐχθροῖς ἀποδοτέον ὅτι ἂν τύχῃ ὀφειλόμενον;
Παντάπασι μὲν οὖν, ἔφη, ὅ γε ὀφείλεται αὐτοῖς· ὀφείλεται
δέ γε, οἶμαι, παρά γε τοῦ ἐχθροῦ τῷ ἐχθρῷ ὅπερ καὶ
προσήκει, κακόν τι.
Ἠινίξατο ἄρα, ἦν δ' ἐγώ, ὡς ἔοικεν, ὁ Σιμωνίδης
c ποιητικῶς τὸ δίκαιον ὃ εἴη. διενοεῖτο μὲν γάρ, ὡς φαίνεται,
ὅτι τοῦτ' εἴη δίκαιον, τὸ προσῆκον ἑκάστῳ ἀποδιδόναι, τοῦτο
δὲ ὠνόμασεν ὀφειλόμενον.
Ἀλλὰ τί οἴει; ἔφη.

331d8 ἔφη ἐγώ AD: ἐγὼ ἔφη F

331d8

'So am I, Polemarchus,' he said, 'not heir to what is yours?'

'Certainly you are', replied Cephalus with a laugh, and he promptly went off to the sacrifice. [d10]

[e1] 'So tell me', I said, 'you who are heir to the discussion, what is it that Simonides says about justice which you think is correct?'

'That it is just' he replied, 'to give back to every person what he is owed; it's in saying this that he seems right, to me at least.'

[e5] 'Well, it is certainly not easy to doubt Simonides' I said, 'for he was a wise and inspired man; but exactly what he means by it perhaps you know, Polemarchus, but I don't. For obviously he doesn't mean what we were saying just now, to return anything deposited with us by anyone, even if the person asking for it back is not in his right mind. 332 And yet what he lent to us is surely owed to him. Isn't that right?'

'Yes'.

'But if anyone demanded it back when not in their right mind, it should in no circumstances be returned?' [a5]

'True', he replied.

'Then Simonides means something other than this, it seems, by saying that it is just to give back what is owed.'

'He certainly does, by Zeus' he replied; 'for he thinks that friends owe it to friends to do them something good, nothing evil.' [a10]

'I see', I said; 'you mean that, if two people are friends, and one gives back to the other a deposit of gold when the return and acceptance is going to cause harm to the recipient, [b1] the returner is not giving the other what is owed to him – isn't that what you claim Simonides is saying?'

'Certainly.'

'But how about this – oughtn't enemies to be repaid whatever happens to be owed to them?' [b5]

'Yes indeed, of course they should get what is owed to them', he said; 'and what is owed is, I believe, also exactly what is appropriate from one enemy to another – something bad.'

'So', I said, 'Simonides, it seems, was defining the just in riddles, like a poet. [c1] For he meant, it appears, that what is just can be defined in this way – giving each person what is appropriate to him – but he called this "what he is owed"'.

'Yes, what do you think he meant?' he said.

5 Πρὸς Διός, ἦν δ' ἐγώ, εἰ οὖν τις αὐτὸν ἤρετο· "Ὦ
Σιμωνίδη, ἡ τίσιν οὖν τί ἀποδιδοῦσα ὀφειλόμενον καὶ
προσῆκον τέχνη ἰατρικὴ καλεῖται;" τί ἂν οἴει ἡμῖν αὐτὸν
ἀποκρίνασθαι;
Δῆλον ὅτι, ἔφη, ἡ σώμασιν φάρμακά τε καὶ σιτία καὶ ποτά.
10 Ἡ δὲ τίσιν τί ἀποδιδοῦσα ὀφειλόμενον καὶ προσῆκον τέχνη
μαγειρικὴ καλεῖται;
d Ἡ τοῖς ὄψοις τὰ ἡδύσματα.
Εἶεν· ἡ οὖν δὴ τίσιν τί ἀποδιδοῦσα τέχνη δικαιοσύνη ἂν
καλοῖτο;
Εἰ μέν τι, ἔφη, δεῖ ἀκολουθεῖν, ὦ Σώκρατες, τοῖς
5 ἔμπροσθεν εἰρημένοις, ἡ τοῖς φίλοις τε καὶ ἐχθροῖς ὠφελίας
τε καὶ βλάβας ἀποδιδοῦσα.
Τὸ τοὺς φίλους ἄρα εὖ ποιεῖν καὶ τοὺς ἐχθροὺς κακῶς
δικαιοσύνην λέγει;
Δοκεῖ μοι.
10 Τίς οὖν δυνατώτατος κάμνοντας φίλους εὖ ποιεῖν καὶ
ἐχθροὺς κακῶς πρὸς νόσον καὶ ὑγίειαν;
e Ἰατρός.
Τίς δὲ πλέοντας πρὸς τὸν τῆς θαλάττης κίνδυνον;
Κυβερνήτης.
Τί δὲ ὁ δίκαιος; ἐν τίνι πράξει καὶ πρὸς τί ἔργον
δυνατώτατος φίλους ὠφελεῖν καὶ ἐχθροὺς βλάπτειν;
5 Ἐν τῷ προσπολεμεῖν καὶ ἐν τῷ συμμαχεῖν, ἔμοιγε δοκεῖ.
Εἶεν· μὴ κάμνουσί γε μήν, ὦ φίλε Πολέμαρχε, ἰατρὸς
ἄχρηστος.
Ἀληθῆ.
Καὶ μὴ πλέουσι δὴ κυβερνήτης.
10 Ναί.
Ἆρα καὶ τοῖς μὴ πολεμοῦσιν ὁ δίκαιος ἄχρηστος;
Οὐ πάνυ μοι δοκεῖ τοῦτο.
333 Χρήσιμον ἄρα καὶ ἐν εἰρήνῃ δικαιοσύνη;
Χρήσιμον.
Καὶ γὰρ γεωργία· ἢ οὔ;

332c5
[c5] 'But in Zeus' name' I said, 'what if someone were to ask him: "Simonides, what then gives medical skill its name – what does it render that is owed and appropriate, and to what things?" How do you think he would reply to us?'

'Obviously', he said, 'it is the skill which gives medicine, food and drink to bodies.'

[c10] 'And what gives the skill of cookery its name – what does it give which is owed and appropriate, and to what things?'

'It is a skill which gives flavour to food.' [d1]

'Good. So then, the skill of giving what and to whom could be called justice?'

'If the answer has to be at all consistent with what we said before, Socrates, it must be the skill which renders benefit to friends and harm to enemies.' [d5]

'So he means that justice is to do good to one's friends and harm to one's enemies?'

'I think so.'

'Now in matters of sickness and health, who is best able to do good to friends and harm to enemies when they are ill?' [d10]

'A doctor.'

[e1] 'And to those sailing, in respect of the dangers of the sea?'

'A ship's captain.'

'But what of the just man? By what action and in what activity is he most able to benefit friends and harm enemies?'

[e5] 'In making war and alliances, I would think.'

'Very well; but when someone is not ill, my dear Polemarchus, a doctor is useless.'

'True.'

'And likewise, when people are not at sea, a ship's captain is useless.'

[e10] 'Yes.'

'So can we assert that for those not fighting a war the just man is useless?'

'Oh no, that doesn't seem true to me at all'.

333 'So justice is useful also in peace?

'It is.'

'Yes, and so is farming, isn't it?'

Ναί.
5 Πρός γε καρποῦ κτῆσιν;
Ναί.
Καὶ μὴν καὶ σκυτοτομική;
Ναί.
Πρός γε ὑποδημάτων ἄν, οἶμαι, φαίης κτῆσιν;
10 Πάνυ γε.
Τί δὲ δή; τὴν δικαιοσύνην πρὸς τίνος χρείαν ἢ κτῆσιν ἐν
εἰρήνῃ φαίης ἂν χρήσιμον εἶναι;
Πρὸς τὰ συμβόλαια, ὦ Σώκρατες.
Συμβόλαια δὲ λέγεις κοινωνήματα ἤ τι ἄλλο;
15 Κοινωνήματα δῆτα.
b Ἆρ᾽ οὖν ὁ δίκαιος ἀγαθὸς καὶ χρήσιμος κοινωνὸς εἰς
πεττῶν θέσιν, ἢ ὁ πεττευτικός;
Ὁ πεττευτικός.
Ἀλλ᾽ εἰς πλίνθων καὶ λίθων θέσιν ὁ δίκαιος χρησιμώτερός
5 τε καὶ ἀμείνων κοινωνὸς τοῦ οἰκοδομικοῦ;
Οὐδαμῶς.
Ἀλλ᾽ εἰς τίνα δὴ κοινωνίαν ὁ δίκαιος ἀμείνων κοινωνὸς τοῦ
κιθαριστικοῦ, ὥσπερ ὁ κιθαριστικὸς τοῦ δικαίου εἰς κρου-
μάτων;
10 Εἰς ἀργυρίου, ἔμοιγε δοκεῖ.
Πλήν γ᾽ ἴσως, ὦ Πολέμαρχε, πρὸς τὸ χρῆσθαι ἀργυρίῳ,
c ὅταν δέῃ ἀργυρίου κοινῇ πρίασθαι ἢ ἀποδόσθαι ἵππον· τότε
δέ, ὡς ἐγὼ οἶμαι, ὁ ἱππικός. ἢ γάρ;
Φαίνεται.
Καὶ μὴν ὅταν γε πλοῖον, ὁ ναυπηγὸς ἢ ὁ κυβερνήτης;
5 Ἔοικεν.
Ὅταν οὖν τί δέῃ ἀργυρίῳ ἢ χρυσίῳ κοινῇ χρῆσθαι, ὁ
δίκαιος χρησιμώτερος τῶν ἄλλων;
Ὅταν παρακαταθέσθαι καὶ σῶν εἶναι, ὦ Σώκρατες.
Οὐκοῦν λέγεις ὅταν μηδὲν δέῃ αὐτῷ χρῆσθαι ἀλλὰ κεῖσθαι;
10 Πάνυ γε.
Ὅταν ἄρα ἄχρηστον ᾖ ἀργύριον, τότε χρήσιμος ἐπ᾽ αὐτῷ ἡ
d δικαιοσύνη;

333b8 κιθαριστικοῦ AF: οἰκοδομικοῦ τε καὶ κιθαριστικοῦ D

'Yes.'

[a5] 'For providing crops?'

'Yes.'

'And likewise, shoemaking?'

'Yes'.

'I presume you would say, for providing shoes?

[a10] 'Of course.'

'So what about justice, now? For what need, or for providing what, would you say it was useful in peacetime?'

'It's useful in connection with business contracts, Socrates.'

'By business contracts you mean partnerships, or something else?'

[a15] 'Yes, I mean partnerships.'

[b1] Now, when it comes to playing draughts, is the just man a good and useful partner, or someone skilled in playing draughts?'

'The person skilled in playing draughts.'

'And in the laying of bricks and stones is the just man a better and more useful partner than the builder?' [b5]

'Of course not.'

'Well then, in what association is the just man a better partner than the lyre-player, just as the lyre-player is better than the just man at striking the chords?'

'Where money is involved, I suppose.' [b10]

'Except perhaps, Polemarchus, in using money when you need jointly to buy or sell a horse; then, I presume, you need a horseman; isn't that so?' [c1]

'Apparently.'

'And again, when it comes to a ship, the shipbuilder or captain?'

[c5] 'It seems so'.

'So what then is the occasion for the joint use of silver or gold at which the just man is a more useful partner than others?'

'When it is to be put on deposit and kept safe, Socrates.'

'In fact, you mean, when we have no need to use it at all, but to put it by?'

[c10] 'Exactly.'

'So when money is useless – that's when justice is useful in relation to it?' [d1]

Κινδυνεύει.

Καὶ ὅταν δὴ δρέπανον δέῃ φυλάττειν, ἡ δικαιοσύνη χρήσιμος καὶ κοινῇ καὶ ἰδίᾳ· ὅταν δὲ χρῆσθαι, ἡ ἀμπελουρ-
5 γική;

Φαίνεται.

Φήσεις δὲ καὶ ἀσπίδα καὶ λύραν ὅταν δέῃ φυλάττειν καὶ μηδὲν χρῆσθαι, χρήσιμον εἶναι τὴν δικαιοσύνην, ὅταν δὲ χρῆσθαι, τὴν ὁπλιτικὴν καὶ τὴν μουσικήν;
10 Ἀνάγκη.

Καὶ περὶ τἆλλα δὴ πάντα ἡ δικαιοσύνη ἑκάστου ἐν μὲν χρήσει ἄχρηστος, ἐν δὲ ἀχρηστίᾳ χρήσιμος;

Κινδυνεύει.

e Οὐκ ἂν οὖν, ὦ φίλε, πάνυ γέ τι σπουδαῖον εἴη ἡ δικαιοσύνη, εἰ πρὸς τὰ ἄχρηστα χρήσιμον ὂν τυγχάνει. τόδε δὲ σκεψώ-μεθα. ἆρ᾽ οὐχ ὁ πατάξαι δεινότατος ἐν μάχῃ εἴτε πυκτικῇ εἴτε τινὶ καὶ ἄλλῃ, οὗτος καὶ φυλάξασθαι;
5 Πάνυ γε.

Ἆρ᾽ οὖν καὶ νόσον ὅστις δεινὸς φυλάξασθαι, καὶ λαθεῖν οὗτος δεινότατος ἐμποιήσας;

Ἔμοιγε δοκεῖ.

334 Ἀλλὰ μὴν στρατοπέδου γε ὁ αὐτὸς φύλαξ ἀγαθὸς ὅσπερ καὶ τὰ τῶν πολεμίων κλέψαι καὶ βουλεύματα καὶ τὰς ἄλλας πράξεις;

Πάνυ γε.
5 Ὅτου τις ἄρα δεινὸς φύλαξ, τούτου καὶ φὼρ δεινός.

Ἔοικεν.

Εἰ ἄρα ὁ δίκαιος ἀργύριον δεινὸς φυλάττειν, καὶ κλέπτειν δεινός.

Ὡς γοῦν ὁ λόγος, ἔφη, σημαίνει.
10 Κλέπτης ἄρα τις ὁ δίκαιος, ὡς ἔοικεν, ἀναπέφανται, καὶ κινδυνεύεις παρ᾽ Ὁμήρου μεμαθηκέναι αὐτό· καὶ γὰρ ἐκεῖνος
b τὸν τοῦ Ὀδυσσέως πρὸς μητρὸς πάππον Αὐτόλυκον ἀγαπᾷ τε καὶ φησιν αὐτὸν πάντας ἀνθρώπους κεκάσθαι κλε-πτοσύνῃ θ᾽ ὅρκῳ τε. ἔοικεν οὖν ἡ δικαιοσύνη καὶ κατὰ σὲ καὶ καθ᾽ Ὅμηρον καὶ κατὰ Σιμωνίδην κλεπτική τις εἶναι,
5 ἐπ᾽ ὠφελίᾳ μέντοι τῶν φίλων καὶ ἐπὶ βλάβῃ τῶν ἐχθρῶν. οὐχ οὕτως ἔλεγες;

333d2
'It looks that way.'

'And so when a pruning-knife needs to be kept safe, justice is useful both in the community and in private life; but when you need to use it you turn to the skill of pruning vines?' [d5]

'It seems so.'

'And so will you say that when you need a shield or a lyre to be kept safe without using it, justice is useful, but when they need to be used you turn to the skill of the hoplite or the musician?'

[d10] 'That follows.'

'So in all other cases, too, justice is useless when each thing is being used, but useful when it is not?'

'It seems so.'

[e1] 'Then, my friend, justice cannot be anything very important, if it turns out to be useful for things only when they are out of use. But let's consider this point: isn't the person who is most formidable in striking blows in a fight, whether boxing or any other kind, also the person who is best at guarding against them?'

'Certainly.' [e5]

'And again, the person who is skilled at guarding against disease is the one best able to introduce it undetected?'

'I think so.'

334 'Then again, the same person is good at protecting a military camp and also at detecting the plans of the enemy and stealing a march on him in other ways?'

'Of course.'

[a5] 'So, of whatever someone is a skilful guardian he will also be a skilful thief.'

'I suppose so.'

'If, then, the just person is skilful at guarding money he will also be skilful at stealing it.'

'That, at all events' he said, 'is where the argument is pointing.'

[a10] 'Then it appears that the just man is unveiled as some kind of thief, and you are likely to have learned that from Homer; for I tell you he's fond of Autolycus, the maternal grandfather of Odysseus, [b1] and says that "he exceeded all men in thieving and perjury". So justice, according to you, Homer and Simonides, seems to be some kind of skill at stealing, [b5] with the proviso that it must be for the benefit of friends and to the detriment of enemies. Isn't that what you meant?'

Οὐ μὰ τὸν Δί', ἔφη, ἀλλ' οὐκέτι οἶδα ἔγωγε ὅτι ἔλεγον. τοῦτο μέντοι ἔμοιγε δοκεῖ ἔτι, ὠφελεῖν μὲν τοὺς φίλους ἡ δικαιοσύνη, βλάπτειν δὲ τοὺς ἐχθρούς.

c   Φίλους δὲ λέγεις εἶναι πότερον τοὺς δοκοῦντας ἑκάστῳ χρηστοὺς εἶναι, ἢ τοὺς ὄντας, κἂν μὴ δοκῶσι, καὶ ἐχθροὺς ὡσαύτως;

Εἰκὸς μέν, ἔφη, οὓς ἄν τις ἡγῆται χρηστοὺς φιλεῖν, οὓς δ'
5 ἂν πονηροὺς μισεῖν.

Ἆρ' οὖν οὐχ ἁμαρτάνουσιν οἱ ἄνθρωποι περὶ τοῦτο, ὥστε δοκεῖν αὐτοῖς πολλοὺς μὲν χρηστοὺς εἶναι μὴ ὄντας, πολλοὺς δὲ τοὐναντίον;

Ἁμαρτάνουσιν.
10 Τούτοις ἄρα οἱ μὲν ἀγαθοὶ ἐχθροί, οἱ δὲ κακοὶ φίλοι;

Πάνυ γε.

Ἀλλ' ὅμως δίκαιον τότε τούτοις τοὺς μὲν πονηροὺς ὠφελεῖν, τοὺς δὲ ἀγαθοὺς βλάπτειν;

Φαίνεται.

d   Ἀλλὰ μὴν οἵ γε ἀγαθοὶ δίκαιοί τε καὶ οἷοι μὴ ἀδικεῖν;

Ἀληθῆ.

Κατὰ δὴ τὸν σὸν λόγον τοὺς μηδὲν ἀδικοῦντας δίκαιον κακῶς ποιεῖν.
5 Μηδαμῶς, ἔφη, ὦ Σώκρατες· πονηρὸς γὰρ ἔοικεν εἶναι ὁ λόγος.

Τοὺς ἀδίκους ἄρα, ἦν δ' ἐγώ, δίκαιον βλάπτειν, τοὺς δὲ δικαίους ὠφελεῖν;

Οὗτος ἐκείνου καλλίων φαίνεται.
10 Πολλοῖς ἄρα, ὦ Πολέμαρχε, συμβήσεται, ὅσοι διημαρτή-
e κασιν τῶν ἀνθρώπων, δίκαιον εἶναι τοὺς μὲν φίλους βλάπτειν, πονηροὶ γὰρ αὐτοῖς εἰσιν, τοὺς δ' ἐχθροὺς ὠφελεῖν, ἀγαθοὶ γάρ· καὶ οὕτως ἐροῦμεν αὐτὸ τοὐναντίον ἢ τὸν Σιμωνίδην ἔφαμεν λέγειν.
5 Καὶ μάλα, ἔφη, οὕτω συμβαίνει. ἀλλὰ μεταθώμεθα· κινδυνεύομεν γὰρ οὐκ ὀρθῶς τὸν φίλον καὶ ἐχθρὸν θέσθαι.

Πῶς θέμενοι, ὦ Πολέμαρχε;

Τὸν δοκοῦντα χρηστόν, τοῦτον φίλον εἶναι.

Νῦν δὲ πῶς, ἦν δ' ἐγώ, μεταθώμεθα;
10 Τὸν δοκοῦντά τε, ἦ δ' ὅς, καὶ τὸν ὄντα χρηστὸν φίλον· τὸν

'Certainly not, by Zeus,' he said, 'but I no longer know what I did mean. Yet this I still think – that justice is helping friends and harming enemies.'

[c1] 'But do you reckon that a person's friends are those who *seem* worthy to each individual, or those who really are, even if they don't seem so, and similarly with enemies?'

'It is likely', he said, 'that someone will love those he thinks worthy and dislike those he thinks bad.' [c5]

'But then, don't people make mistakes about this, so that many people seem good to them when they aren't, and *vice versa*?'

'They do.'

[c10] 'For these people, then, the good are their enemies and the bad their friends?'

'Yes, indeed.'

'But is it nevertheless just in that case for them to help the bad and harm the good?'

'It would seem so.'

[d1] 'But surely good people are just and cannot do wrong?'

'True.'

'So according to your argument it is just to do harm to those who do no injustice.'

[d5] 'No, no, Socrates', he said, 'the argument seems to be a bad one.'

'Then', I said, 'it must be just to harm the unjust and help the just?'

'That seems a better conclusion than the other.'

[d10] 'So, for the many people who misjudge their fellows, [e1] it will turn out to be just to harm their friends, who are bad as far as they are concerned, and help their enemies, who are good. And thus we will be saying the very opposite of what we claimed Simonides meant.'

[e5] 'It certainly does work out like that', he said. 'But let us change our ground; for it looks as if we didn't define the friend and the enemy correctly.'

'In what way, Polemarchus?'

'When we said that the person who seems worthy is our friend.'

'But how are we to change it now?' I asked.

[e10] 'By stating' he said 'that a friend is the one who both seems and is good;

335 δὲ δοκοῦντα μέν, ὄντα δὲ μή, δοκεῖν ἀλλὰ μὴ εἶναι φίλον. καὶ
περὶ τοῦ ἐχθροῦ δὲ ἡ αὐτὴ θέσις.
Φίλος μὲν δή, ὡς ἔοικε, τούτῳ τῷ λόγῳ ὁ ἀγαθὸς ἔσται,
ἐχθρὸς δὲ ὁ πονηρός.
5 Ναί.
Κελεύεις δὴ ἡμᾶς προσθεῖναι τῷ δικαίῳ ἢ ὡς τὸ πρῶτον
ἐλέγομεν, λέγοντες δίκαιον εἶναι τὸν μὲν φίλον εὖ ποιεῖν, τὸν
δ' ἐχθρὸν κακῶς, νῦν πρὸς τούτῳ ὧδε λέγειν, τὸν μὲν φίλον
ἀγαθὸν ὄντα εὖ ποιεῖν, τὸν δ' ἐχθρὸν κακὸν ὄντα βλάπτειν;
b Πάνυ μὲν οὖν, ἔφη, οὕτως ἄν μοι δοκεῖ καλῶς λέγεσθαι.
Ἔστιν ἄρα, ἦν δ' ἐγώ, δικαίου ἀνδρὸς βλάπτειν καὶ
ὁντινοῦν ἀνθρώπων;
Καὶ πάνυ γε, ἔφη· τούς γε πονηρούς τε καὶ ἐχθροὺς δεῖ
5 βλάπτειν.
Βλαπτόμενοι δ' ἵπποι βελτίους ἢ χείρους γίγνονται;
Χείρους.
Ἆρα εἰς τὴν τῶν κυνῶν ἀρετήν, ἢ εἰς τὴν τῶν ἵππων;
Εἰς τὴν τῶν ἵππων.
10 Ἆρ' οὖν καὶ κύνες βλαπτόμενοι χείρους γίγνονται εἰς τὴν
τῶν κυνῶν ἀλλ' οὐκ εἰς τὴν τῶν ἵππων ἀρετήν;
c Ἀνάγκη.
Ἀνθρώπους δέ, ὦ ἑταῖρε, μὴ οὕτω φῶμεν, βλαπτομένους
εἰς τὴν ἀνθρωπείαν ἀρετὴν χείρους γίγνεσθαι;
Πάνυ μὲν οὖν.
5 Ἀλλ' ἡ δικαιοσύνη οὐκ ἀνθρωπεία ἀρετή;
Καὶ τοῦτ' ἀνάγκη.
Καὶ τοὺς βλαπτομένους ἄρα, ὦ φίλε, τῶν ἀνθρώπων
ἀνάγκη ἀδικωτέρους γίγνεσθαι.
Ἔοικεν.
Ἆρ' οὖν τῇ μουσικῇ οἱ μουσικοὶ ἀμούσους δύνανται ποιεῖν;
10 Ἀδύνατον.
Ἀλλὰ τῇ ἱππικῇ οἱ ἱππικοὶ ἀφίππους;
Οὐκ ἔστιν.
Ἀλλὰ τῇ δικαιοσύνῃ δὴ οἱ δίκαιοι ἀδίκους; ἢ καὶ
d συλλήβδην ἀρετῇ οἱ ἀγαθοὶ κακούς;

335a8 λέγειν F: λέγειν ὅτι ἔστιν δίκαιον AD

while the one who seems so but in reality is not, is not our friend, though he may seem so. **335** And the same argument applies to an enemy.'

'Then by this argument, it seems, the good person will be our friend, and the bad one our enemy.'

[a5] 'Yes.'

'So you are stipulating that we must add to our idea of the just person, as we first defined it, when we said that it was just to do good to a friend and harm to an enemy – now we are to add to this as follows: that it is just to do good to a friend if he is good, and harm to an enemy if he is bad?'

[b1] 'Certainly', he replied, 'that seems a good way of putting it.'

'But is it part of being a just man,' I asked, 'to harm any human being at all?'

'Yes, indeed,' he replied, 'he ought to harm those who are both bad and his enemies.' [b5]

'When horses are harmed, do they become better or worse?'

'Worse.'

'By the standard of excellence of dogs or that of horses?'

'Of horses.'

[b10] 'And dogs, too, if harmed, become worse by the standard of excellence of dogs and not that of horses?'

'That follows.'

[c1] 'But of humans, my friend, mustn't we say that, when harmed, they become worse by the standard of human excellence?'

'Certainly.'

'And is not justice a human excellence?'

[c5] 'That also follows.'

'So, my friend, those men who are harmed necessarily become more unjust.'

'So it seems.'

'Well, are musicians through their musical skill able to make people unmusical?'

[c10] 'Impossible.'

'Or horsemen through their skill in riding able to make people bad riders?'

'No'.

'Well, is it by justice, then, that the just make people unjust, or, in short, is it by their excellence that the good make people bad?' [d1]

Ἀλλὰ ἀδύνατον.

Οὐ γὰρ θερμότητος, οἶμαι, ἔργον ψύχειν ἀλλὰ τοῦ ἐναντίου.

5 Ναί.

Οὐδὲ ξηρότητος ὑγραίνειν ἀλλὰ τοῦ ἐναντίου.

Πάνυ γε.

Οὐδὲ δὴ τοῦ ἀγαθοῦ βλάπτειν ἀλλὰ τοῦ ἐναντίου.

Φαίνεται.

10 Ὁ δέ γε δίκαιος ἀγαθός;

Πάνυ γε.

Οὐκ ἄρα τοῦ δικαίου βλάπτειν ἔργον, ὦ Πολέμαρχε, οὔτε φίλον οὔτ' ἄλλον οὐδένα, ἀλλὰ τοῦ ἐναντίου, τοῦ ἀδίκου.

e   Παντάπασί μοι δοκεῖς ἀληθῆ λέγειν, ἔφη, ὦ Σώκρατες.

Εἰ ἄρα τὰ ὀφειλόμενα ἑκάστῳ ἀποδιδόναι φησίν τις δίκαιον εἶναι, τοῦτο δὲ δὴ νοεῖ αὐτῷ τοῖς μὲν ἐχθροῖς βλάβην ὀφείλεσθαι παρὰ τοῦ δικαίου ἀνδρός, τοῖς δὲ φίλοις ὠφελίαν,

5 οὐκ ἦν σοφὸς ὁ ταῦτα εἰπών. οὐ γὰρ ἀληθῆ ἔλεγεν· οὐδαμοῦ γὰρ δίκαιον οὐδένα ἡμῖν ἐφάνη ὂν βλάπτειν.

Συγχωρῶ, ἦ δ' ὅς.

Μαχούμεθα ἄρα, ἦν δ' ἐγώ, κοινῇ ἐγώ τε καὶ σύ, ἐάν τις αὐτὸ φῇ ἢ Σιμωνίδην ἢ Βίαντα ἢ Πιττακὸν εἰρηκέναι ἤ τιν'

10 ἄλλον τῶν σοφῶν τε καὶ μακαρίων ἀνδρῶν.

Ἐγὼ γοῦν, ἔφη, ἕτοιμός εἰμι κοινωνεῖν τῆς μάχης.

336   Ἀλλ' οἶσθα, ἦν δ' ἐγώ, οὗ μοι δοκεῖ εἶναι τὸ ῥῆμα, τὸ φάναι δίκαιον εἶναι τοὺς μὲν φίλους ὠφελεῖν, τοὺς δ' ἐχθροὺς βλάπτειν;

Τίνος; ἔφη.

5   Οἶμαι αὐτὸ Περιάνδρου εἶναι ἢ Περδίκκου ἢ Ξέρξου ἢ Ἰσμηνίου τοῦ Θηβαίου ἤ τινος ἄλλου μέγα οἰομένου δύνασθαι πλουσίου ἀνδρός.

Ἀληθέστατα, ἔφη, λέγεις.

Εἶεν, ἦν δ' ἐγώ· ἐπειδὴ δὲ οὐδὲ τοῦτο ἐφάνη ἡ δικαιοσύνη

10 ὂν οὐδὲ τὸ δίκαιον, τί ἂν ἄλλο τις αὐτὸ φαίη εἶναι;

b   Καὶ ὁ Θρασύμαχος πολλάκις μὲν καὶ διαλεγομένων ἡμῶν μεταξὺ ὥρμα ἀντιλαμβάνεσθαι τοῦ λόγου, ἔπειτα ὑπὸ τῶν παρακαθημένων διεκωλύετο βουλομένων διακοῦσαι τὸν λόγον· ὡς δὲ διεπαυσάμεθα καὶ ἐγὼ ταῦτ' εἶπον, οὐκέτι

335d2

'No, that cannot be.'

'No, for it is not, I assume, the function of heat to cool things, but of its opposite.'

[d5] 'Yes.'

'Nor of dryness to make things wet, but of its opposite.'

'Of course.'

'Nor indeed is it the function of the good person to do harm but of his opposite.'

'So it appears.'

[d10] 'And is not the just person good?'

'Of course.'

'Then, Polemarchus, it is not the function of the just person to harm either a friend or anyone else, but that of his opposite, the unjust person.'

[e1] 'I think you are entirely right, Socrates,' he said.

'So if anyone claims that it is just to render to each what is owed, and by that he actually means that harm is due from the just man to his enemies, and benefit to his friends, the man who said this was not wise. For what he said is not true; [e5] it has become apparent to us that it is in no way just to harm anyone.'

'I concede that,' he said.

'So you and I,' I said, 'will fight together against anyone who claims that this view was put forward by Simonides or Bias or Pittacus, or any other of the blessed sages.' [e10]

'Well,' he said, '*I'm* ready enough to join in the fight.'

336 'But do you know', I said, 'whose saying I think it is – the one which says that it is just to benefit friends, but harm enemies?'

'Whose?' he asked.

[a5] 'I think it must be from Periander or Perdiccas or Xerxes or Ismenias of Thebes or some other rich man with a great belief in his capabilities.

'That's very true,' he said.

'Well then,' I said, since it has become apparent that neither justice nor the just consists in this, what else can anyone suggest it is?' [a10]

[b1] Now Thrasymachus, even while we were talking, had many times been eagerly trying to get between us and take hold of the argument, but up to this point had been restrained by those sitting near him who wanted to hear the argument out. But when we came to a pause and I had asked my question, he could no longer

5 ἡσυχίαν ἦγεν, ἀλλὰ συστρέψας ἑαυτὸν ὥσπερ θηρίον ἦκεν
ἐφ᾽ ἡμᾶς ὡς διαρπασόμενος. καὶ ἐγώ τε καὶ ὁ Πολέμαρχος
δείσαντες διεπτοήθημεν· ὁ δ᾽ εἰς τὸ μέσον φθεγξάμενος, Τίς,

c ἔφη, ὑμᾶς πάλαι φλυαρία ἔχει, ὦ Σώκρατες; καὶ τί εὐηθίζε-
σθε πρὸς ἀλλήλους ὑποκατακλινόμενοι ὑμῖν αὐτοῖς; ἀλλ᾽ εἴπερ
ὡς ἀληθῶς βούλει εἰδέναι τὸ δίκαιον ὅτι ἐστί, μὴ μόνον ἐρώτα
μηδὲ φιλοτιμοῦ ἐλέγχων ἐπειδάν τίς τι ἀποκρίνηται,

5 ἐγνωκὼς τοῦτο, ὅτι ῥᾷον ἐρωτᾶν ἢ ἀποκρίνεσθαι, ἀλλὰ καὶ
αὐτὸς ἀπόκριναι καὶ εἰπὲ τί φὴς εἶναι τὸ δίκαιον. καὶ ὅπως

d μοι μὴ ἐρεῖς ὅτι τὸ δέον ἐστὶν μηδ᾽ ὅτι τὸ ὠφέλιμον μηδ᾽ ὅτι
τὸ λυσιτελοῦν μηδ᾽ ὅτι τὸ κερδαλέον μηδ᾽ ὅτι τὸ συμφέρον,
ἀλλὰ σαφῶς μοι καὶ ἀκριβῶς λέγε ὅτι ἂν λέγῃς· ὡς ἐγὼ οὐκ
ἀποδέξομαι ἐὰν ὕθλους τοιούτους λέγῃς.

5 Καὶ ἐγὼ ἀκούσας ἐξεπλάγην καὶ προσβλέπων αὐτὸν
ἐφοβούμην, καί μοι δοκῶ, εἰ μὴ πρότερος ἑωράκη αὐτὸν ἢ
᾽κεῖνος ἐμέ, ἄφωνος ἂν γενέσθαι. νῦν δὲ ἡνίκα ὑπὸ τοῦ λόγου
ἤρχετο ἐξαγριαίνεσθαι, προσέβλεψα αὐτὸν πρότερος, ὥστε

e αὐτῷ οἷός τ᾽ ἐγενόμην ἀποκρίνασθαι, καὶ εἶπον ὑποτρέμων·
Ὦ Θρασύμαχε, μὴ χαλεπὸς ἡμῖν ἴσθι· εἰ γὰρ ἐξαμαρτάνομεν
ἐν τῇ τῶν λόγων σκέψει ἐγώ τε καὶ ὅδε, εὖ ἴσθι ὅτι ἄκοντες
ἁμαρτάνομεν. μὴ γὰρ δὴ οἴου, εἰ μὲν χρυσίον ἐζητοῦμεν, οὐκ

5 ἄν ποτε ἡμᾶς ἑκόντας εἶναι ὑποκατακλίνεσθαι ἀλλήλοις ἐν τῇ
ζητήσει καὶ διαφθείρειν τὴν εὕρεσιν αὐτοῦ, δικαιοσύνην δὲ
ζητοῦντας, πρᾶγμα πολλῶν χρυσίων τιμιώτερον, ἔπειθ᾽
οὕτως ἀνοήτως ὑπείκειν ἀλλήλοις καὶ οὐ σπουδάζειν ὅτι
μάλιστα φανῆναι αὐτό· οἴου γε σύ, ὦ φίλε. ἀλλ᾽, οἶμαι, οὐ

337 δυνάμεθα. ἐλεεῖσθαι οὖν ἡμᾶς πολὺ μᾶλλον εἰκός ἐστίν που
ὑπὸ ὑμῶν τῶν δεινῶν ἢ χαλεπαίνεσθαι.

Καὶ ὃς ἀκούσας ἀνεκάγχασέ τε μάλα σαρδάνιον καὶ εἶπεν·
Ὦ Ἡράκλεις, ἔφη, αὕτη ᾽κείνη ἡ εἰωθυῖα εἰρωνεία Σωκρά-

5 τους, καὶ ταῦτ᾽ ἐγὼ ᾔδη τε καὶ τούτοις προύλεγον, ὅτι σὺ
ἀποκρίνασθαι μὲν οὐκ ἐθελήσοις, εἰρωνεύσοιο δὲ καὶ πάντα
μᾶλλον ποιήσοις ἢ ἀποκρινοῖο, εἴ τίς τί σ᾽ ἐρωτᾷ.

Σοφὸς γὰρ εἶ, ἦν δ᾽ ἐγώ, ὦ Θρασύμαχε· εὖ οὖν ᾔδησθα ὅτι

b εἴ τινα ἔροιο ὁπόσα ἐστὶν τὰ δώδεκα, καὶ ἐρόμενος προείποις
αὐτῷ· ᾽ ᾽Ὅπως μοι, ὦ ἄνθρωπε, μὴ ἐρεῖς ὅτι ἐστὶν τὰ δώδεκα
δὶς ἓξ μηδ᾽ ὅτι τρὶς τέτταρα μηδ᾽ ὅτι ἑξάκις δύο μηδ᾽ ὅτι
τετράκις τρία· ὡς οὐκ ἀποδέξομαί σου ἐὰν τοιαῦτα φλυαρῇς᾽,

336e9 οἵου γε Bekker: οἵου τε ADF

336b5

keep quiet, [b5] but, gathering himself up like a wild beast, he sprang on us as if he wanted to tear us in pieces.

Polemarchus and I were panic stricken as he bawled out into our midst, 'What rubbish is this you've been talking all this time, Socrates? [c1] And why do you play the fool, deferring to each other like this? If you really wish to know what justice is, Socrates, don't just ask questions or show off by refuting anyone who answers you, since you know full well that it is easier to ask than to answer. [c5] So give an answer yourself and say what you claim justice is. And you – don't you be telling me that it is [d1] the obligatory or the beneficial or the advantageous or the profitable or the expedient, but make your definition clear and precise; for I won't take that sort of drivel from you.'

[d5] Hearing him I was panic-stricken and looking at him I was filled with fear, and I believe that if I had not caught sight of him before he looked at me I would have been rendered speechless. But at the very moment when he began to be exasperated by the argument I glanced at him before he looked at me, so that I was capable of answering him, [e1] and I said, trembling a little: 'Don't be harsh with us, Thrasymachus. For if I and my friend have made any mistakes in our consideration of the argument, rest assured that it was not deliberate error on our part. For don't imagine that, if we were looking for a piece of gold [e5] we would never willingly defer to each other in the search and ruin our chances of finding it, yet in searching for justice, an objective more valuable than masses of gold, we would be so foolish as to give way to each other and not seriously do our very best to bring it to light. Believe me that we are serious, my friend. But I think it's the ability we lack; **337** so it is surely far more reasonable for us to be pitied by clever fellows like you rather than be victims of your anger.'

Hearing this he burst into loud sarcastic laughter and said: 'Heracles! Here we have that habitual ironic evasion of Socrates; [a5] I knew it and predicted to these people that you would not be willing to answer but would sham ignorance and do anything to avoid answering, if anyone asked you anything.'

'That's because you're clever, Thrasymachus', I said; 'so you knew very well that if you were to enquire of anyone how many are twelve, and in putting the question you warned him: [b1] "Be sure not to tell me, my good fellow, that twelve is twice six or three times four or six times two or four times three, because I will not accept that kind of nonsense from you" – you saw very clearly, I think, that nobody would

5 δῆλον, οἶμαι, σοι ἦν ὅτι οὐδεὶς ἀποκρινοῖτο οὕτως πυνθανο-
μένῳ. ἀλλ᾽ εἴ σοι εἶπεν· "Ὦ Θρασύμαχε, πῶς λέγεις; μὴ
ἀποκρίνωμαι ὧν προεῖπες μηδέν; πότερον, ὦ θαυμάσιε, μηδ᾽
εἰ τούτων τι τυγχάνει ὄν, ἀλλ᾽ ἕτερον εἴπω τι τοῦ ἀληθοῦς; ἢ
c πῶς λέγεις;" τί ἂν αὐτῷ εἶπες πρὸς ταῦτα;
Εἶεν, ἔφη· ὡς δὴ ὅμοιον τοῦτο ἐκείνῳ.
Οὐδέν γε κωλύει, ἦν δ᾽ ἐγώ· εἰ δ᾽ οὖν καὶ μὴ ἔστιν ὅμοιον,
φαίνεται δὲ τῷ ἐρωτηθέντι τοιοῦτον, ἧττόν τι αὐτὸν οἴει
5 ἀποκρινεῖσθαι τὸ φαινόμενον ἑαυτῷ, ἐάντε ἡμεῖς ἀπαγορεύω-
μεν ἐάντε μή;
Ἄλλο τι οὖν, ἔφη, καὶ σὺ οὕτω ποιήσεις; ὧν ἐγὼ ἀπεῖπον,
τούτων τι ἀποκρινῇ;
Οὐκ ἂν θαυμάσαιμι, ἦν δ᾽ ἐγώ, εἴ μοι σκεψαμένῳ οὕτω
10 δόξειεν.
d Τί οὖν, ἔφη, ἂν ἐγὼ δείξω ἑτέραν ἀπόκρισιν παρὰ πάσας
ταύτας περὶ δικαιοσύνης, βελτίω τούτων; τί ἀξιοῖς παθεῖν;
Τί ἄλλο, ἦν δ᾽ ἐγώ, ἢ ὅπερ προσήκει πάσχειν τῷ μὴ εἰδότι;
προσήκει δέ που μαθεῖν παρὰ τοῦ εἰδότος. καὶ ἐγὼ οὖν τοῦτο
5 ἀξιῶ παθεῖν.
Ἡδὺς γὰρ εἶ, ἔφη· ἀλλὰ πρὸς τῷ μαθεῖν καὶ ἀπότεισον
ἀργύριον.
Οὐκοῦν ἐπειδάν μοι γένηται, εἶπον.
Ἀλλ᾽ ἔστιν, ἔφη ὁ Γλαύκων. ἀλλ᾽ ἕνεκα ἀργυρίου, ὦ
10 Θρασύμαχε, λέγε· πάντες γὰρ ἡμεῖς Σωκράτει εἰσοίσομεν.
e Πάνυ γε οἶμαι, ἦ δ᾽ ὅς, ἵνα Σωκράτης τὸ εἰωθὸς δια-
πράξηται· αὐτὸς μὲν μὴ ἀποκρίνηται, ἄλλου δ᾽ ἀποκρινομένου
λαμβάνῃ λόγον καὶ ἐλέγχῃ.
Πῶς γὰρ ἄν, ἔφην ἐγώ, ὦ βέλτιστε, τις ἀποκρίναιτο
5 πρῶτον μὲν μὴ εἰδὼς μηδὲ φάσκων εἰδέναι, ἔπειτα, εἴ τι
καὶ οἴεται, περὶ τούτων ἀπειρημένον αὐτῷ εἴη ὅπως μηδὲν
ἐρεῖ ὧν ἡγεῖται ὑπ᾽ ἀνδρὸς οὐ φαύλου; ἀλλὰ σὲ δὴ μᾶλλον
338 εἰκὸς λέγειν· σὺ γὰρ δὴ φῂς εἰδέναι καὶ ἔχειν εἰπεῖν. μὴ οὖν
ἄλλως ποίει, ἀλλὰ ἐμοί τε χαρίζου ἀποκρινόμενος καὶ μὴ
φθονήσῃς καὶ Γλαύκωνα τόνδε διδάξαι καὶ τοὺς ἄλλους.
Εἰπόντος δέ μου ταῦτα ὅ τε Γλαύκων καὶ οἱ ἄλλοι ἐδέοντο
5 αὐτοῦ μὴ ἄλλως ποιεῖν. καὶ ὁ Θρασύμαχος φανερὸς μὲν ἦν
ἐπιθυμῶν εἰπεῖν ἵν᾽ εὐδοκιμήσειεν, ἡγούμενος ἔχειν ἀπόκρισιν
παγκάλην· προσεποιεῖτο δὲ φιλονικεῖν πρὸς τὸ ἐμὲ εἶναι τὸν
b ἀποκρινόμενον. τελευτῶν δὲ συνεχώρησεν, κἄπειτα, Αὕτη δή,
ἔφη, ἡ Σωκράτους σοφία· αὐτὸν μὲν μὴ ἐθέλειν διδάσκειν,

337b5

answer a question put like that. [b5] But if he had said to you: "What do you mean, Thrasymachus? May I not reply with any of the answers you have mentioned? Even if it really is one of these, my dear fellow, must I still say something other than the truth? What do you mean?" What would your answer be to him?' [c1]

'Well, well,' he replied, 'how alike your example is to mine, to be sure!'

'I can see nothing against it', I said, 'but even assuming the examples are not alike, but yet appear so to the person questioned, do you think he is any less likely to answer with what appears correct to him, whether we forbid him or not?' [c5]

'So that is what you're planning to do as well, is it?', he said; 'you're going to give one of the answers I've forbidden?'

'I wouldn't be surprised,' I said, 'if on reflection I decided to do that.' [c10]

[d1] 'So what if I demonstrate that there is an answer about justice which is different from all these, and better? What penalty ought you to suffer?'

'What else', I said, 'than what is fitting for the ignorant? One should surely learn from the knowledgeable. So that's what I propose for my penalty.' [d5]

'You play the innocent!', he said, 'but along with the learning you must pay me some money too.'

'Sure!, whenever I get some', I said.

'Oh, he has it,' said Glaucon; 'if money is the problem, Thrasymachus, go ahead, for we'll all chip in for Socrates.' [d10]

[e1] 'Oh yes, I'm sure you will,' he said, 'so that Socrates can do his usual trick, not answer himself, but cross-examine and refute someone else's attempt.'

'Yes, my dear fellow,' I said, 'for how could anyone answer if in the first place he had no knowledge and was making no claim to it, [e5] and secondly, even if he had an opinion, he had been forbidden by a man of no mean reputation to say anything of what he believed? But actually it's more reasonable for you to speak; **338** you're the one who claims to know and can inform us. So don't hesitate, but gratify me by answering, and don't begrudge your teaching to Glaucon here and the others.'

When I said this, Glaucon and the others begged him do as I asked. [a5] It was clear that Thrasymachus was keen to speak in order to shine, since he believed he had a brilliant answer; but he went on pretending to compete by making me the one to answer. Finally he gave way, and then said: [b1] 'There you are, this is the wisdom of Socrates; he's not willing himself to teach but goes about learning from

παρὰ δὲ τῶν ἄλλων περιιόντα μανθάνειν καὶ τούτων μηδὲ
χάριν ἀποδιδόναι.

5   Ὅτι μέν, ἦν δ᾽ ἐγώ, μανθάνω παρὰ τῶν ἄλλων, ἀληθῆ
εἶπες, ὦ Θρασύμαχε, ὅτι δὲ οὔ με φῇς χάριν ἐκτίνειν, ψεύδῃ·
ἐκτίνω γὰρ ὅσην δύναμαι. δύναμαι δὲ ἐπαινεῖν μόνον·
χρήματα γὰρ οὐκ ἔχω. ὡς δὲ προθύμως τοῦτο δρῶ, ἐάν τίς
μοι δοκῇ εὖ λέγειν, εὖ εἴσῃ αὐτίκα δὴ μάλα, ἐπειδὰν
c   ἀποκρίνῃ· οἶμαι γάρ σε εὖ ἐρεῖν.
    Ἄκουε δή, ἦ δ᾽ ὅς. φημὶ γὰρ ἐγὼ εἶναι τὸ δίκαιον οὐκ ἄλλο
τι ἢ τὸ τοῦ κρείττονος συμφέρον. ἀλλὰ τί οὐκ ἐπαινεῖς; ἀλλ᾽
οὐκ ἐθελήσεις.

5   Ἐὰν μάθω γε πρῶτον, ἔφην, τί λέγεις· νῦν γὰρ οὔπω οἶδα.
τὸ τοῦ κρείττονος φῇς συμφέρον δίκαιον εἶναι. καὶ τοῦτο, ὦ
Θρασύμαχε, τί ποτε λέγεις; οὐ γάρ που τό γε τοιόνδε φῇς· εἰ
Πουλυδάμας ἡμῶν κρείττων ὁ παγκρατιαστὴς καὶ αὐτῷ
συμφέρει τὰ βόεια κρέα πρὸς τὸ σῶμα, τοῦτο τὸ σιτίον
d   εἶναι καὶ ἡμῖν τοῖς ἥττοσιν ἐκείνου συμφέρον ἅμα καὶ δίκαιον.
    Βδελυρὸς γὰρ εἶ, ἔφη, ὦ Σώκρατες, καὶ ταύτῃ ὑπολαμβά-
νεις ᾗ ἂν κακουργήσαις μάλιστα τὸν λόγον.
    Οὐδαμῶς, ὦ ἄριστε, ἦν δ᾽ ἐγώ· ἀλλὰ σαφέστερον εἰπὲ τί
5   λέγεις.
    Εἶτ᾽ οὐκ οἶσθ᾽, ἔφη, ὅτι τῶν πόλεων αἱ μὲν τυραννοῦνται, αἱ
δὲ δημοκρατοῦνται, αἱ δὲ ἀριστοκρατοῦνται;
    Πῶς γὰρ οὔ;
    Οὐκοῦν τοῦτο κρατεῖ ἐν ἑκάστῃ πόλει, τὸ ἄρχον;
10   Πάνυ γε.
e   Τίθεται δέ γε τοὺς νόμους ἑκάστη ἡ ἀρχὴ πρὸς τὸ αὑτῇ
συμφέρον, δημοκρατία μὲν δημοκρατικούς, τυραννὶς δὲ τυ-
ραννικούς, καὶ αἱ ἄλλαι οὕτως· θέμεναι δὲ ἀπέφηναν τοῦτο
δίκαιον τοῖς ἀρχομένοις εἶναι, τὸ σφίσι συμφέρον, καὶ τὸν
5   τούτου ἐκβαίνοντα κολάζουσιν ὡς παρανομοῦντά τε καὶ
ἀδικοῦντα. τοῦτ᾽ οὖν ἐστιν, ὦ βέλτιστε, ὃ λέγω ἐν ἁπάσαις
339   ταῖς πόλεσιν ταὐτὸν εἶναι δίκαιον, τὸ τῆς καθεστηκυίας
ἀρχῆς συμφέρον· αὕτη δέ που κρατεῖ, ὥστε συμβαίνει τῷ
ὀρθῶς λογιζομένῳ πανταχοῦ εἶναι τὸ αὐτὸ δίκαιον, τὸ τοῦ
κρείττονος συμφέρον.
5   Νῦν, ἦν δ᾽ ἐγώ, ἔμαθον ὃ λέγεις· εἰ δὲ ἀληθὲς ἢ μή,
πειράσομαι μαθεῖν. τὸ συμφέρον μὲν οὖν, ὦ Θρασύμαχε,

others and does not even show gratitude.'

[b5] 'When you said I learn from others, Thrasymachus,' I said, 'that's true; but you are mistaken when you claim that I'm not grateful in return; for I pay back as much as I can. But I can only bestow praise; for money I lack. How readily I do this when anyone appears to give a good answer, you will find out the very moment you give your reply; for I think you will speak well.' [c1]

'Hear this then,' he said: 'for I say that justice is nothing other than what is advantageous to the stronger. Well, why don't you praise me? You just won't do it.'

[c5] 'I will,' I said, 'provided that I first understand what you mean, because at the moment I'm not yet clear. You say that what is advantageous to the stronger is just. But whatever do you mean by this, Thrasymachus? For I can't imagine you're claiming something like this: if Polydamas the pancratiast is stronger than we are, and it's to his advantage to eat beef to keep fit, that this diet is advantageous and just for us who are weaker than he is.' [d1]

'You're disgusting, Socrates,' he said; 'you take my statement in the sense most likely to damage it.'

'Not at all, my dear fellow,' I said; 'just explain more clearly what you mean.' [d5]

'Do you mean to say' he said, 'that you don't know that some cities are governed by tyrannies, some by democracies and some by aristocracies?'

'Of course.'

'And so isn't the element which wields power in each city the one which rules?'

[d10] 'Certainly.'

[e1] 'But each ruling power passes laws with a view to its own advantage, a democracy democratic laws, a tyranny tyrannical ones, and so on; in passing them, the rulers proclaim that what is to their own advantage is just for those who are ruled by them, and if anyone deviates from this they punish him as a lawbreaker and wrongdoer. [e5] So that is what I mean, my dear fellow, when I say that justice is the same in all cities: that which is to the advantage of the established rule. **339** This, surely, exercises dominant power, so that to anyone who reasons correctly justice is the same everywhere, namely the advantage of the stronger.'

[a5] 'Now,' I said, 'I grasp your meaning; but I will try to discover whether you are right or not. You yourself have answered that what is just is what is advantageous, O Thrasymachus;

καὶ σὺ ἀπεκρίνω δίκαιον εἶναι, καίτοι ἔμοιγε ἀπηγόρευες
b   ὅπως μὴ τοῦτο ἀποκρινοίμην· πρόσεστιν δὲ δὴ αὐτόθι τὸ "τοῦ
κρείττονος."
Σμικρά γε ἴσως, ἔφη, προσθήκη.
Οὔπω δῆλον οὐδ᾽ εἰ μεγάλη· ἀλλ᾽ ὅτι μὲν τοῦτο σκεπτέον εἰ
5   ἀληθῆ λέγεις, δῆλον. ἐπειδὴ γὰρ συμφέρον γέ τι εἶναι καὶ ἐγὼ
ὁμολογῶ τὸ δίκαιον, σὺ δὲ προστίθης καὶ αὐτὸ φὴς εἶναι τὸ
τοῦ κρείττονος, ἐγὼ δὲ ἀγνοῶ, σκεπτέον δή.
Σκόπει, ἔφη.
Ταῦτ᾽ ἔσται, ἦν δ᾽ ἐγώ. καί μοι εἰπέ· οὐ καὶ πείθεσθαι
10 μέντοι τοῖς ἄρχουσιν δίκαιον φὴς εἶναι;
Ἔγωγε.
c   Πότερον δὲ ἀναμάρτητοί εἰσιν οἱ ἄρχοντες ἐν ταῖς πόλεσιν
ἑκάσταις ἢ οἷοί τι καὶ ἁμαρτεῖν;
Πάντως που, ἔφη, οἷοί τι καὶ ἁμαρτεῖν.
Οὐκοῦν ἐπιχειροῦντες νόμους τιθέναι τοὺς μὲν ὀρθῶς
5   τιθέασιν, τοὺς δέ τινας οὐκ ὀρθῶς;
Οἶμαι ἔγωγε.
Τὸ δὲ ὀρθῶς ἆρα τὸ τὰ συμφέροντά ἐστι τίθεσθαι ἑαυτοῖς,
τὸ δὲ μὴ ὀρθῶς ἀσύμφορα; ἢ πῶς λέγεις;
Οὕτως.
10 Ἃ δ᾽ ἂν θῶνται ποιητέον τοῖς ἀρχομένοις, καὶ τοῦτό ἐστι
τὸ δίκαιον;
Πῶς γὰρ οὔ;
d   Οὐ μόνον ἄρα δίκαιόν ἐστιν κατὰ τὸν σὸν λόγον τὸ τοῦ
κρείττονος συμφέρον ποιεῖν ἀλλὰ καὶ τοὐναντίον, τὸ μὴ
συμφέρον.
Τί λέγεις σύ; ἔφη.
5   Ἃ σὺ λέγεις, ἔμοιγε δοκῶ· σκοπῶμεν δὲ βέλτιον. οὐχ
ὡμολόγηται τοὺς ἄρχοντας τοῖς ἀρχομένοις προστάττοντας
ποιεῖν ἄττα ἐνίοτε διαμαρτάνειν τοῦ ἑαυτοῖς βελτίστου, ἃ δ᾽
ἂν προστάττωσιν οἱ ἄρχοντες δίκαιον εἶναι τοῖς ἀρχομένοις
ποιεῖν; ταῦτ᾽ οὐχ ὡμολόγηται;
10 Οἶμαι ἔγωγε, ἔφη.
e   Οἴου τοίνυν, ἦν δ᾽ ἐγώ, καὶ τὸ ἀσύμφορα ποιεῖν τοῖς
ἄρχουσί τε καὶ κρείττοσι δίκαιον εἶναι ὡμολογῆσθαί σοι·

339a7

and yet this was a reply you forbade me to give; but you immediately added the qualification "to the stronger". [b1]

'A trivial addition, I suppose!' he said.

'Well, it's not yet clear if it might be significant. But what is clear is that we must enquire whether what you say is true. [b5] That what is just is some kind of advantage is a thesis with which I too am in agreement; but you go further and say that it is the advantage of the stronger person, and this is what I don't know about. We really must look into it.'

'Go ahead,' he said.

'I'll do so,' I said. Tell me, don't you claim, too, that obeying rulers is just?' [b10]

'I do.'

[c1] Are the rulers in the various cities infallible or can they sometimes make mistakes?'

'Of course', he said; 'doubtless they can make mistakes.'

'Therefore in attempting to legislate, some laws they make rightly and some not?' [c5]

'I suppose so.'

'Making them rightly implies doing it to their own advantage, and wrongly, to their disadvantage, doesn't it? Is that what you mean?'

'Precisely.'

[c10] 'But whatever they legislate must be acted on by their subjects, and that is justice?'

'Of course'.

[d1] 'Then by your argument it is just to do not only what is to the advantage of the stronger, but also the opposite, what is to their disadvantage.'

'What do you mean?', he replied.

[d5] 'The same as you, I think; but let's take a closer look at it. Is it not agreed that rulers in legislating for their subjects sometimes make mistakes over what is best for themselves, but at the same time it is just for subjects to do whatever their rulers order. Was that not agreed?'

[d10] 'I suppose so', he said.

[e1] 'Therefore', I said, 'you have to suppose that you have also conceded that it is just for the rulers and those who are stronger to do what is to their disadvantage;

ὅταν οἱ μὲν ἄρχοντες ἄκοντες κακὰ αὑτοῖς προστάττωσιν,
τοῖς δὲ δίκαιον εἶναι φῇς ταῦτα ποιεῖν ἃ ἐκεῖνοι προσέταξαν,
5 ἆρα τότε, ὦ σοφώτατε Θρασύμαχε, οὐκ ἀναγκαῖον συμβαίνειν αὐτὸ οὑτωσί, δίκαιον εἶναι ποιεῖν τοὐναντίον ἢ ὃ σὺ
λέγεις; τὸ γὰρ τοῦ κρείττονος ἀσύμφορον δήπου προστάττε-
ται τοῖς ἥττοσιν ποιεῖν.
340 Ναὶ μὰ Δί', ἔφη, ὦ Σώκρατες, ὁ Πολέμαρχος, σαφέστατά
γε.
Ἐὰν σύ γ', ἔφη, αὐτῷ μαρτυρήσῃς, ὁ Κλειτοφῶν ὑπο-
λαβών.
5 Καὶ τί, ἔφη, δεῖται μάρτυρος; αὐτὸς γὰρ Θρασύμαχος
ὁμολογεῖ τοὺς μὲν ἄρχοντας ἐνίοτε ἑαυτοῖς κακὰ προστάτ-
τειν, τοῖς δὲ δίκαιον εἶναι ταῦτα ποιεῖν.
Τὸ γὰρ τὰ κελευόμενα ποιεῖν, ὦ Πολέμαρχε, ὑπὸ τῶν
ἀρχόντων δίκαιον εἶναι ἔθετο Θρασύμαχος.
10 Καὶ γὰρ τὸ τοῦ κρείττονος, ὦ Κλειτοφῶν, συμφέρον
b δίκαιον εἶναι ἔθετο. ταῦτα δὲ ἀμφότερα θέμενος ὡμολόγησεν
αὖ ἐνίοτε τοὺς κρείττους τὰ αὑτοῖς ἀσύμφορα κελεύειν τοὺς
ἥττους τε καὶ ἀρχομένους ποιεῖν. ἐκ δὲ τούτων τῶν ὁμολο-
γιῶν οὐδὲν μᾶλλον τὸ τοῦ κρείττονος συμφέρον δίκαιον ἂν εἴη
5 ἢ τὸ μὴ συμφέρον.
Ἀλλ', ἔφη ὁ Κλειτοφῶν, τὸ τοῦ κρείττονος συμφέρον
ἔλεγεν ὃ ἡγοῖτο ὁ κρείττων αὑτῷ συμφέρειν· τοῦτο ποιητέον
εἶναι τῷ ἥττονι, καὶ τὸ δίκαιον τοῦτο ἐτίθετο.
Ἀλλ' οὐχ οὕτως, ἦ δ' ὃς ὁ Πολέμαρχος, ἐλέγετο.
c Οὐδέν, ἦν δ' ἐγώ, ὦ Πολέμαρχε, διαφέρει, ἀλλ' εἰ νῦν οὕτω
λέγει Θρασύμαχος, οὕτως αὐτοῦ ἀποδεχώμεθα. Καί μοι εἰπέ,
ὦ Θρασύμαχε· τοῦτο ἦν ὃ ἐβούλου λέγειν τὸ δίκαιον, τὸ τοῦ
κρείττονος συμφέρον δοκοῦν εἶναι τῷ κρείττονι, ἐάντε συμ-
5 φέρῃ ἐάντε μή; οὕτω σε φῶμεν λέγειν;
Ἥκιστά γε, ἔφη· ἀλλὰ κρείττω με οἴει καλεῖν τὸν
ἐξαμαρτάνοντα ὅταν ἐξαμαρτάνῃ;
Ἔγωγε, εἶπον, ᾤμην σε τοῦτο λέγειν ὅτε τοὺς ἄρχοντας
d ὡμολόγεις οὐκ ἀναμαρτήτους εἶναι ἀλλά τι καὶ ἐξαμαρτάνειν.
Συκοφάντης γὰρ εἶ, ἔφη, ὦ Σώκρατες, ἐν τοῖς λόγοις· ἐπεὶ
αὐτίκα ἰατρὸν καλεῖς σὺ τὸν ἐξαμαρτάνοντα περὶ τοὺς
κάμνοντας κατ' αὐτὸ τοῦτο ὃ ἐξαμαρτάνει; ἢ λογιστικόν, ὃς
5 ἂν ἐν λογισμῷ ἁμαρτάνῃ, τότε ὅταν ἁμαρτάνῃ, κατὰ ταύτην

339e3

whenever the rulers unintentionally order what is bad for themselves, and you claim that it is just for the ruled to do what the rulers have ordered, [e5] in that case doesn't the conclusion inevitably follow, O most clever Thrasymachus, that it is just to do the opposite of what you assert? For the weaker are commanded to perform what is to the disadvantage of the stronger.'

340 'By Zeus, Socrates,' said Polemarchus, 'nothing could be more obvious.'

'Of course,' said Cleitophon, interrupting, 'if you are his witness.'

[a5] 'And why do we need a witness?', he replied. 'Thrasymachus himself admits that rulers sometimes give orders which are harmful to themselves, and it is just for the ruled to obey them.'

'Yes, Polemarchus, because Thrasymachus proposed that it is just to carry out the orders of the rulers.'

[a10] 'Yes, Cleitophon, and he also took the position that the advantage of the stronger was just. [b1] And having proposed both of these, he again made a concession, that the stronger sometimes order the weaker and ruled to do what is not to their (the stronger's) advantage. And from these admissions it follows that the advantage of the stronger would no more be just than what is to their disadvantage.' [b5]

'But,' Cleitophon objected, 'by the advantage of the stronger he meant what the stronger *believe* to be to their advantage; this is what the weaker must do, and that is what he claimed was just.'

'Well, that wasn't what was said,' replied Polemarchus.

[c1] 'It doesn't matter, Polemarchus,' I said, 'but if that is now what Thrasymachus maintains, let us accept it as it is. So tell me, Thrasymachus, was this how you wanted to define justice: that it is the advantage of the stronger as it appears to the stronger, whether it really *is* to their advantage or not? Is that how we are to take what you said?' [c5]

'Not in the least,' he replied; 'do you really imagine I call someone who is in error stronger at the moment when he is making his mistake?'

'Well I thought you meant that,' I said, 'when you agreed that rulers are not infallible but can sometimes make mistakes.' [d1]

'That's because you browbeat people in arguments, Socrates; just to give an immediate example, do you call a person who is mistaken about the sick a doctor in respect of that very error? Or in the case of a mathematician who makes a mistake in calculation, do you call him a mathematician at the moment when he makes the mistake and in respect of that error? [d5] We express it like this, I suppose, saying that

τὴν ἁμαρτίαν; ἀλλ', οἶμαι, λέγομεν τῷ ῥήματι οὕτως, ὅτι ὁ
ἰατρὸς ἐξήμαρτεν καὶ ὁ λογιστὴς ἐξήμαρτεν καὶ ὁ γραμμα-
τιστής· τὸ δ' οἶμαι ἕκαστος τούτων, καθ' ὅσον τοῦτ' ἔστιν ὃ
e προσαγορεύομεν αὐτόν, οὐδέποτε ἁμαρτάνει. ὥστε κατὰ τὸν
ἀκριβῆ λόγον, ἐπειδὴ καὶ σὺ ἀκριβολογῇ, οὐδεὶς τῶν
δημιουργῶν ἁμαρτάνει. ἐπιλιπούσης γὰρ ἐπιστήμης ὁ ἁμαρ-
τάνων ἁμαρτάνει, ἐν ᾧ οὐκ ἔστι δημιουργός· ὥστε δημιουρ-
5 γὸς ἢ σοφὸς ἢ ἄρχων οὐδεὶς ἁμαρτάνει τότε ὅταν ἄρχων ᾖ,
ἀλλὰ πᾶς γ' ἂν εἴποι ὅτι ὁ ἰατρὸς ἥμαρτεν καὶ ὁ ἄρχων
ἥμαρτεν. τοιοῦτον οὖν δή σοι καὶ ἐμὲ ὑπόλαβε νυνδὴ
ἀποκρίνεσθαι· τὸ δὲ ἀκριβέστατον ἐκεῖνο τυγχάνει ὄν, τὸν
341 ἄρχοντα, καθ' ὅσον ἄρχων ἐστίν, μὴ ἁμαρτάνειν, μὴ ἁμαρτά-
νοντα δὲ τὸ αὑτῷ βέλτιστον τίθεσθαι, τοῦτο δὲ τῷ ἀρχομένῳ
ποιητέον. ὥστε, ὅπερ ἐξ ἀρχῆς ἔλεγον, δίκαιον λέγω τὸ τοῦ
κρείττονος ποιεῖν συμφέρον.
5   Εἶεν, ἦν δ' ἐγώ, ὦ Θρασύμαχε· δοκῶ σοι συκοφαντεῖν;
Πάνυ μὲν οὖν, ἔφη.
Οἴει γάρ με ἐξ ἐπιβουλῆς ἐν τοῖς λόγοις κακουργοῦντά σε
ἐρέσθαι ὡς ἠρόμην;
Εὖ μὲν οὖν οἶδα, ἔφη. καὶ οὐδέν γέ σοι πλέον ἔσται· οὔτε
b γὰρ ἄν με λάθοις κακουργῶν, οὔτε μὴ λαθὼν βιάσασθαι τῷ
λόγῳ δύναιο.
Οὐδέ γ' ἂν ἐπιχειρήσαιμι, ἦν δ' ἐγώ, ὦ μακάριε. ἀλλ', ἵνα
μὴ αὖθις ἡμῖν τοιοῦτον ἐγγένηται, διόρισαι ποτέρως λέγεις
5 τὸν ἄρχοντά τε καὶ τὸν κρείττονα, τὸν ὡς ἔπος εἰπεῖν ἢ τὸν
ἀκριβεῖ λόγῳ, ὃ νυνδὴ ἔλεγες, οὗ τὸ συμφέρον κρείττονος
ὄντος δίκαιον ἔσται τῷ ἥττονι ποιεῖν.
Τὸν τῷ ἀκριβεστάτῳ, ἔφη, λόγῳ ἄρχοντα ὄντα. πρὸς
ταῦτα κακούργει καὶ συκοφάντει, εἴ τι δύνασαι· οὐδέν σου
c παρίεμαι. ἀλλ' οὐ μὴ οἷός τ' ᾖς.
Οἴει γὰρ ἄν με, εἶπον, οὕτω μανῆναι ὥστε ξυρεῖν ἐπιχειρεῖν
λέοντα καὶ συκοφαντεῖν Θρασύμαχον;
Νῦν γοῦν, ἔφη, ἐπεχείρησας, οὐδὲν ὢν καὶ ταῦτα.
5   Ἅδην, ἦν δ' ἐγώ, τῶν τοιούτων. ἀλλ' εἰπέ μοι· ὁ τῷ ἀκριβεῖ
λόγῳ ἰατρός, ὃν ἄρτι ἔλεγες, πότερον χρηματιστής ἐστιν ἢ
τῶν καμνόντων θεραπευτής; καὶ λέγε τὸν τῷ ὄντι ἰατρὸν
ὄντα.
Τῶν καμνόντων, ἔφη, θεραπευτής.

340e3 ἐπιλιπούσης AD Stobaeus: ἐπιλειπούσης F

340d6

the doctor has made a mistake, and the mathematician and the teacher likewise; but in fact, I don't think that any of these ever makes a mistake, in terms of what we call him. [e1] Consequently, according to strict logic, since you yourself insist on it, no skilled professional makes a mistake. For it is when his knowledge has deserted him that he who goes wrong goes wrong, and to that extent he is not a skilled professional; [e5] so that no skilled professional, wise man or ruler, makes a mistake at the moment when he is a ruler, even though everybody might use the expression that the doctor or the ruler made a mistake. This is the way, then, that you should take the answer I gave you just now. But to speak really strictly one should say that the ruler, **341** inasmuch as he is a ruler, does not make mistakes, and in his infallibility he ordains what is best for himself, and this his subjects must perform. Consequently, as I said from the start, I repeat: justice is to do what is to the advantage of the stronger.'

[a5] 'Well now, so you think I'm browbeating you, Thrasymachus?'

'I certainly do.'

'Because you think I asked my questions with the intention of doing you down in argument?'

'I'm perfectly sure of it' he said. 'And you won't get the upper hand, for you won't harm me by stealth, [b1] nor, failing that, could you use argument to take me by force.'

'My dear fellow, I wouldn't even dream of trying', I said. 'But to avoid this sort of thing happening to us again, distinguish in which way you understand the ruler and the stronger, [b5] whether in general terms or in strict logic as you were saying just now, in whose interest, as the stronger, it will be just for the weaker to act'.

'I mean the ruler in the strictest sense,' he replied. Try out your evil tricks and browbeating arguments on that, if you can; I'm not asking to be excused. But there's really no chance of your succeeding.' [c1]

'What, do you imagine,' I said, 'that I would be so mad as to attempt to shave a lion and browbeat Thrasymachus?'

'Well you did try just now,' he said, 'though you were no good even then.'

[c5] 'Enough of that sort of talk', I said. 'But tell me; this precisely-defined doctor whom you have just been speaking about, is he a man of business or a carer of the sick? Be sure to speak about the man who really is a doctor.'

'He is a carer of the sick', he replied.

10 Τί δὲ κυβερνήτης; ὁ ὀρθῶς κυβερνήτης ναυτῶν ἄρχων
ἐστὶν ἢ ναύτης;
d Ναυτῶν ἄρχων.
Οὐδὲν οἶμαι τοῦτο ὑπολογιστέον, ὅτι πλεῖ ἐν τῇ νηΐ, οὐδ᾽
ἐστὶν κλητέος ναύτης· οὐ γὰρ κατὰ τὸ πλεῖν κυβερνήτης
καλεῖται, ἀλλὰ κατὰ τὴν τέχνην καὶ τὴν τῶν ναυτῶν ἀρχήν.
5 Ἀληθῆ, ἔφη.
Οὐκοῦν ἑκάστῳ τούτων ἔστιν τι συμφέρον;
Πάνυ γε.
Οὐ καὶ ἡ τέχνη, ἦν δ᾽ ἐγώ, ἐπὶ τούτῳ πέφυκεν, ἐπὶ τῷ τὸ
συμφέρον ἑκάστῳ ζητεῖν τε καὶ ἐκπορίζειν;
10 Ἐπὶ τούτῳ, ἔφη.
Ἆρ᾽ οὖν καὶ ἑκάστῃ τῶν τεχνῶν ἔστιν τι συμφέρον ἄλλο ἢ
ὅτι μάλιστα τελέαν εἶναι;
e Πῶς τοῦτο ἐρωτᾷς;
Ὥσπερ, ἔφην ἐγώ, εἴ με ἔροιο εἰ ἐξαρκεῖ σώματι εἶναι
σώματι ἢ προσδεῖταί τινος, εἴποιμ᾽ ἂν ὅτι "Παντάπασι μὲν
οὖν προσδεῖται. διὰ ταῦτα καὶ ἡ τέχνη ἐστὶν ἡ ἰατρικὴ νῦν
5 ηὑρημένη, ὅτι σῶμά ἐστιν πονηρὸν καὶ οὐκ ἐξαρκεῖ αὐτῷ
τοιούτῳ εἶναι. τούτῳ οὖν ὅπως ἐκπορίζῃ τὰ συμφέροντα, ἐπὶ
τοῦτο παρεσκευάσθη ἡ τέχνη." ἢ ὀρθῶς σοι δοκῶ, ἔφην, ἂν
εἰπεῖν οὕτω λέγων, ἢ οὔ;
342 Ὀρθῶς, ἔφη.
Τί δὲ δή; αὐτὴ ἡ ἰατρική ἐστιν πονηρά, ἢ ἄλλη τις τέχνη
ἔσθ᾽ ὅτι προσδεῖταί τινος ἀρετῆς, ὥσπερ ὀφθαλμοὶ ὄψεως καὶ
ὦτα ἀκοῆς, καὶ διὰ ταῦτα ἐπ᾽ αὐτοῖς δεῖ τινος τέχνης τῆς τὸ
5 συμφέρον εἰς ταῦτα σκεψομένης τε καὶ ἐκποριούσης, ἆρα καὶ
ἐν αὐτῇ τῇ τέχνῃ ἔνι τις πονηρία, καὶ δεῖ ἑκάστῃ τέχνῃ ἄλλης
τέχνης ἥτις αὐτῇ τὸ συμφέρον σκέψεται, καὶ τῇ σκοπουμένῃ
ἑτέρας αὖ τοιαύτης, καὶ τοῦτ᾽ ἔστιν ἀπέραντον; ἢ αὐτὴ αὑτῇ
b τὸ συμφέρον σκέψεται; ἢ οὔτε αὑτῆς οὔτε ἄλλης προσδεῖται
ἐπὶ τὴν αὑτῆς πονηρίαν τὸ συμφέρον σκοπεῖν· οὔτε γὰρ
πονηρία οὔτε ἁμαρτία οὐδεμία οὐδεμιᾷ τέχνῃ πάρεστιν,
οὐδὲ προσήκει τέχνῃ ἄλλῳ τὸ συμφέρον ζητεῖν ἢ ᾽κείνῳ οὗ
5 τέχνη ἐστίν, αὐτὴ δὲ ἀβλαβὴς καὶ ἀκέραιός ἐστιν ὀρθὴ οὖσα,
ἕωσπερ ἂν ᾖ ἑκάστη ἀκριβὴς ὅλη ἥπερ ἐστίν; καὶ σκόπει
ἐκείνῳ τῷ ἀκριβεῖ λόγῳ· οὕτως ἢ ἄλλως ἔχει;
Οὕτως, ἔφη, φαίνεται.

341c10

And what of the ship's captain? Is the captain, rightly so-called, a sailor or a commander of sailors?' [c10]

[d1] 'A commander of sailors.'

'We shouldn't, I think, take into account merely that he sails on the ship, nor should he be called a sailor for that reason; for it is not in respect of his sailing that he is called a captain, but by virtue of his skill and command of the crew.'

[d5] 'True', he said.

'Then, do these people each have something to their advantage?'

'Yes.'

'And', I said, 'does not the skill they possess exist naturally in seeking and providing for each of them what is to their advantage?'

[d10] 'It does,' he said.

'So for each of the skills is anything else advantageous than being as perfect as possible?'

[e1] 'What do you mean by that?'

'It is just as if', I said, 'you were to ask me whether the body is self-sufficient or whether it has need of something else. In that case I should reply: "It certainly does have needs. That is why the skill of medicine has now been invented, [e5] because the body is defective and as such is not self-sufficient. So the skill was developed for the very purpose of providing for the advantage of the body." Do you think my reasoning would be correct when I said this, or not?'

342 'It would be correct,' he replied.

'Then what about this? Is the skill of medicine itself defective, and does any other skill need any excellence to perfect it – just as the eyes need sight and the ears hearing, and for this reason they have need of some skill over them which will watch over and provide for their advantage to achieve these ends – [a5] is there any defect in a skill as such, and does each skill require another skill which will provide for its advantage, and again another one for that one, and so on *ad infinitum*? Or will each consider its own advantage? [b1] No, it has no need either of itself or any other skill to remedy its defects or consider what is advantageous for it. For there is no defect or flaw present in any skill, nor does it belong to its nature to seek the advantage of anything else other than its own subject-matter; [b5] and when it is correct, is it faultless and pure, so long as each skill remains precisely and wholly what it is? Consider this in that precise sense of yours – is it so or not?'

'It appears to be so,' he said.

c Οὐκ ἄρα, ἦν δ' ἐγώ, ἰατρικὴ ἰατρικῇ τὸ συμφέρον σκοπεῖ
ἀλλὰ σώματι.
Ναί, ἔφη.
Οὐδὲ ἱππικὴ ἱππικῇ ἀλλ' ἵπποις· οὐδὲ ἄλλη τέχνη οὐδεμία
5 ἑαυτῇ, οὐδὲ γὰρ προσδεῖται, ἀλλ' ἐκείνῳ οὗ τέχνη ἐστίν.
Φαίνεται, ἔφη, οὕτως.
Ἀλλὰ μὴν, ὦ Θρασύμαχε, ἄρχουσί γε αἱ τέχναι καὶ
κρατοῦσιν ἐκείνου οὗπέρ εἰσιν τέχναι.
Συνεχώρησεν ἐνταῦθα καὶ μάλα μόγις.
10 Οὐκ ἄρα ἐπιστήμη γε οὐδεμία τὸ τοῦ κρείττονος συμφέρον
d σκοπεῖ οὐδ' ἐπιτάττει, ἀλλὰ τὸ τοῦ ἥττονός τε καὶ ἀρχομένου
ὑπὸ ἑαυτῆς.
Συνωμολόγησε μὲν καὶ ταῦτα τελευτῶν, ἐπεχείρει δὲ περὶ
αὐτὰ μάχεσθαι· ἐπειδὴ δὲ ὡμολόγησεν, Ἄλλο τι οὖν, ἦν δ'
5 ἐγώ, οὐδὲ ἰατρὸς οὐδείς, καθ' ὅσον ἰατρός, τὸ τῷ ἰατρῷ
συμφέρον σκοπεῖ οὐδ' ἐπιτάττει, ἀλλὰ τὸ τῷ κάμνοντι;
ὡμολόγηται γὰρ ὁ ἀκριβὴς ἰατρὸς σωμάτων εἶναι ἄρχων
ἀλλ' οὐ χρηματιστής. ἢ οὐχ ὡμολόγηται;
Συνέφη.
10 Οὐκοῦν καὶ ὁ κυβερνήτης ὁ ἀκριβὴς ναυτῶν εἶναι ἄρχων
e ἀλλ' οὐ ναύτης;
Ὡμολόγηται.
Οὐκ ἄρα ὅ γε τοιοῦτος κυβερνήτης τε καὶ ἄρχων τὸ τῷ
κυβερνήτῃ συμφέρον σκέψεταί τε καὶ προστάξει, ἀλλὰ τὸ τῷ
5 ναύτῃ τε καὶ ἀρχομένῳ.
Συνέφησε μόγις.
Οὐκοῦν, ἦν δ' ἐγώ, ὦ Θρασύμαχε, οὐδὲ ἄλλος οὐδεὶς ἐν
οὐδεμιᾷ ἀρχῇ, καθ' ὅσον ἄρχων ἐστίν, τὸ αὑτῷ συμφέρον
σκοπεῖ οὐδ' ἐπιτάττει, ἀλλὰ τὸ τῷ ἀρχομένῳ καὶ ᾧ ἂν αὐτὸς
10 δημιουργῇ, καὶ πρὸς ἐκεῖνο βλέπων καὶ τὸ ἐκείνῳ συμφέρον
καὶ πρέπον, καὶ λέγει ἃ λέγει καὶ ποιεῖ ἃ ποιεῖ ἅπαντα.
343 Ἐπειδὴ οὖν ἐνταῦθα ἦμεν τοῦ λόγου καὶ πᾶσι καταφανὲς
ἦν ὅτι ὁ τοῦ δικαίου λόγος εἰς τοὐναντίον περιειστήκει, ὁ
Θρασύμαχος ἀντὶ τοῦ ἀποκρίνεσθαι, Εἰπέ μοι, ἔφη, ὦ
Σώκρατες, τίτθη σοι ἔστιν;
5 Τί δέ; ἦν δ' ἐγώ· οὐκ ἀποκρίνεσθαι χρῆν μᾶλλον ἢ τοιαῦτα
ἐρωτᾶν;

342c1

[c1] 'So', I said, 'medical skill looks not to its own advantage but to that of the body.'

'Yes,' he replied.

And the skill of horsemanship not to its own advantage but to that of horses. Nor does any other skill look to its own advantage – for it has no need – but to the advantage of that for which it exists as a skill.' [c5]

'So it seems,' he said.

'But then again, Thrasymachus, skills surely also rule and hold sway over that of which they are the skills.'

At this point he conceded, but very reluctantly.

[c10] 'So no body of knowledge considers or regulates the advantage of the stronger, but that of the weaker subjected to it.' [d1]

He finally agreed to this, too, though he tried to make a fight of it; when he gave way, I said: 'So surely no doctor, in his capacity as a doctor, looks to or orders anything to his own advantage but rather to that of his patient? [d5] For it was agreed that the doctor, precisely defined, is a ruler of bodies and not in the business of making money. Was that not agreed?'

He assented.

[d10] 'And that the captain, precisely defined, is a commander of sailors but not a sailor?' [e1]

'Agreed.'

'And so that sort of captain and ruler will not consider and give orders to his own advantage, but to that of the sailor who is ruled by him.' [e5]

He assented reluctantly.

'And so it follows, Thrasymachus,' I said, 'that nobody at all in any ruling position, in his capacity as a ruler, looks to or orders what is to his own advantage, but that of the ruled and the person on whose behalf he exercises his skill, [e10] and it is by looking to that, and to what is advantageous and appropriate to it, that he says all that he says and does all that he does.'

343 Now when we had come to this point in the discussion, and it was obvious to everybody that his thesis on justice had been turned around into its opposite, Thrasymachus, instead of replying, said: 'Tell me, Socrates, do you have a wet-nurse?'

[a5] 'What do you mean?' I replied; 'shouldn't you have answered me rather than asking that sort of thing?'

Ὅτι τοί σε, ἔφη, κορυζῶντα περιορᾷ καὶ οὐκ ἀπομύττει
δεόμενον, ὅς γε αὐτῇ οὐδὲ πρόβατα οὐδὲ ποιμένα γιγνώσκεις.
Ὅτι δὴ τί μάλιστα; ἦν δ' ἐγώ.

b Ὅτι οἴει τοὺς ποιμένας ἢ τοὺς βουκόλους τὸ τῶν προβάτων ἢ τὸ τῶν βοῶν ἀγαθὸν σκοπεῖν καὶ παχύνειν αὐτοὺς
καὶ θεραπεύειν πρὸς ἄλλο τι βλέποντας ἢ τὸ τῶν δεσποτῶν
ἀγαθὸν καὶ τὸ αὑτῶν, καὶ δὴ καὶ τοὺς ἐν ταῖς πόλεσιν
5 ἄρχοντας, οἳ ὡς ἀληθῶς ἄρχουσιν, ἄλλως πως ἡγῇ διανοεῖ-
σθαι πρὸς τοὺς ἀρχομένους ἢ ὥσπερ ἄν τις πρὸς πρόβατα
διατεθείη, καὶ ἄλλο τι σκοπεῖν αὐτοὺς διὰ νυκτὸς καὶ ἡμέρας
c ἢ τοῦτο, ὅθεν αὐτοὶ ὠφελήσονται. καὶ οὕτω πόρρω εἶ περί τε
τοῦ δικαίου καὶ δικαιοσύνης καὶ ἀδίκου τε καὶ ἀδικίας, ὥστε
ἀγνοεῖς ὅτι ἡ μὲν δικαιοσύνη καὶ τὸ δίκαιον ἀλλότριον ἀγαθὸν
τῷ ὄντι, τοῦ κρείττονός τε καὶ ἄρχοντος συμφέρον, οἰκεία δὲ
5 τοῦ πειθομένου τε καὶ ὑπηρετοῦντος βλάβη, ἡ δὲ ἀδικία
τοὐναντίον, καὶ ἄρχει τῶν ὡς ἀληθῶς εὐηθικῶν τε καὶ
δικαίων, οἱ δ' ἀρχόμενοι ποιοῦσιν τὸ ἐκείνου συμφέρον
κρείττονος ὄντος, καὶ εὐδαίμονα ἐκεῖνον ποιοῦσιν ὑπηρετοῦν-
d τες αὐτῷ, ἑαυτοὺς δὲ οὐδ' ὁπωστιοῦν.
    Σκοπεῖσθαι δέ, ὦ εὐηθέστατε Σώκρατες, οὑτωσὶ χρή, ὅτι
δίκαιος ἀνὴρ ἀδίκου πανταχοῦ ἔλαττον ἔχει· πρῶτον μὲν ἐν
τοῖς πρὸς ἀλλήλους συμβολαίοις, ὅπου ἂν ὁ τοιοῦτος τῷ
5 τοιούτῳ κοινωνήσῃ, οὐδαμοῦ ἂν εὕροις ἐν τῇ διαλύσει τῆς
κοινωνίας πλέον ἔχοντα τὸν δίκαιον τοῦ ἀδίκου ἀλλ' ἔλαττον·
ἔπειτα ἐν τοῖς πρὸς τὴν πόλιν, ὅταν τέ τινες εἰσφοραὶ ὦσιν, ὁ
μὲν δίκαιος ἀπὸ τῶν ἴσων πλέον εἰσφέρει, ὁ δ' ἔλαττον, ὅταν
e τε λήψεις, ὁ μὲν οὐδέν, ὁ δὲ πολλὰ κερδαίνει. καὶ γὰρ ὅταν
ἀρχήν τινα ἄρχῃ ἑκάτερος, τῷ μὲν δικαίῳ ὑπάρχει, καὶ εἰ
μηδεμία ἄλλη ζημία, τά γε οἰκεῖα δι' ἀμέλειαν μοχθηροτέρως
ἔχειν, ἐκ δὲ τοῦ δημοσίου μηδὲν ὠφελεῖσθαι διὰ τὸ δίκαιον
5 εἶναι, πρὸς δὲ τούτοις ἀπεχθέσθαι τοῖς τε οἰκείοις καὶ τοῖς
γνωρίμοις, ὅταν μηδὲν ἐθέλῃ αὐτοῖς ὑπηρετεῖν παρὰ τὸ
δίκαιον· τῷ δὲ ἀδίκῳ πάντα τούτων τἀναντία ὑπάρχει.

344 λέγω γὰρ ὅνπερ νυνδὴ ἔλεγον, τὸν μεγάλα δυνάμενον πλεο-
νεκτεῖν· τοῦτον οὖν σκόπει, εἴπερ βούλει κρίνειν πόσῳ μᾶλλον
συμφέρει ἰδίᾳ αὑτῷ ἄδικον εἶναι ἢ τὸ δίκαιον.
    Πάντων δὲ ῥᾷστα μαθήσῃ, ἐὰν ἐπὶ τὴν τελεωτάτην ἀδικίαν
5 ἔλθῃς, ἣ τὸν μὲν ἀδικήσαντα εὐδαιμονέστατον ποιεῖ, τοὺς δὲ

344a3 ἄδικον...ἢ τὸ δίκαιον AD: τῶν ἀδίκων...ἢ τῶν δικαίων F

343a7

'Because I'm telling you', he said, 'she's turning a blind eye at your snivelling nose and doesn't wipe your face though you need it – who can't even get you to recognise the difference between sheep and shepherd.'

'And why exactly do you say that?' I asked.

[b1] 'Because you imagine that shepherds or herdsmen are considering the good of their flocks or herds and that they fatten and tend them with something in view other than the good of their masters and themselves, and what's more, you think that the attitude of those who govern cities (those who really are rulers) [b5] towards those who are governed is somehow different from the way one might be disposed towards sheep, and that they think of anything else night and day than this: how to make a profit out of them. [c1] And you are so far out in understanding about what is just and justice and what is unjust and injustice, that you don't know that justice and the just are in reality someone else's good, the advantage of the stronger and the ruler, whereas the harm suffered by the subject who obeys and is subservient is all his own. [c5] But injustice is the opposite of this, and rules over those who are truly simple-minded and just; and, being ruled, they serve the advantage of the one who is the stronger, and by serving him they promote his happiness, to the total exclusion of their own. [d1]

You must look at the matter, my most simple-minded Socrates, thus: that the just man everywhere comes off worse than the unjust. To begin with, in business relations, wherever one person collaborates with another, nowhere would you find, [d5] when the association is concluded, that the just person has come off better than the unjust, but worse. Then again, in relations with the city, when there are taxes to be paid, the just person contributes more and the unjust less out of equal resources, and when there are hand-outs the latter gains much, but the former nothing. [e1] And so, when each of them holds any office, the just person, even if he suffers no other penalty, will see his private affairs becoming comparatively worse through neglect and, because he is just, he will gain no profit from his office; [e5] and on top of that he will be hated by his family and friends, when he is not willing to do them a service unjustly. But with the unjust person all this is exactly the opposite. 344 I'm referring to the person I spoke of just now, the one who is able to go to excess on a large scale; now this is the man to watch if you want to judge how much more he is personally benefited by being unjust than by being just.

However, you will understand this matter most easily if you turn to the most complete injustice, which makes the person who has been unjust most happy, [a5]

ἀδικηθέντας καὶ ἀδικῆσαι οὐκ ἂν ἐθέλοντας ἀθλιωτάτους.
ἔστιν δὲ τοῦτο τυραννίς, ἣ οὐ κατὰ σμικρὸν τἀλλότρια καὶ
λάθρᾳ καὶ βίᾳ ἀφαιρεῖται, καὶ ἱερὰ καὶ ὅσια καὶ ἴδια καὶ
b δημόσια, ἀλλὰ συλλήβδην· ὧν ἐφ' ἑκάστῳ μέρει ὅταν τις
ἀδικήσας μὴ λάθῃ, ζημιοῦταί τε καὶ ὀνείδη ἔχει τὰ μέγιστα·
καὶ γὰρ ἱερόσυλοι καὶ ἀνδραποδισταὶ καὶ τοιχωρύχοι καὶ
ἀποστερηταὶ καὶ κλέπται οἱ κατὰ μέρη ἀδικοῦντες τῶν
5 τοιούτων κακουργημάτων καλοῦνται. ἐπειδὰν δέ τις πρὸς
τοῖς τῶν πολιτῶν χρήμασιν καὶ αὐτοὺς ἀνδραποδισάμενος
δουλώσηται, ἀντὶ τούτων τῶν αἰσχρῶν ὀνομάτων εὐδαίμονες
c καὶ μακάριοι κέκληνται, οὐ μόνον ὑπὸ τῶν πολιτῶν ἀλλὰ καὶ
ὑπὸ τῶν ἄλλων ὅσοι ἂν πύθωνται αὐτὸν τὴν ὅλην ἀδικίαν
ἠδικηκότα· οὐ γὰρ τὸ ποιεῖν τὰ ἄδικα ἀλλὰ τὸ πάσχειν
φοβούμενοι ὀνειδίζουσιν οἱ ὀνειδίζοντες τὴν ἀδικίαν.
5 Οὕτως, ὦ Σώκρατες, καὶ ἰσχυρότερον καὶ ἐλευθεριώτερον
καὶ δεσποτικώτερον ἀδικία δικαιοσύνης ἐστὶν ἱκανῶς γιγνομένη, καὶ ὅπερ ἐξ ἀρχῆς ἔλεγον, τὸ μὲν τοῦ κρείττονος
συμφέρον τὸ δίκαιον τυγχάνει ὄν, τὸ δ' ἄδικον ἑαυτῷ
λυσιτελοῦν τε καὶ συμφέρον.
d Ταῦτα εἰπὼν ὁ Θρασύμαχος ἐν νῷ εἶχεν ἀπιέναι, ὥσπερ
βαλανεὺς ἡμῶν καταντλήσας κατὰ τῶν ὤτων ἀθρόον καὶ
πολὺν τὸν λόγον· οὐ μὴν εἴασάν γε αὐτὸν οἱ παρόντες, ἀλλ'
ἠνάγκασαν ὑπομεῖναί τε καὶ παρασχεῖν τῶν εἰρημένων λόγον.
5 καὶ δὴ ἔγωγε καὶ αὐτὸς πάνυ ἐδεόμην τε καὶ εἶπον· Ὦ
δαιμόνιε Θρασύμαχε, οἷον ἐμβαλὼν λόγον ἐν νῷ ἔχεις ἀπιέναι
πρὶν διδάξαι ἱκανῶς ἢ μαθεῖν εἴτε οὕτως εἴτε ἄλλως ἔχει. ἢ
e σμικρὸν οἴει ἐπιχειρεῖν πρᾶγμα διορίζεσθαι, ἀλλ' οὐ βίου
διαγωγήν, ᾗ ἂν διαγόμενος ἕκαστος ἡμῶν λυσιτελεστάτην
ζωὴν ζῴη;
Ἐγὼ γὰρ οἶμαι, ἔφη ὁ Θρασύμαχος, τουτὶ ἄλλως ἔχειν;
5 Ἔοικας, ἦν δ' ἐγώ, ἤτοι ἡμῶν γε οὐδὲν κήδεσθαι, οὐδέ τι
φροντίζειν εἴτε χεῖρον εἴτε βέλτιον βιωσόμεθα ἀγνοοῦντες ὃ
σὺ φὴς εἰδέναι. ἀλλ', ὠγαθέ, προθυμοῦ καὶ ἡμῖν ἐνδείξασθαι·
345 οὔ τοι κακῶς σοι κείσεται ὅτι ἂν ἡμᾶς τοσούσδε ὄντας
εὐεργετήσῃς. ἐγὼ γὰρ δή σοι λέγω τό γ' ἐμόν, ὅτι οὐ πείθομαι
οὐδ' οἶμαι ἀδικίαν δικαιοσύνης κερδαλεώτερον εἶναι, οὐδ' ἐὰν
ἐᾷ τις αὐτὴν καὶ μὴ διακωλύῃ πράττειν ἃ βούλεται. ἀλλ',
5 ὠγαθέ, ἔστω μὲν ἄδικος, δυνάσθω δὲ ἀδικεῖν ἢ τῷ λανθάνειν

344e1   ἀλλ' οὐ AD: ὅλου F

344a6
and those who have been wronged and would be unwilling to commit a crime most miserable. I'm talking about tyranny, which secretly and by force appropriates others' possessions, sacred and secular, private and public, and not on a small scale but wholesale. [b1] When people are caught committing unjust acts like these in isolation, they are fined and incur the greatest disgrace – I'm talking about temple-robbers, kidnappers, burglars, fraudsters, thieves, as people who commit these isolated forms of villainy are called. [b5] But whenever someone kidnaps and enslaves the citizens themselves in addition to their property, instead of those shameful names such people are called happy and fortunate, not only by the citizens [c1] but also by everyone else who hears about the person who has committed such out-and-out injustice; for those who censure injustice do so not because they fear doing, but rather because they fear being the victims of, unjust acts.

[c5] Thus, Socrates, injustice when it occurs on a sufficiently large scale is both stronger and freer and more masterful than justice, and, as I said at the beginning, justice is in fact the advantage of the stronger, but injustice is profitable and advantageous to oneself.'

[d1] After this Thrasymachus was intending to depart, having, like a bath-attendant, emptied over our ears an incessant and copious flood of words. However those present would not let him, but compelled him to remain behind and defend what he had just said.

[d5] Indeed I too was particularly insistent in asking him to stay, saying: 'My dear Thrasymachus, surely you don't intend to launch such an argument at us and then go away before explaining it adequately or finding out whether it is correct or not? [e1] Do you think it's a minor matter you are attempting to define, and not the course of a life which each of us should follow in order to live it most profitably?'

'Of course; do you imagine I think otherwise?' retorted Thrasymachus.

[e5] 'You seem to', I replied,' or else you don't care about us, and you don't feel any concern whether we are going to live worse or better lives in ignorance of what you claim to know. Come on, my friend, show willingness to demonstrate it to us too; whatever benefit you can bestow on so many of us won't be a bad investment. **345** For I can tell you that as far as I'm concerned you haven't convinced me, and I don't think that injustice is more profitable than justice, not even if one allows it a free hand and does not prevent it from doing what it wants. [a5] No, my friend: granted

ἢ τῷ διαμάχεσθαι, ὅμως ἐμέγε οὐ πείθει ὡς ἔστι τῆς
b δικαιοσύνης κερδαλεώτερον. ταῦτ᾽ οὖν καὶ ἕτερος ἴσως τις
ἡμῶν πέπονθεν, οὐ μόνος ἐγώ· πεῖσον οὖν, ὦ μακάριε, ἱκανῶς
ἡμᾶς ὅτι οὐκ ὀρθῶς βουλευόμεθα δικαιοσύνην ἀδικίας περὶ
πλείονος ποιούμενοι.
5 Καὶ πῶς, ἔφη, σὲ πείσω; εἰ γὰρ οἷς νυνδὴ ἔλεγον μὴ
πέπεισαι, τί σοι ἔτι ποιήσω; ἢ εἰς τὴν ψυχὴν φέρων ἐνθῶ
τὸν λόγον;
Μὰ Δί᾽, ἦν δ᾽ ἐγώ, μὴ σύ γε· ἀλλὰ πρῶτον μέν, ἃ ἂν εἴπῃς,
ἔμμενε τούτοις, ἢ ἐὰν μετατιθῇ, φανερῶς μετατίθεσο καὶ
c ἡμᾶς μὴ ἐξαπάτα. νῦν δὲ ὁρᾷς, ὦ Θρασύμαχε, ἔτι γὰρ τὰ
ἔμπροσθεν ἐπισκεψώμεθα, ὅτι τὸν ὡς ἀληθῶς ἰατρὸν τὸ
πρῶτον ὁριζόμενος τὸν ὡς ἀληθῶς ποιμένα οὐκέτι ᾤου δεῖν
ὕστερον ἀκριβῶς φυλάξαι, ἀλλὰ πιαίνειν οἴει αὐτὸν τὰ
5 πρόβατα, καθ᾽ ὅσον ποιμήν ἐστιν, οὐ πρὸς τὸ τῶν προβάτων
βέλτιστον βλέποντα ἀλλ᾽, ὥσπερ δαιτυμόνα τινὰ καὶ μέλ-
λοντα ἑστιάσεσθαι, πρὸς τὴν εὐωχίαν, ἢ αὖ πρὸς τὸ ἀποδό-
d σθαι, ὥσπερ χρηματιστὴν ἀλλ᾽ οὐ ποιμένα. τῇ δὲ ποιμενικῇ
οὐ δήπου ἄλλου του μέλει ἢ ἐφ᾽ ᾧ τέτακται, ὅπως τούτῳ τὸ
βέλτιστον ἐκποριεῖ· ἐπεὶ τά γε αὐτῆς ὥστ᾽ εἶναι βελτίστη
ἱκανῶς δήπου ἐκπεπόρισται, ἕως γ᾽ ἂν μηδὲν ἐνδέῃ τοῦ
5 ποιμενικὴ εἶναι. οὕτω δὴ ᾤμην ἔγωγε νυνδὴ ἀναγκαῖον
εἶναι ἡμῖν ὁμολογεῖν πᾶσαν ἀρχήν, καθ᾽ ὅσον ἀρχή, μηδενὶ
ἄλλῳ τὸ βέλτιστον σκοπεῖσθαι ἢ ἐκείνῳ, τῷ ἀρχομένῳ τε καὶ
e θεραπευομένῳ, ἔν τε πολιτικῇ καὶ ἰδιωτικῇ ἀρχῇ. σὺ δὲ τοὺς
ἄρχοντας ἐν ταῖς πόλεσιν, τοὺς ὡς ἀληθῶς ἄρχοντας, ἑκόντας
οἴει ἄρχειν;
Μὰ Δί᾽ οὔκ, ἔφη, ἀλλ᾽ εὖ οἶδα.
5 Τί δέ, ἦν δ᾽ ἐγώ, ὦ Θρασύμαχε; τὰς ἄλλας ἀρχὰς οὐκ
ἐννοεῖς ὅτι οὐδεὶς ἐθέλει ἄρχειν ἑκών, ἀλλὰ μισθὸν αἰτοῦσιν,
ὡς οὐχὶ αὐτοῖσιν ὠφελίαν ἐσομένην ἐκ τοῦ ἄρχειν ἀλλὰ τοῖς
346 ἀρχομένοις; ἐπεὶ τοσόνδε εἰπέ· οὐχὶ ἑκάστην μέντοι φαμὲν
ἑκάστοτε τῶν τεχνῶν τούτῳ ἑτέραν εἶναι, τῷ ἑτέραν τὴν
δύναμιν ἔχειν; καί, ὦ μακάριε, μὴ παρὰ δόξαν ἀποκρίνου, ἵνα
τι καὶ περαίνωμεν.
5 Ἀλλὰ τούτῳ, ἔφη, ἑτέρα.

345c4   πιαίνειν A Eusebius: ποιμαίνειν A (lectio in margine scripta) D: παχύνειν F

345a6
the unjust person, and let him have the power to act unjustly either undetected or by
fighting it out openly, he still doesn't persuade me for my part that injustice is a more
profitable thing than justice. [b1] And there may well be someone else among
us who feels the same, and not just myself; so then, my dear fellow, make an
adequate job of persuading us that we are not on the right track in valuing justice
above injustice.'

[b5] 'And how am I to persuade you?' he said. 'For if you are not convinced by
what I have just been saying, what more can I do for you? Must I take the argument
and implant it in your soul?'

'Certainly I don't want that from you, by Zeus', I said; 'but in the first place, do
stand by whatever you say, or if you shift your ground, make your move openly
and don't deceive us. [c1] Now then, Thrasymachus, let's continue to look at your
previous examples: you see that while you began by defining a doctor in the true
sense, you didn't subsequently think it necessary to maintain your precision where
the true shepherd was concerned. You suppose that, in his capacity as a shepherd,
[c5] he fattens up the flocks, not with an eye to their best interests but, like some
banqueter about to enjoy a good meal and good company, or again with a view
to selling them like a businessman, but not as a shepherd. [d1] But the skill of
shepherding is surely directed only towards how to provide what is best for that
which is in its charge, since, I imagine, it has sufficiently provided what concerns
itself with a view to being at its best, as long as it in no way falls short of being
the shepherd's skill. [d5] And so I thought just now that agreement among us was
inevitable that every form of rule, seen purely as rule, considers what is best for
nothing other than those governed and under its care, in both public and private
situations. [e1] But do you think that rulers in cities, rulers in the true sense, hold
office willingly?'

'By Zeus,' he replied, 'I don't think it; I know they do.'

[e5] 'But what of this, Thrasymachus?' I said. 'Have you not considered that in the
case of other forms of rule nobody willingly chooses authority, but people demand
payment, on the grounds that no benefit from their rule will come to themselves,
but to those ruled? **346** And tell me this: don't we usually say that each of the skills
is different from others because it has a different function? And, my good fellow,
don't answer contrary to your real belief, so that we may make some progress.'

[a5] 'Well yes,' he replied, 'that is where they differ.'

Οὐκοῦν καὶ ὠφελίαν ἑκάστη ἰδίαν τινὰ ἡμῖν παρέχεται ἀλλ᾽
οὐ κοινήν, οἷον ἰατρικὴ μὲν ὑγίειαν, κυβερνητικὴ δὲ σωτηρίαν
ἐν τῷ πλεῖν, καὶ αἱ ἄλλαι οὕτω;
Πάνυ γε.

b　Οὐκοῦν καὶ μισθωτικὴ μισθόν; αὕτη γὰρ αὑτῆς ἡ δύναμις·
ἢ τὴν ἰατρικὴν σὺ καὶ τὴν κυβερνητικὴν τὴν αὐτὴν καλεῖς; ἢ
ἐάνπερ βούλῃ ἀκριβῶς διορίζειν, ὥσπερ ὑπέθου, οὐδέν τι
μᾶλλον, ἐάν τις κυβερνῶν ὑγιὴς γίγνηται διὰ τὸ συμφέρειν
5　αὐτῷ πλεῖν ἐν τῇ θαλάττῃ, ἕνεκα τούτου καλεῖς μᾶλλον αὐτὴν
ἰατρικήν;
Οὐ δῆτα, ἔφη.
Οὐδέ γ᾽, οἶμαι, τὴν μισθωτικήν, ἐὰν ὑγιαίνῃ τις μισθαρ-
νῶν.
10　Οὐ δῆτα.
Τί δέ; τὴν ἰατρικὴν μισθαρνητικήν, ἐὰν ἰώμενός τις μι-
σθαρνῇ;
c　Οὐκ ἔφη.
Οὐκοῦν τήν γε ὠφελίαν ἑκάστης τῆς τέχνης ἰδίαν ὡμο-
λογήσαμεν εἶναι;
Ἔστω, ἔφη.
5　Ἥντινα ἄρα ὠφελίαν κοινῇ ὠφελοῦνται πάντες οἱ δημιουρ-
γοί, δῆλον ὅτι κοινῇ τινι τῷ αὐτῷ προσχρώμενοι ἀπ᾽ ἐκείνου
ὠφελοῦνται.
Ἔοικεν, ἔφη.
Φαμὲν δέ γε τὸ μισθὸν ἀρνυμένους ὠφελεῖσθαι τοὺς
10　δημιουργοὺς ἀπὸ τοῦ προσχρῆσθαι τῇ μισθωτικῇ τέχνῃ
γίγνεσθαι αὐτοῖς.
Συνέφη μόγις.
d　Οὐκ ἄρα ἀπὸ τῆς αὑτοῦ τέχνης ἑκάστῳ αὕτη ἡ ὠφελία
ἐστίν, ἡ τοῦ μισθοῦ λῆψις, ἀλλ᾽, εἰ δεῖ ἀκριβῶς σκοπεῖσθαι, ἡ
μὲν ἰατρικὴ ὑγίειαν ποιεῖ, ἡ δὲ μισθαρνητικὴ μισθόν, καὶ ἡ
μὲν οἰκοδομικὴ οἰκίαν, ἡ δὲ μισθαρνητικὴ αὐτῇ ἑπομένη
5　μισθόν, καὶ αἱ ἄλλαι πᾶσαι οὕτως τὸ αὑτῆς ἑκάστη ἔργον
ἐργάζεται καὶ ὠφελεῖ ἐκεῖνο ἐφ᾽ ᾧ τέτακται. ἐὰν δὲ μὴ μισθὸς
αὐτῇ προσγίγνηται, ἔσθ᾽ ὅτι ὠφελεῖται ὁ δημιουργὸς ἀπὸ τῆς
τέχνης;
Οὐ φαίνεται, ἔφη.
e　Ἆρ᾽ οὖν οὐδ᾽ ὠφελεῖ τότε, ὅταν προῖκα ἐργάζηται;

346b4　ξυμφέρειν F: ξυμφέρον AD

'So doesn't each of them give us some unique benefit not common to the others: for example, medicine gives us health, navigation safety in sailing, and so on? 'Yes.'

[b1] 'So doesn't the skill of wage-earning give us wages? For that is its function; or would you call the doctor's and the captain's skill the same? Or, if you wish to discriminate precisely, as you proposed, are you any more likely to call navigation medicine simply because some ship's captain recovers his health through the beneficial effect of a voyage? [b5]

'No, of course not,' he replied.

'Any more, I imagine, than you would call wage-earning medicine if someone regains health while earning money.'

[b10] 'No, indeed.'

'What about this, then? Is medicine to be called wage-earning if someone earns money while administering treatment?'

[c1] He said it wasn't.

'So are we agreed that each skill has its own particular benefit?'

'Let it be so,' he said.

[c5] 'So any common benefit all skilled professionals enjoy they clearly derive from the use of some additional thing they have in common.'

'It seems so,' he said.

'And we say, don't we, that skilled professionals earning wages benefit from exercising the wage-earning skill in addition to their own.' [c10]

He agreed reluctantly.

[d1] 'So this benefit, the receiving of wages, does not come to each person from his own skill, but, if we must be precise, medicine produces health, wage-earning wages, and house-building a house, but it is the addition of wage-earning which produces the wages, [d5] and with all the other skills likewise: each has its own function and benefits that over which it has charge. But if no wages are added to the skill, can the skilled professional benefit from his skill?'

'Apparently not', he said.

[e1] 'But does he confer no benefit either, on the occasions when he works for nothing?'

Οἶμαι ἔγωγε.

Οὐκοῦν, ὦ Θρασύμαχε, τοῦτο ἤδη δῆλον, ὅτι οὐδεμία τέχνη οὐδὲ ἀρχὴ τὸ αὑτῇ ὠφέλιμον παρασκευάζει, ἀλλ᾽, ὅπερ πάλαι ἐλέγομεν, τὸ τῷ ἀρχομένῳ καὶ παρασκευάζει καὶ ἐπιτάττει, τὸ ἐκείνου συμφέρον ἥττονος ὄντος σκοποῦσα, ἀλλ᾽ οὐ τὸ τοῦ κρείττονος. διὰ δὴ ταῦτα ἔγωγε, ὦ φίλε Θρασύμαχε, καὶ ἄρτι ἔλεγον μηδένα ἐθέλειν ἑκόντα ἄρχειν καὶ τὰ ἀλλότρια κακὰ μεταχειρίζεσθαι ἀνορθοῦντα, ἀλλὰ μισθὸν αἰτεῖν, ὅτι ὁ μέλλων καλῶς τῇ τέχνῃ πράξειν οὐδέποτε αὑτῷ τὸ βέλτιστον πράττει οὐδ᾽ ἐπιτάττει κατὰ τὴν τέχνην ἐπιτάττων, ἀλλὰ τῷ ἀρχομένῳ· ὧν δὴ ἕνεκα, ὡς ἔοικε, μισθὸν δεῖν ὑπάρχειν τοῖς μέλλουσιν ἐθελήσειν ἄρχειν, ἢ ἀργύριον ἢ τιμήν, ἢ ζημίαν ἐὰν μὴ ἄρχῃ.

Πῶς τοῦτο λέγεις, ὦ Σώκρατες; ἔφη ὁ Γλαύκων· τοὺς μὲν γὰρ δύο μισθοὺς γιγνώσκω, τὴν δὲ ζημίαν ἥντινα λέγεις καὶ ὡς ἐν μισθοῦ μέρει εἴρηκας, οὐ συνῆκα.

Τὸν τῶν βελτίστων ἄρα μισθόν, ἔφην, οὐ συνίης, δι᾽ ὃν ἄρχουσιν οἱ ἐπιεικέστατοι, ὅταν ἐθέλωσιν ἄρχειν. ἢ οὐκ οἶσθα ὅτι τὸ φιλότιμόν τε καὶ φιλάργυρον εἶναι ὄνειδος λέγεταί τε καὶ ἔστιν;

Ἔγωγε, ἔφη.

Διὰ ταῦτα τοίνυν, ἦν δ᾽ ἐγώ, οὔτε χρημάτων ἕνεκα ἐθέλουσιν ἄρχειν οἱ ἀγαθοὶ οὔτε τιμῆς· οὔτε γὰρ φανερῶς πραττόμενοι τῆς ἀρχῆς ἕνεκα μισθὸν μισθωτοὶ βούλονται κεκλῆσθαι, οὔτε λάθρᾳ αὐτοὶ ἐκ τῆς ἀρχῆς λαμβάνοντες κλέπται. οὐδ᾽ αὖ τιμῆς ἕνεκα· οὐ γάρ εἰσι φιλότιμοι. δεῖ δὴ αὐτοῖς ἀνάγκην προσεῖναι καὶ ζημίαν, εἰ μέλλουσιν ἐθέλειν ἄρχειν· ὅθεν κινδυνεύει τὸ ἑκόντα ἐπὶ τὸ ἄρχειν ἰέναι ἀλλὰ μὴ ἀνάγκην περιμένειν αἰσχρὸν νενομίσθαι. τῆς δὲ ζημίας μεγίστη τὸ ὑπὸ πονηροτέρου ἄρχεσθαι, ἐὰν μὴ αὐτὸς ἐθέλῃ ἄρχειν· ἣν δείσαντές μοι φαίνονται ἄρχειν, ὅταν ἄρχωσιν, οἱ ἐπιεικεῖς. καὶ τότε ἔρχονται ἐπὶ τὸ ἄρχειν, οὐχ ὡς ἐπ᾽ ἀγαθόν τι ἰόντες οὐδ᾽ ὡς εὐπαθήσοντες ἐν αὐτῷ, ἀλλ᾽ ὡς ἐπ᾽ ἀναγκαῖον, καὶ οὐκ ἔχοντες ἑαυτῶν βελτίοσιν ἐπιτρέψαι οὐδὲ ὁμοίοις. ἐπεὶ κινδυνεύει πόλις ἀνδρῶν ἀγαθῶν εἰ γένοιτο, περιμάχητον ἂν εἶναι τὸ μὴ ἄρχειν ὥσπερ νυνὶ τὸ ἄρχειν, καὶ ἐνταῦθ᾽ ἂν καταφανὲς γενέσθαι ὅτι τῷ ὄντι ἀληθινὸς ἄρχων οὐ πέφυκε τὸ αὑτῷ συμφέρον σκοπεῖσθαι ἀλλὰ τὸ τῷ ἀρχομένῳ· ὥστε πᾶς ἂν ὁ γιγνώσκων τὸ ὠφελεῖσθαι μᾶλλον ἕλοιτο ὑπ᾽ ἄλλου ἢ ἄλλον ὠφελῶν

346e2
'I think he does.'

'So, Thrasymachus, it is by now apparent that no skill or rule provides for its own benefit, but, as we said long ago, [e5] it provides for and orders for the benefit of those who are governed, looking to the advantage of the weaker, and not that of the stronger. That is why, my dear Thrasymachus, I made a point of saying just now that nobody willingly chooses to govern and get involved in setting right other peoples' wrongs, but they demand payment, **347** because whoever intends to exercise his skill well will never act or order to his own best advantage (if he practises according to his art) but will act in the interests of those who are ruled; and it is for this reason, it seems, that those who intend to choose to rule must be paid, either with money or honours, or incur a penalty if they refuse.' [a5]

'What do you mean by that, Socrates?' said Glaucon; 'the first two rewards I recognise, but what penalty you mean and in what sense you describe it as replacing wages – that I don't understand.'

[b1] 'Then you don't understand the reward of the best men,' I replied, 'for which the most estimable govern, when they are willing to do so. Don't you know that to be keen on honour and money is said to be, and actually is, discreditable?'

[b5] 'I do', he replied.

'That's the reason, therefore,' I said, 'why the good are not willing to rule for the sake of money or honour; for they don't wish to be called hired workers for openly doing the work of governing for pay, nor thieves for secretly extracting money from their office. Nor do they wish to serve for honour, for they are not ambitious. [c1] So they must have imposed on them an obligation and in addition a penalty, if they are going to consent to rule – which is probably why it is considered shameful to be willing to accept office and not wait to be compelled. But the greatest penalty, if they are not themselves willing, is to be ruled by someone worse. [c5] It is fear of this, it seems to me, that impels the estimable to rule, when they do consent, and even then they go into it not as to something good, nor as to something which they expect to enjoy, but as to something they have to do, [d1] because they cannot put it into the hands of anyone better than themselves or equal to them. For it is likely that in a city of good men, were it to exist, there would be as much in-fighting to avoid political power as there now is to gain it, thereby making it plain that the person who is really and truly a ruler [d5] does not naturally consider his own interest, but that of the ruled; so that every person of understanding would choose to

πράγματα ἔχειν. τοῦτο μὲν οὖν ἔγωγε οὐδαμῇ συγχωρῶ
e Θρασυμάχῳ, ὡς τὸ δίκαιόν ἐστιν τὸ τοῦ κρείττονος συμφέρον. ἀλλὰ τοῦτο μὲν δὴ καὶ εἰς αὖθις σκεψόμεθα· πολὺ δέ
μοι δοκεῖ μεῖζον εἶναι ὃ νῦν λέγει Θρασύμαχος, τὸν τοῦ
ἀδίκου βίον φάσκων εἶναι κρείττω ἢ τὸν τοῦ δικαίου. σὺ
5 οὖν ποτέρως, ἦν δ' ἐγώ, ὦ Γλαύκων, αἱρῇ; καὶ πότερον
ἀληθεστέρως δοκεῖ σοι λέγεσθαι;
        Τὸν τοῦ δικαίου ἔγωγε λυσιτελέστερον βίον εἶναι.
348   Ἤκουσας οὖν, ἦν δ' ἐγώ, ὅσα ἄρτι Θρασύμαχος ἀγαθὰ
διῆλθεν τῷ τοῦ ἀδίκου;
        Ἤκουσα, ἔφη, ἀλλ' οὐ πείθομαι.
        Βούλει οὖν αὐτὸν πείθωμεν, ἂν δυνώμεθά πῃ ἐξευρεῖν, ὡς
5 οὐκ ἀληθῆ λέγει;
        Πῶς γὰρ οὐ βούλομαι; ἦ δ' ὅς.
        Ἂν μὲν τοίνυν, ἦν δ' ἐγώ, ἀντικατατείναντες λέγωμεν
αὐτῷ λόγον παρὰ λόγον, ὅσα αὖ ἀγαθὰ ἔχει τὸ δίκαιον
εἶναι, καὶ αὖθις οὗτος, καὶ ἄλλον ἡμεῖς, ἀριθμεῖν δεήσει
b τἀγαθὰ καὶ μετρεῖν ὅσα ἑκάτεροι ἐν ἑκατέρῳ λέγομεν, καὶ
ἤδη δικαστῶν τινων τῶν διακρινούντων δεησόμεθα· ἂν δὲ
ὥσπερ ἄρτι ἀνομολογούμενοι πρὸς ἀλλήλους σκοπῶμεν, ἅμα
αὐτοί τε δικασταὶ καὶ ῥήτορες ἐσόμεθα.
5   Πάνυ μὲν οὖν, ἔφη.
        Ποτέρως οὖν σοι, ἦν δ' ἐγώ, ἀρέσκει;
        Οὕτως, ἔφη.
        Ἴθι δή, ἦν δ' ἐγώ, ὦ Θρασύμαχε, ἀπόκριναι ἡμῖν ἐξ ἀρχῆς.
τὴν τελέαν ἀδικίαν τελέας οὔσης δικαιοσύνης λυσιτελεστέραν
10 φῂς εἶναι;
c   Πάνυ μὲν οὖν καὶ φημί, ἔφη, καὶ δι' ἅ, εἴρηκα.
        Φέρε δή, τὸ τοιόνδε περὶ αὐτῶν πῶς λέγεις; τὸ μέν που
ἀρετὴν αὐτοῖν καλεῖς, τὸ δὲ κακίαν;
        Πῶς γὰρ οὔ;
5   Οὐκοῦν τὴν μὲν δικαιοσύνην ἀρετήν, τὴν δὲ ἀδικίαν
κακίαν;
        Εἰκός γ', ἔφη, ὦ ἥδιστε, ἐπειδή γε καὶ λέγω ἀδικίαν μὲν
λυσιτελεῖν, δικαιοσύνην δ' οὔ.
        Ἀλλὰ τί μήν;

347d5
be benefited by another rather than to have the bother of being the one who confers
the benefit on him. So on that point, then, I totally disagree with Thrasymachus [e1]
when he claims that justice is the advantage of the stronger. But that is a question
which we will examine later; of much greater significance, it seems to me, is what
Thrasymachus was saying just now, when he asserted that the life of the unjust
person is better than that of the just. Now which of these do you choose, Glaucon?'
I said, [e5] 'and which of us do you think is nearer the truth?'

'I say that the life of the just person is more profitable.'

348 'Did you hear,' I said, 'how many good things in the life of the unjust person
Thrasymachus has just listed?'

'I did', he said, 'but I'm not convinced.'

'Then if we can find a way, do you want us to persuade him that he is not right?'
[a5]

'Of course I want us to', he said.

'Well then,' I said, 'if we set out our argument directly counter to his, enumerating
all the good things to come from justice, and then he does the same, and then we
reply to him, we will have to count up and measure all the good things listed by
each of us, [b1] and we will soon need some judges to decide between us. But if
we carry on the enquiry by mutual agreement, as we have done up to this point,
we will be both judges and advocates ourselves.

[b5] 'Certainly', he said.

'So which method,' I asked, 'do you prefer?'

'The latter,' he replied.

'Come then, Thrasymachus,' I said, 'go back to the beginning and answer us. You
claim that perfect injustice is more profitable than justice in its perfect state?'
[b10]

[c1] 'That's exactly what I do say,' he replied, 'and I have told you why.'

'Well then, what do you say about them on this point: you call one of them, I
presume, an excellence and the other a vice?'

'Of course.'

[c5] 'So justice is the excellence and injustice the vice?'

'That's very likely, isn't it' he said, 'you simpleton, when I actually say that injustice
is profitable and justice isn't?'

'Well, what do you say then?'

10 Τοὐναντίον, ἦ δ' ὅς.
Ἦ τὴν δικαιοσύνην κακίαν;
Οὔκ, ἀλλὰ πάνυ γενναίαν εὐήθειαν.

d Τὴν ἀδικίαν ἄρα κακοήθειαν καλεῖς;
Οὔκ, ἀλλ' εὐβουλίαν, ἔφη.

Ἦ καὶ φρόνιμοί σοι, ὦ Θρασύμαχε, δοκοῦσιν εἶναι καὶ
ἀγαθοὶ οἱ ἄδικοι;

5 Οἵ γε τελέως, ἔφη, οἷοί τε ἀδικεῖν, πόλεις τε καὶ ἔθνη
δυνάμενοι ἀνθρώπων ὑφ' ἑαυτοὺς ποιεῖσθαι· σὺ δὲ οἴει με
ἴσως τοὺς τὰ βαλλάντια ἀποτέμνοντας λέγειν. λυσιτελεῖ μὲν
οὖν, ἦ δ' ὅς, καὶ τὰ τοιαῦτα, ἐάνπερ λανθάνῃ· ἔστι δὲ οὐκ ἄξια
λόγου, ἀλλ' ἃ νυνδὴ ἔλεγον.

e Τοῦτο μέν, ἔφην, οὐκ ἀγνοῶ ὃ βούλει λέγειν, ἀλλὰ τόδε
ἐθαύμασα, εἰ ἐν ἀρετῆς καὶ σοφίας τίθης μέρει τὴν ἀδικίαν,
τὴν δὲ δικαιοσύνην ἐν τοῖς ἐναντίοις.
Ἀλλὰ πάνυ οὕτω τίθημι.

5 Τοῦτο, ἦν δ' ἐγώ, ἤδη στερεώτερον, ὦ ἑταῖρε, καὶ οὐκέτι
ῥᾴδιον ἔχειν ὅτι τις εἴπῃ. εἰ γὰρ λυσιτελεῖν μὲν τὴν ἀδικίαν
ἐτίθεσο, κακίαν μέντοι ἢ αἰσχρὸν αὐτὸ ὡμολόγεις εἶναι
ὥσπερ ἄλλοι τινές, εἴχομεν ἄν τι λέγειν κατὰ τὰ νομιζόμενα
λέγοντες. νῦν δὲ δῆλος εἶ ὅτι φήσεις αὐτὸ καὶ καλὸν καὶ
349 ἰσχυρὸν εἶναι καὶ τἆλλα αὐτῷ πάντα προσθήσεις ἃ ἡμεῖς τῷ
δικαίῳ προσετίθεμεν, ἐπειδή γε καὶ ἐν ἀρετῇ αὐτὸ καὶ σοφίᾳ
ἐτόλμησας θεῖναι.
Ἀληθέστατα, ἔφη, μαντεύῃ.

5 Ἀλλ' οὐ μέντοι, ἦν δ' ἐγώ, ἀποκνητέον γε τῷ λόγῳ
ἐπεξελθεῖν σκοπούμενον, ἕως ἄν σε ὑπολαμβάνω λέγειν
ἅπερ διανοῇ. ἐμοὶ γὰρ δοκεῖς σύ, ὦ Θρασύμαχε, ἀτεχνῶς
νῦν οὐ σκώπτειν, ἀλλὰ τὰ δοκοῦντα περὶ τῆς ἀληθείας λέγειν.
Τί δέ σοι, ἔφη, τοῦτο διαφέρει, εἴτε μοι δοκεῖ εἴτε μή, ἀλλ'
10 οὐ τὸν λόγον ἐλέγχεις;

b Οὐδέν, ἦν δ' ἐγώ. ἀλλὰ τόδε μοι πειρῶ ἔτι πρὸς τούτοις
ἀποκρίνασθαι· ὁ δίκαιος τοῦ δικαίου δοκεῖ τί σοι ἂν ἐθέλειν
πλέον ἔχειν;
Οὐδαμῶς, ἔφη· οὐ γὰρ ἂν ἦν ἀστεῖος, ὥσπερ νῦν, καὶ
5 εὐήθης.
Τί δέ; τῆς δικαίας πράξεως;

348c10

[c10] 'The opposite,' he replied.

'Are you saying justice is the vice?'

'No, but a most high-minded good nature.'

[d1] 'Then are you calling injustice the opposite – bad nature?'

'No; rather, good judgement,' he replied.

'So you think that the unjust are intelligent, good people, Thrasymachus?'

[d5] 'Certainly,' he said, 'those who are capable of complete injustice, and have the power to subject cities and tribes of people to themselves. But you perhaps imagine I'm talking of people who snatch purses. To be sure,' he said, 'things like that can be profitable too, if they go undetected; but they are insignificant compared with what I have just described.'

[e1] 'I'm not unaware of what you mean by that,' I said, 'but I am surprised, if you put injustice in the category of excellence and wisdom, and justice in the opposite.'

'Well, that is just what I do.'

[e5] 'That takes us on to a much stiffer proposition, my friend, 'I said, 'and it's no longer easy to produce a reply. For if you had proposed that injustice was profitable, but nevertheless conceded that it was a vice and shameful, as some others do, we would be able to discuss the matter along generally accepted lines. As it is, you are obviously going to claim that it is fine and strong **349** and will ascribe to it all the other qualities with which we were categorising justice, since you have not flinched from putting it alongside even excellence and wisdom.'

'You are a most accurate prophet,' he said.

'Yes,' I said, 'but we mustn't hesitate from working through the logic of the enquiry [a5] as long as I can take it for granted that you are saying what you think. For I believe, Thrasymachus, that you are not now simply mocking us, but saying what you believe to be the truth'

'What difference does it make to you,' he replied, 'whether *I* believe it or not, if you avoid testing my argument?' [a10]

[b1] 'None,' I replied, 'but still try to give me an answer to this question: do you think that a just person would wish to outdo another just person?'

'Certainly not,' he said, 'otherwise he would not be the civilised, good-natured fellow we've just been talking about.' [b5]

'And would he go beyond the just action?'

Οὐδὲ ⟨ταύ⟩της [δικαίας], ἔφη.

Τοῦ δὲ ἀδίκου πότερον ἀξιοῖ ἂν πλεονεκτεῖν καὶ ἡγοῖτο
δίκαιον εἶναι, ἢ οὐκ ἂν ἡγοῖτο;

10   Ἡγοῖτ᾽ ἄν, ἦ δ᾽ ὅς, καὶ ἀξιοῖ, ἀλλ᾽ οὐκ ἂν δύναιτο.

c   Ἀλλ᾽ οὐ τοῦτο, ἦν δ᾽ ἐγώ, ἐρωτῶ, ἀλλ᾽ εἰ τοῦ μὲν δικαίου
μὴ ἀξιοῖ πλέον ἔχειν μηδὲ βούλεται ὁ δίκαιος, τοῦ δὲ ἀδίκου;
Ἀλλ᾽ οὕτως, ἔφη, ἔχει.

Τί δὲ δὴ ὁ ἄδικος; ἆρα ἀξιοῖ τοῦ δικαίου πλεονεκτεῖν καὶ
5   τῆς δικαίας πράξεως;

Πῶς γὰρ οὔκ; ἔφη, ὅς γε πάντων πλέον ἔχειν ἀξιοῖ;

Οὐκοῦν καὶ ἀδίκου ἀνθρώπου τε καὶ πράξεως ὁ ἄδικος
πλεονεκτήσει, καὶ ἁμιλλήσεται ὡς ἁπάντων πλεῖστον αὐτὸς
λάβῃ;

10   Ἔστι ταῦτα.

Ὧδε δὴ λέγωμεν, ἔφην· ὁ δίκαιος τοῦ μὲν ὁμοίου οὐ

d   πλεονεκτεῖ, τοῦ δὲ ἀνομοίου, ὁ δὲ ἄδικος τοῦ τε ὁμοίου καὶ
τοῦ ἀνομοίου;

Ἄριστα, ἔφη, εἴρηκας.

Ἔστιν δέ γε, ἔφην, φρόνιμός τε καὶ ἀγαθὸς ὁ ἄδικος, ὁ δὲ
5   δίκαιος οὐδέτερα;

Καὶ τοῦτ᾽, ἔφη, εὖ.

Οὐκοῦν, ἦν δ᾽ ἐγώ, καὶ ἔοικε τῷ φρονίμῳ καὶ τῷ ἀγαθῷ ὁ
ἄδικος, ὁ δὲ δίκαιος οὐκ ἔοικεν;

Πῶς γὰρ οὐ μέλλει, ἔφη, ὁ τοιοῦτος ὢν καὶ ἐοικέναι τοῖς
10   τοιούτοις, ὁ δὲ μὴ ἐοικέναι;

Καλῶς. τοιοῦτος ἄρα ἐστὶν ἑκάτερος αὐτῶν οἷσπερ ἔοικεν;
Ἀλλὰ τί μέλλει; ἔφη.

e   Εἶεν, ὦ Θρασύμαχε· μουσικὸν δέ τινα λέγεις, ἕτερον δὲ
ἄμουσον;

Ἔγωγε.

Πότερον φρόνιμον καὶ πότερον ἄφρονα;

5   Τὸν μὲν μουσικὸν δήπου φρόνιμον, τὸν δὲ ἄμουσον ἄφρονα.

Οὐκοῦν ἅπερ φρόνιμον, ἀγαθόν, ἃ δὲ ἄφρονα, κακόν;

349b7   ταύτης Slings: τῆς ADF Stobaeus: δικαίας ADF Stobaeus: secl. Wilamowitz: δικαίας
πράξεως Stallbaum

'Not that either,' he replied.

'But what of the unjust person – would the just consider outdoing him and think it right to do so, or not?'

[b10] 'He would consider it and think it right, but he would not be able to.'

[c1] 'That's not what I'm asking,' I said, 'but whether a just person does not think it right to outdo another just person, and doesn't wish to do so, but would wish to in the case of an unjust person?'

'Yes, that is so,' he replied.

'Well then, what about the unjust person? Will he think it right to outdo the just person and go beyond acting justly?' [c5]

'How could he not', he replied, 'seeing that he considers it right to have more than his fair share of everything?'

'Therefore the unjust person will outdo the unjust fellow too in action and will struggle to get the largest share of all himself?'

[c10] 'That is so.'

'Let's put it this way then', I said. 'The just person does not outdo his like but his unlike, but the unjust outdoes both.' [d1]

'Very well put,' he said.

'Yet the unjust is intelligent and good, and the just neither?'

[d5] 'Well put again,' he said.

'So,' I said, 'the unjust resembles the intelligent and good, but the just does not?'

'Yes, for being such as he is, how could he not resemble those of his kind, while the just person is unlike them?' [d10]

'Excellent. So each is the same sort as those he resembles?'

'So, what then?' he said.

'Let's see, Thrasymachus; do you call one person musical and another not?' [e1]

'I do.'

'Which is the intelligent and which the unintelligent?'

'The musical is intelligent, I suppose, and the unmusical not so.' [e5]

'And is he not good in the things in which he is intelligent and bad where he lacks intelligence?'

Ναί.

Τί δὲ ἰατρικόν; οὐχ οὕτως;

Οὕτως.

10 Δοκεῖ ἂν οὖν τίς σοι, ὦ ἄριστε, μουσικὸς ἀνὴρ ἁρμοττό-
μενος λύραν ἐθέλειν μουσικοῦ ἀνδρὸς ἐν τῇ ἐπιτάσει καὶ
ἀνέσει τῶν χορδῶν πλεονεκτεῖν ἢ ἀξιοῦν πλέον ἔχειν;

Οὐκ ἔμοιγε.

Τί δέ; ἀμούσου;

15 Ἀνάγκη, ἔφη.

350 Τί δὲ ἰατρικός; ἐν τῇ ἐδωδῇ ἢ πόσει ἐθέλειν ἄν τι ἰατρικοῦ
πλεονεκτεῖν ἢ ἀνδρὸς ἢ πράγματος;

Οὐ δῆτα.

Μὴ ἰατρικοῦ δέ;

5 Ναί.

Περὶ πάσης δὴ ὅρα ἐπιστήμης τε καὶ ἀνεπιστημοσύνης εἴ
τίς σοι δοκεῖ ἐπιστήμων ὁστισοῦν πλείω ἂν ἐθέλειν αἱρεῖσθαι
ἢ ὅσα ἄλλος ἐπιστήμων ἢ πράττειν ἢ λέγειν, καὶ οὐ ταὐτὰ τῷ
ὁμοίῳ ἑαυτῷ εἰς τὴν αὐτὴν πρᾶξιν.

10 Ἀλλ' ἴσως, ἔφη, ἀνάγκη τοῦτό γε οὕτως ἔχειν.

Τί δὲ ὁ ἀνεπιστήμων; οὐχὶ ὁμοίως μὲν ἐπιστήμονος
b πλεονεκτήσειεν ἄν, ὁμοίως δὲ ἀνεπιστήμονος;

Ἴσως.

Ὁ δὲ ἐπιστήμων σοφός;

Φημί.

5 Ὁ δὲ σοφὸς ἀγαθός;

Φημί.

Ὁ ἄρα ἀγαθός τε καὶ σοφὸς τοῦ μὲν ὁμοίου οὐκ ἐθελήσει
πλεονεκτεῖν, τοῦ δὲ ἀνομοίου τε καὶ ἐναντίου.

Ἔοικεν, ἔφη.

10 Ὁ δὲ κακός τε καὶ ἀμαθὴς τοῦ τε ὁμοίου καὶ τοῦ ἐναντίου.

Φαίνεται.

Οὐκοῦν, ὦ Θρασύμαχε, ἦν δ' ἐγώ, ὁ ἄδικος ἡμῖν τοῦ

'Yes.'

'What of a doctor; doesn't the same apply?'

'It does.'

[e10] 'Then do you think, my friend, that in tuning a lyre a musical person would want to outdo another in tightening and loosening the strings, or think he ought to exceed him?'

'I don't think so.'

'But would he, with an unmusical person?'

[e15] 'Of course', he replied.

350 'And what of a doctor? In prescribing food and drink would he wish to outdo another doctor in any way, either the person or what he does?'

'Certainly not.'

'But he would a non-doctor?'

[a5] 'Yes.'

'In the whole field of knowledge and ignorance, consider whether you think any knowledgeable person whatever would want to choose to do or say more than another knowledgeable person, and not rather do and say the same as his colleague in the same activity.'

[a10] 'Well,' he said, 'perhaps it must be so in these cases.'

'But what of the person without knowledge? Won't he wish to outdo the knowledgeable and the ignorant alike?' [b1]

'Perhaps.'

'But the knowledgeable person is wise?'

'Yes.'

[b5] 'And the wise person is good?'

'I agree.'

'So the good and wise person will not wish to outdo his like but only the opposite, his unlike.'

'It appears so,' he said.

[b10] 'But the bad and ignorant will wish to outdo both his like and unlike.'

'So it seems.'

'Therefore, Thrasymachus,' I said, 'our unjust person outdoes both unlike and

ἀνομοίου τε καὶ ὁμοίου πλεονεκτεῖ; ἢ οὐχ οὕτως ἔλεγες;
Ἔγωγε, ἔφη.

c Ὁ δέ γε δίκαιος τοῦ μὲν ὁμοίου οὐ πλεονεκτήσει, τοῦ δὲ
ἀνομοίου;
Ναί.
Ἔοικεν ἄρα, ἦν δ᾽ ἐγώ, ὁ μὲν δίκαιος τῷ σοφῷ καὶ ἀγαθῷ,
5 ὁ δὲ ἄδικος τῷ κακῷ καὶ ἀμαθεῖ.
Κινδυνεύει.
Ἀλλὰ μὴν ὡμολογοῦμεν, ᾧ γε ὅμοιος ἑκάτερος εἴη,
τοιοῦτον καὶ ἑκάτερον εἶναι.
Ὡμολογοῦμεν γάρ.
10 Ὁ μὲν ἄρα δίκαιος ἡμῖν ἀναπέφανται ὢν ἀγαθός τε καὶ
σοφός, ὁ δὲ ἄδικος ἀμαθής τε καὶ κακός.

Ὁ δὲ Θρασύμαχος ὡμολόγησε μὲν πάντα ταῦτα, οὐχ ὡς
d ἐγὼ νῦν ῥᾳδίως λέγω, ἀλλ᾽ ἑλκόμενος καὶ μόγις, μετὰ
ἱδρῶτος θαυμαστοῦ ὅσου, ἅτε καὶ θέρους ὄντος· τότε καὶ
εἶδον ἐγώ, πρότερον δὲ οὔπω, Θρασύμαχον ἐρυθριῶντα.
ἐπειδὴ δὲ οὖν διωμολογησάμεθα τὴν δικαιοσύνην ἀρετὴν
5 εἶναι καὶ σοφίαν, τὴν δὲ ἀδικίαν κακίαν τε καὶ ἀμαθίαν, Εἶεν,
ἦν δ᾽ ἐγώ, τοῦτο μὲν ἡμῖν οὕτω κείσθω, ἔφαμεν δὲ δὴ καὶ
ἰσχυρὸν εἶναι τὴν ἀδικίαν. ἢ οὐ μέμνησαι, ὦ Θρασύμαχε;
Μέμνημαι, ἔφη, ἀλλ᾽ ἔμοιγε οὐδὲ ἃ νῦν λέγεις ἀρέσκει, καὶ
ἔχω περὶ αὐτῶν λέγειν. εἰ οὖν λέγοιμι, εὖ οἶδ᾽ ὅτι δημηγορεῖν
e ἄν με φαίης. ἢ οὖν ἔα με εἰπεῖν ὅσα βούλομαι, ἤ, εἰ βούλει
ἐρωτᾶν, ἐρώτα· ἐγὼ δέ σοι, ὥσπερ ταῖς γραυσὶν ταῖς τοὺς
μύθους λεγούσαις, "εἶεν" ἐρῶ καὶ κατανεύσομαι καὶ ἀνανεύ-
σομαι.
5 Μηδαμῶς, ἦν δ᾽ ἐγώ, παρά γε τὴν σαυτοῦ δόξαν.
Ὥστε σοί, ἔφη, ἀρέσκειν, ἐπειδήπερ οὐκ ἐᾷς λέγειν. καίτοι
τί ἄλλο βούλει;
Οὐδὲν μὰ Δία, ἦν δ᾽ ἐγώ, ἀλλ᾽ εἴπερ τοῦτο ποιήσεις, ποίει·
ἐγὼ δὲ ἐρωτήσω.
10 Ἐρώτα δή.
Τοῦτο τοίνυν ἐρωτῶ, ὅπερ ἄρτι, ἵνα καὶ ἑξῆς διασκεψώ-
351 μεθα τὸν λόγον, ὁποῖόν τι τυγχάνει ὂν δικαιοσύνη πρὸς
ἀδικίαν. ἐλέχθη γάρ που ὅτι καὶ δυνατώτερον καὶ ἰσχυρότερον εἴη ἀδικία δικαιοσύνης· νῦν δέ γ᾽, ἔφην, εἴπερ σοφία τε
καὶ ἀρετή ἐστιν δικαιοσύνη, ῥᾳδίως, οἶμαι, φανήσεται καὶ
5 ἰσχυρότερον ἀδικίας, ἐπειδήπερ ἐστὶν ἀμαθία ἡ ἀδικία· οὐδεὶς
ἂν ἔτι τοῦτο ἀγνοήσειεν. ἀλλ᾽ οὔ τι οὕτως ἁπλῶς, ὦ

350b13

like? Did you not say that?'

'Yes, I did,' he replied.

[c1] 'But the just person will not outdo his like but his unlike?'

'Yes.'

'So the just person is like the wise and good, and the unjust person the bad and ignorant.' [c5]

'I suppose so.'

'But further, we agreed that each of them is of the same kind as that which he is like.'

'Yes, we did.'

[c10] 'So the just person has turned out by our argument to be good and wise, and the unjust person ignorant and bad.'

Now Thrasymachus' agreement to all this did not come easily, as I now narrate, but had to be dragged out of him reluctantly, [d1] with a remarkable quantity of sweat – for it *was* hot – and then I saw what I had never seen before: Thrasymachus blushing. So when we did reach agreement that justice is excellence and wisdom, [d5] injustice badness and ignorance, I said: 'Well, let us now take that as settled. But we also said that injustice is strong. Don't you remember that, Thrasymachus?'

'I do', he said; but I'm not even happy with what you're now saying, and I have something to say about it. Now if I were to say it, I know very well that you would accuse me of ranting. [e1] So either allow me to say as much as I want, or if you prefer to question me, ask away; but, like someone listening to old women telling their tales, I'll only answer you 'Right ho', and nod or shake my head.

[e5] 'No, don't do that', I said, 'contrary to what you believe.'

'Yes, I will,' he replied, 'to please you, since in fact you won't allow me to make a speech. But what else do you want?'

'Nothing, by Zeus,' I said, 'but if that's what you plan to do, go ahead and do it, and I will ask the questions.'

[e10] 'Ask on, then.'

'Then I'll ask, as I did before, so that we may consider the argument in sequence: 351 how does the nature of justice relate to injustice? For it was stated, I believe, that injustice is a more powerful and stronger thing than justice. Now', I said, 'if indeed justice is wisdom and excellence, I think it can easily be shown to be also a stronger thing than injustice, seeing that injustice is ignorance – [a5] nobody could now fail to recognise that. But I've no desire to put it simply like that,

100   PLATO

Θρασύμαχε, ἔγωγε ἐπιθυμῶ, ἀλλὰ τῇδέ πῃ σκέψασθαι·
b πόλιν φαίης ἂν ἄδικον εἶναι καὶ ἄλλας πόλεις ἐπιχειρεῖν
δουλοῦσθαι ἀδίκως καὶ καταδεδουλῶσθαι, πολλὰς δὲ καὶ
ὑφ' ἑαυτῇ ἔχειν δουλωσαμένην;
Πῶς γὰρ οὔκ; ἔφη. καὶ τοῦτό γε ἡ ἀρίστη μάλιστα ποιήσει
5 καὶ τελεώτατα οὖσα ἄδικος.
Μανθάνω, ἔφην, ὅτι σὸς οὗτος ἦν ὁ λόγος. ἀλλὰ τόδε περὶ
αὐτοῦ σκοπῶ· πότερον ἡ κρείττων γιγνομένη πόλις πόλεως
ἄνευ δικαιοσύνης τὴν δύναμιν ταύτην ἕξει, ἢ ἀνάγκη αὐτῇ
μετὰ δικαιοσύνης;
c Εἰ μέν, ἔφη, ὡς σὺ ἄρτι ἔλεγες [ἔχει], ἡ δικαιοσύνη σοφία,
μετὰ δικαιοσύνης· εἰ δ' ὡς ἐγὼ ἔλεγον, μετ' ἀδικίας.
Πάνυ ἄγαμαι, ἦν δ' ἐγώ, ὦ Θρασύμαχε, ὅτι οὐκ ἐπινεύεις
μόνον καὶ ἀνανεύεις, ἀλλὰ καὶ ἀποκρίνῃ πάνυ καλῶς.
5 Σοὶ γάρ, ἔφη, χαρίζομαι.
Εὖ γε σὺ ποιῶν· ἀλλὰ δὴ καὶ τόδε μοι χάρισαι καὶ λέγε·
δοκεῖς ἂν ἢ πόλιν ἢ στρατόπεδον ἢ λῃστὰς ἢ κλέπτας ἢ ἄλλο
τι ἔθνος, ὅσα κοινῇ ἐπί τι ἔρχεται ἀδίκως, πρᾶξαι ἄν τι
δύνασθαι, εἰ ἀδικοῖεν ἀλλήλους;
10 Οὐ δῆτα, ἦ δ' ὅς.
d Τί δ' εἰ μὴ ἀδικοῖεν; οὐ μᾶλλον;
Πάνυ γε.
Στάσεις γάρ που, ὦ Θρασύμαχε, ἥ γε ἀδικία καὶ μίση καὶ
μάχας ἐν ἀλλήλοις παρέχει, ἡ δὲ δικαιοσύνη ὁμόνοιαν καὶ
5 φιλίαν. ἦ γάρ;
Ἔστω, ἦ δ' ὅς, ἵνα σοι μὴ διαφέρωμαι.
Ἀλλ' εὖ γε σὺ ποιῶν, ὦ ἄριστε. τόδε δέ μοι λέγε· ἆρα εἰ
τοῦτο ἔργον ἀδικίας, μῖσος ἐμποιεῖν ὅπου ἂν ἐνῇ, οὐ καὶ ἐν
ἐλευθέροις τε καὶ δούλοις ἐγγιγνομένη μισεῖν ποιήσει ἀλλή-
e λους καὶ στασιάζειν καὶ ἀδυνάτους εἶναι κοινῇ μετ' ἀλλήλων
πράττειν;
Πάνυ γε.
Τί δὲ ἂν ἐν δυοῖν ἐγγένηται; οὐ διοίσονται καὶ μισήσουσιν
5 καὶ ἐχθροὶ ἔσονται ἀλλήλοις τε καὶ τοῖς δικαίοις;
Ἔσονται, ἔφη.
Ἐὰν δὲ δή, ὦ θαυμάσιε, ἐν ἑνὶ ἐγγένηται ἀδικία, μῶν μὴ
ἀπολεῖ τὴν αὐτῆς δύναμιν, ἢ οὐδὲν ἧττον ἕξει;

351c1 ἔχει ADF Stobaeus: secl. Tucker

351a7

Thrasymachus, but consider it from this angle: [b1] would you say that a city is unjust to try to enslave other cities unjustly, and to succeed in that, and keep many of them which it has enslaved in its power?'

'Yes, of course' he replied. 'And this is what the best city, being most complete in its injustice, will do its utmost to achieve.' [b5]

'I am learning,' I said, 'that that was your thesis. But the point I am considering is this: will the city which has become stronger than another without justice have this capability, or must it include justice?'

[c1] 'If,' he replied, 'as you have just maintained, justice is wisdom, then justice must be included; but if it is as I have argued, it will need injustice.'

'I really admire you, Thrasymachus,' I said, 'for not just nodding and shaking your head, but also giving very good answers.'

[c5] 'I'm doing it' he said, 'to oblige you.'

'And well done you! But now do me this favour and tell me whether you think that a city or an army or bandits or thieves or any other group which sets about any unjust action together, could achieve anything if they wronged one another?'

[c10] 'Certainly not,' he replied.

[d1] 'But what if they didn't wrong each other? Wouldn't their prospects be better?'

'Yes, indeed.'

'Yes, for injustice surely breeds dissension, hatreds and fighting among each other, whereas justice brings concord and friendship; isn't that so?' [d5]

'Let it be so,' he replied, 'to avoid my contradicting you.'

'How kind of you, my friend. But tell me this: if it is the function of injustice to engender hatred wherever it is found, when it arises among free or slave, won't it cause them to hate each other and quarrel and be unable to act in concert?' [e1]

'Indeed, yes.'

'What if injustice arises between two people? Won't they quarrel and hate each other and be at odds both with each other and with those who are just?' [e5]

'They will,' he replied.

'But, my dear fellow, what if injustice arises within one person; surely it won't lose its power, but rather retain it undiminished?'

Μηδὲν ἧττον ἐχέτω, ἔφη.

10 Οὐκοῦν τοιάνδε τινὰ φαίνεται ἔχουσα τὴν δύναμιν, οἵαν, ᾧ
ἂν ἐγγένηται, εἴτε πόλει τινὶ εἴτε γένει εἴτε στρατοπέδῳ εἴτε
352 ἄλλῳ ὁτῳοῦν, πρῶτον μὲν ἀδύνατον αὐτὸ ποιεῖν πράττειν
μεθ᾽ αὑτοῦ διὰ τὸ στασιάζειν καὶ διαφέρεσθαι, ἔτι δ᾽ ἐχθρὸν
εἶναι ἑαυτῷ τε καὶ τῷ ἐναντίῳ παντὶ καὶ τῷ δικαίῳ; οὐχ
οὕτως;

5 Πάνυ γε.

Καὶ ἐν ἑνὶ δή, οἶμαι, ἐνοῦσα ταὐτὰ ταῦτα ποιήσει ἅπερ
πέφυκεν ἐργάζεσθαι· πρῶτον μὲν ἀδύνατον αὐτὸν πράττειν
ποιήσει στασιάζοντα καὶ οὐχ ὁμονοοῦντα αὐτὸν ἑαυτῷ,
ἔπειτα ἐχθρὸν καὶ ἑαυτῷ καὶ τοῖς δικαίοις. ἦ γάρ;

10 Ναί.

Δίκαιοι δέ γ᾽ εἰσίν, ὦ φίλε, καὶ οἱ θεοί;

b Ἔστω, ἔφη.

Καὶ θεοῖς ἄρα ἐχθρὸς ἔσται ὁ ἄδικος, ὦ Θρασύμαχε, ὁ δὲ
δίκαιος φίλος.

Εὐωχοῦ τοῦ λόγου, ἔφη, θαρρῶν· οὐ γὰρ ἔγωγέ σοι
5 ἐναντιώσομαι, ἵνα μὴ τοῖσδε ἀπέχθωμαι.

Ἴθι δή, ἦν δ᾽ ἐγώ, καὶ τὰ λοιπά μοι τῆς ἑστιάσεως
ἀποπλήρωσον, ἀποκρινόμενος ὥσπερ καὶ νῦν. ὅτι μὲν γὰρ
καὶ σοφώτεροι καὶ ἀμείνους καὶ δυνατώτεροι πράττειν οἱ
δίκαιοι φαίνονται, οἱ δὲ ἄδικοι οὐδὲν πράττειν μετ᾽ ἀλλήλων
c οἷοί τε, ἀλλὰ δὴ καὶ οὓς φαμεν ἐρρωμένως πώποτέ τι μετ᾽
ἀλλήλων κοινῇ πρᾶξαι ἀδίκους ὄντας, τοῦτο οὐ παντάπασιν
ἀληθὲς λέγομεν· οὐ γὰρ ἂν ἀπείχοντο ἀλλήλων κομιδῇ ὄντες
ἄδικοι, ἀλλὰ δῆλον ὅτι ἐνῆν τις αὐτοῖς δικαιοσύνη, ἣ αὐτοὺς
5 ἐποίει μή τοι καὶ ἀλλήλους γε καὶ ἐφ᾽ οὓς ᾖσαν ἅμα ἀδικεῖν,
δι᾽ ἣν ἔπραξαν ἃ ἔπραξαν, ὥρμησαν δὲ ἐπὶ τὰ ἄδικα ἀδικίᾳ
ἡμιμόχθηροι ὄντες, ἐπεὶ οἵ γε παμπόνηροι καὶ τελέως ἄδικοι
d τελέως εἰσὶ καὶ πράττειν ἀδύνατοι. ταῦτα μὲν οὖν ὅτι οὕτως
ἔχει μανθάνω, ἀλλ᾽ οὐχ ὡς σὺ τὸ πρῶτον ἐτίθεσο· εἰ δὲ καὶ
ἄμεινον ζῶσιν οἱ δίκαιοι τῶν ἀδίκων καὶ εὐδαιμονέστεροί
εἰσιν, ὅπερ τὸ ὕστερον προυθέμεθα σκέψασθαι, σκεπτέον.
5 φαίνονται μὲν οὖν καὶ νῦν, ὥς γέ μοι δοκεῖ, ἐξ ὧν εἰρήκαμεν·
ὅμως δ᾽ ἔτι βέλτιον σκεπτέον. οὐ γὰρ περὶ τοῦ ἐπιτυχόντος ὁ
λόγος, ἀλλὰ περὶ τοῦ ὅντινα τρόπον χρὴ ζῆν.

Σκόπει δή, ἔφη.

351e9

'Let's say it will retain it,' he replied.

[e10] 'Therefore does it not appear to have the kind of power that, in whatever it arises, whether in a city, a family, an army camp or anywhere else, **352** it makes that body firstly incapable of co-operation with itself owing to factions and quarrels, and secondly makes it hostile both to itself and to what is in every way opposed to it, including what is just? Isn't that so?'

[a5] 'Certainly.'

'And so dwelling in a single person, I think, it will bring about those very same effects which it naturally produces: it will make him firstly unable to act through strife and lack of agreement within himself, and secondly he will be hostile both to himself and to those who are just. True?'

[a10] 'Yes.'

'But, my friend, the gods too are just?'

[b1] 'Let it be so,' he replied.

'So then, Thrasymachus, the unjust person will be an enemy to the gods, but the just will be their friend.'

'Go on, feast on your argument with good cheer,' he said; 'for I won't oppose you in case I annoy these people here.' [b5]

'Come then,' I said, 'satisfy me in what remains of my feast by answering as you have done up to now. The fact is that the just appear to be wiser and better and more capable of action, while the unjust cannot even cooperate with each other; [c1] in fact if we say that people have ever taken common action with each other effectively, despite being unjust, we are not altogether truthful, for if they had been entirely unjust, they would never have kept their hands off one another. But it is clear that there was some justice in them which at least prevented them from wronging each other as well as those they were attacking, [c5] and because of which they succeeded in what they attempted and set about their unjust acts only half-corrupted by injustice, since utter villains, men who are completely unjust, are also completely incapable of effective action. [d1] Now this is how I understand the situation, and not as you proposed at first.

But we must now consider the question we proposed to investigate subsequently: whether the just have a better life than the unjust and are happier. Now they manifestly are already, it seems to me, from what we have said; [d5] but all the same we ought to consider the question still more closely. For the discussion is not about an incidental matter, but about the way we ought to live.'

'Enquire away, then,' he said.

Σκοπῶ, ἦν δ᾽ ἐγώ. καί μοι λέγε· δοκεῖ τί σοι εἶναι ἵππου
e ἔργον;
Ἔμοιγε.
Ἆρ᾽ οὖν τοῦτο ἂν θείης καὶ ἵππου καὶ ἄλλου ὁτουοῦν ἔργον,
ὃ ἂν ἢ μόνῳ ἐκείνῳ ποιῇ τις ἢ ἄριστα;
5 Οὐ μανθάνω, ἔφη.
Ἀλλ᾽ ὧδε· ἔσθ᾽ ὅτῳ ἂν ἄλλῳ ἴδοις ἢ ὀφθαλμοῖς;
Οὐ δῆτα.
Τί δέ; ἀκούσαις ἄλλῳ ἢ ὠσίν;
Οὐδαμῶς.
10 Οὐκοῦν δικαίως [ἂν] ταῦτα τούτων φαμὲν ἔργα εἶναι;
Πάνυ γε.
353 Τί δέ; μαχαίρᾳ ἀμπέλου κλῆμα ἀποτέμοις καὶ σμίλῃ καὶ
ἄλλοις πολλοῖς;
Πῶς γὰρ οὔ;
Ἀλλ᾽ οὐδενί γ᾽ ἄν, οἶμαι, οὕτω καλῶς ὡς δρεπάνῳ τῷ ἐπὶ
5 τοῦτο ἐργασθέντι.
Ἀληθῆ.
Ἆρ᾽ οὖν οὐ τοῦτο τούτου ἔργον θήσομεν;
Θήσομεν μὲν οὖν.
Νῦν δή, οἶμαι, ἄμεινον ἂν μάθοις ὃ ἄρτι ἠρώτων, πυνθα-
10 νόμενος εἰ οὐ τοῦτο ἑκάστου εἴη ἔργον ὃ ἂν ἢ μόνον τι ἢ
κάλλιστα τῶν ἄλλων ἀπεργάζηται.
Ἀλλά, ἔφη, μανθάνω τε καί μοι δοκεῖ τοῦτο ἑκάστου
b πράγματος ἔργον εἶναι.
Εἶεν, ἦν δ᾽ ἐγώ· οὐκοῦν καὶ ἀρετὴ δοκεῖ σοι εἶναι ἑκάστῳ
ᾧπερ καὶ ἔργον τι προστέτακται; ἴωμεν δὲ ἐπὶ τὰ αὐτὰ πάλιν·
ὀφθαλμῶν, φαμέν, ἔστι τι ἔργον;
5 Ἔστιν.
Ἆρ᾽ οὖν καὶ ἀρετὴ ὀφθαλμῶν ἔστιν;
Καὶ ἀρετή.
Τί δέ; ὤτων ἦν τι ἔργον;

352e10 ἂν ADF Stobaeus: secl. Adam

352d9

'I will,' I replied. 'So tell me, in your opinion, does a horse have a function?' [e1]

'It does.'

'So would you maintain in the case of a horse or anything else that its function is this: namely that which one can only do or do best with that thing alone?'

[e5] 'I don't understand,' he said.

'Well, look at it like this; is there anything else you can see with except eyes?'

'Of course not.'

'Again, can you hear with anything but ears?'

'Certainly not.'

[e10] 'Therefore do we rightly say that these organs have these functions?'

'Yes.'

353 'So again: you could cut off a vine-shoot with a dagger or carving-knife or many other tools?'

'Of course.'

'But with none so well, I think, as with a pruning-knife made for that purpose.' [a5]

'True.'

'So shall we designate pruning as its function?'

'Yes, let's do that.'

'Well now, I think you can understand better what I was asking just now when I asked if the function of each thing was that which it alone can do, or that which it does better than anything else.' [a10]

'Yes, I do understand,' he said, 'and I think that this is what is meant by the function of each thing.' [b1]

'Good,' I said. 'Therefore don't you think that in the case of everything to which a function has been ascribed, there is also an excellence? Let's go over the same points again: in the case of the eyes, we say there is a function.'

[b5] 'We do.'

'And so they also have an excellence?'

'An excellence too.'

'Again: the ears have a function?'

Ναί.

10 Οὐκοῦν καὶ ἀρετή;

Καὶ ἀρετή.

Τί δὲ πάντων πέρι τῶν ἄλλων; οὐχ οὕτω;

Οὕτω.

Ἔχε δή· ἆρ' ἄν ποτε ὄμματα τὸ αὐτῶν ἔργον καλῶς

c ἀπεργάσαιντο μὴ ἔχοντα τὴν αὐτῶν οἰκείαν ἀρετήν, ἀλλ'
ἀντὶ τῆς ἀρετῆς κακίαν;

Καὶ πῶς ἄν; ἔφη· τυφλότητα γὰρ ἴσως λέγεις ἀντὶ τῆς
ὄψεως.

5 Ἥτις, ἦν δ' ἐγώ, αὐτῶν ἡ ἀρετή· οὐ γάρ πω τοῦτο ἐρωτῶ,
ἀλλ' εἰ τῇ οἰκείᾳ μὲν ἀρετῇ τὸ αὐτῶν ἔργον εὖ ἐργάσεται τὰ
ἐργαζόμενα, κακίᾳ δὲ κακῶς.

Ἀληθές, ἔφη, τοῦτό γε λέγεις.

Οὐκοῦν καὶ ὦτα στερόμενα τῆς αὐτῶν ἀρετῆς κακῶς τὸ

10 αὐτῶν ἔργον ἀπεργάσεται;

Πάνυ γε.

d Τίθεμεν οὖν καὶ τἆλλα πάντα εἰς τὸν αὐτὸν λόγον;

Ἔμοιγε δοκεῖ.

Ἴθι δή, μετὰ ταῦτα τόδε σκέψαι. ψυχῆς ἔστιν τι ἔργον ὃ
ἄλλῳ τῶν ὄντων οὐδ' ἂν ἑνὶ πράξαις; οἷον τὸ τοιόνδε· τὸ

5 ἐπιμελεῖσθαι καὶ ἄρχειν καὶ βουλεύεσθαι καὶ τὰ τοιαῦτα
πάντα, ἔσθ' ὅτῳ ἄλλῳ ἢ ψυχῇ δικαίως ἂν αὐτὰ ἀποδοῖμεν
καὶ φαῖμεν ἴδια ἐκείνης εἶναι;

Οὐδενὶ ἄλλῳ.

Τί δ' αὖ τὸ ζῆν; οὐ ψυχῆς φήσομεν ἔργον εἶναι;

10 Μάλιστά γ', ἔφη.

Οὐκοῦν καὶ ἀρετήν φαμέν τινα ψυχῆς εἶναι;

Φαμέν.

e Ἆρ' οὖν ποτε, ὦ Θρασύμαχε, ψυχὴ τὰ αὐτῆς ἔργα εὖ
ἀπεργάσεται στερομένη τῆς οἰκείας ἀρετῆς, ἢ ἀδύνατον;

Ἀδύνατον.

Ἀνάγκη ἄρα κακῇ ψυχῇ κακῶς ἄρχειν καὶ ἐπιμελεῖσθαι,

'Yes.'

[b10] 'And so an excellence?'

'Yes again'.

'And what about all other things? Is it not the same?'

'It is.'

'Well then: could the eyes ever perform their function well if they didn't have their own particular excellence, [c1] but instead a defect?'

'Why, how could they,' he said; 'for I suppose you mean blindness instead of sight.'

[c5] 'Whatever their excellence may be,' I said; 'for I'm not asking that yet, but only whether anything will perform its function well by virtue of its particular excellence, and badly through its particular defect.'

'That much is certainly true,' he said.

'So the ears too, when they are bereft of their particular excellence, will perform their distinctive function badly?' [c10]

'Yes indeed.'

[d1] And so we can apply the same argument to all other cases?'

'It would appear so.'

'All right then, next consider this: take the soul – does it have a function which you could perform with nothing else in the world, as for example: caring, ruling, deliberating and all things like that: [d5] is there anything else other than the soul to which we could rightly entrust these, and say that they were its particular province?'

'No, no other.'

'But what about living, then? Shall we not say that it is a function of the soul?'

[d10] 'Very definitely,' he replied.

'And do we not say that the soul also has an excellence?'

'We do.'

[e1] 'Now, Thrasymachus, will the soul ever realise its particular function well if it is deprived of its own excellence, or is that impossible?'

'It's impossible.'

'So of necessity, if the soul is bad its rule and care will be badly performed, but

5 τῇ δὲ ἀγαθῇ πάντα ταῦτα εὖ πράττειν.
Ἀνάγκη.
Οὐκοῦν ἀρετήν γε συνεχωρήσαμεν ψυχῆς εἶναι δικαιο-
σύνην, κακίαν δὲ ἀδικίαν;
Συνεχωρήσαμεν γάρ.
10 Ἡ μὲν ἄρα δικαία ψυχὴ καὶ ὁ δίκαιος ἀνὴρ εὖ βιώσεται,
κακῶς δὲ ὁ ἄδικος.
Φαίνεται, ἔφη, κατὰ τὸν σὸν λόγον.
354 Ἀλλὰ μὴν ὅ γε εὖ ζῶν μακάριός τε καὶ εὐδαίμων, ὁ δὲ μὴ
τἀναντία.
Πῶς γὰρ οὔ;
Ὁ μὲν δίκαιος ἄρα εὐδαίμων, ὁ δ' ἄδικος ἄθλιος.
5 Ἔστω, ἔφη.
Ἀλλὰ μὴν ἄθλιόν γε εἶναι οὐ λυσιτελεῖ, εὐδαίμονα δέ.
Πῶς γὰρ οὔ;
Οὐδέποτ' ἄρα, ὦ μακάριε Θρασύμαχε, λυσιτελέστερον
ἀδικία δικαιοσύνης.
10 Ταῦτα δή σοι, ἔφη, ὦ Σώκρατες, εἱστιάσθω ἐν τοῖς
Βενδιδίοις.
Ὑπὸ σοῦ γε, ἦν δ' ἐγώ, ὦ Θρασύμαχε, ἐπειδή μοι πρᾶος
ἐγένου καὶ χαλεπαίνων ἐπαύσω. οὐ μέντοι καλῶς γε εἱστία-
b μαι, δι' ἐμαυτὸν ἀλλ' οὐ διὰ σέ· ἀλλ' ὥσπερ οἱ λίχνοι τοῦ ἀεὶ
παραφερομένου ἀπογεύονται ἁρπάζοντες, πρὶν τοῦ προτέρου
μετρίως ἀπολαῦσαι, καὶ ἐγώ μοι δοκῶ οὕτω, πρὶν ὃ τὸ
πρῶτον ἐσκοποῦμεν εὑρεῖν, τὸ δίκαιον ὅτι ποτ' ἐστίν,
5 ἀφέμενος ἐκείνου ὁρμῆσαι ἐπὶ τὸ σκέψασθαι περὶ αὐτοῦ
εἴτε κακία ἐστὶν καὶ ἀμαθία, εἴτε σοφία καὶ ἀρετή. καὶ
ἐμπεσόντος αὖ ὑστέρου λόγου, ὅτι λυσιτελέστερον ἡ ἀδικία
τῆς δικαιοσύνης, οὐκ ἀπεσχόμην τὸ μὴ οὐκ ἐπὶ τοῦτο ἐλθεῖν
ἀπ' ἐκείνου· ὥστε μοι νυνὶ γέγονεν ἐκ τοῦ διαλόγου μηδὲν
c εἰδέναι· ὁπότε γὰρ τὸ δίκαιον μὴ οἶδα ὅ ἐστιν, σχολῇ εἴσομαι
εἴτε ἀρετή τις οὖσα τυγχάνει εἴτε καὶ οὔ, καὶ πότερον ὁ ἔχων
αὐτὸ οὐκ εὐδαίμων ἐστὶν ἢ εὐδαίμων.

353e5

if it's good, all these things will be well done.' [e5]

'Necessarily.'

'And did we not agree that the excellence of the soul is justice, and its defect injustice?'

'Yes, we did agree.'

[e10] 'So the just soul and the just man will live well, and the unjust badly.'

'It appears so,' he said, 'according to your argument.'

354 'But furthermore, the person who lives well is blessed and happy, and he who does not, the reverse.'

'Of course.'

'So the just person is happy, the unjust miserable.'

[a5] 'So be it', he said.

'Moreover it does not pay to be miserable, but happy.'

'Of course.'

'In that case, my dear Thrasymachus, injustice can never be a more profitable thing than justice.'

[a10] 'Well, let these conclusions be your feast, Socrates,' he replied, 'at the festival of Bendis.'

'Provided by you, Thrasymachus', I said, 'now that you have become gentler and have stopped being angry. I have not feasted well, however, [b1] not because of you, but because of myself; just like greedy banqueters who snatch a taste of each dish as it's served up before they have savoured the previous one properly, that's how I think I too have behaved: before discovering what we were first investigating, what justice is, [b5] I let that subject drop in my rush to consider whether it is badness and ignorance or wisdom and excellence. And again later when the argument burst in on us that injustice is more profitable than justice, I couldn't resist turning to that from the previous argument; so now the current outcome of our enquiry is that I don't know anything. [c1] For as long as I don't know what justice is, I'm hardly likely to discover whether it is actually an excellence or not, and whether the person possessing it is unhappy or happy.'

B II

a Ἐγὼ μὲν οὖν ταῦτα εἰπὼν ᾤμην λόγου ἀπηλλάχθαι· τὸ δ᾽
ἦν ἄρα, ὡς ἔοικε, προοίμιον. ὁ γὰρ Γλαύκων ἀεί τε
ἀνδρειότατος ὢν τυγχάνει πρὸς ἅπαντα, καὶ δὴ καὶ τότε
τοῦ Θρασυμάχου τὴν ἀπόρρησιν οὐκ ἀπεδέξατο, ἀλλ᾽ ἔφη· Ὦ
5 Σώκρατες, πότερον ἡμᾶς βούλει δοκεῖν πεπεικέναι ἢ ὡς
b ἀληθῶς πεῖσαι ὅτι παντὶ τρόπῳ ἄμεινόν ἐστιν δίκαιον εἶναι
ἢ ἄδικον;
Ὡς ἀληθῶς, εἶπον, ἔγωγ᾽ ἂν ἑλοίμην, εἰ ἐπ᾽ ἐμοὶ εἴη.
Οὐ τοίνυν, ἔφη, ποιεῖς ὃ βούλει. λέγε γάρ μοι· ἆρά σοι
5 δοκεῖ τοιόνδε τι εἶναι ἀγαθόν, ὃ δεξαίμεθ᾽ ἂν ἔχειν οὐ τῶν
ἀποβαινόντων ἐφιέμενοι, ἀλλ᾽ αὐτὸ αὑτοῦ ἕνεκα ἀσπαζόμενοι,
οἷον τὸ χαίρειν καὶ αἱ ἡδοναὶ ὅσαι ἀβλαβεῖς καὶ μηδὲν εἰς τὸν
ἔπειτα χρόνον διὰ ταύτας γίγνεται ἄλλο ἢ χαίρειν ἔχοντα;
c Ἔμοιγε, ἦν δ᾽ ἐγώ, δοκεῖ τι εἶναι τοιοῦτον.
Τί δέ, ὃ αὐτό τε αὑτοῦ χάριν ἀγαπῶμεν καὶ τῶν ἀπ᾽ αὐτοῦ
γιγνομένων, οἷον αὖ τὸ φρονεῖν καὶ τὸ ὁρᾶν καὶ τὸ ὑγιαίνειν;
τὰ γὰρ τοιαῦτά που δι᾽ ἀμφότερα ἀσπαζόμεθα.
5 Ναί, εἶπον.
Τρίτον δὲ ὁρᾷς τι, ἔφη, εἶδος ἀγαθοῦ, ἐν ᾧ τὸ γυμνάζεσθαι
καὶ τὸ κάμνοντα ἰατρεύεσθαι καὶ ἰάτρευσίς τε καὶ ὁ ἄλλος
χρηματισμός; ταῦτα γὰρ ἐπίπονα φαῖμεν ἄν, ὠφελεῖν δὲ
ἡμᾶς, καὶ αὐτὰ μὲν ἑαυτῶν ἕνεκα οὐκ ἂν δεξαίμεθα ἔχειν,
d τῶν δὲ μισθῶν τε χάριν καὶ τῶν ἄλλων ὅσα γίγνεται ἀπ᾽
αὐτῶν.
Ἔστιν γὰρ οὖν, ἔφην, καὶ τοῦτο τρίτον. ἀλλὰ τί δή;
Ἐν ποίῳ, ἔφη, τούτων τὴν δικαιοσύνην τίθης;
358 Ἐγὼ μὲν οἶμαι, ἦν δ᾽ ἐγώ, ἐν τῷ καλλίστῳ, ὃ καὶ δι᾽ αὑτὸ
καὶ διὰ τὰ γιγνόμενα ἀπ᾽ αὐτοῦ ἀγαπητέον τῷ μέλλοντι
μακαρίῳ ἔσεσθαι.
Οὐ τοίνυν δοκεῖ, ἔφη, τοῖς πολλοῖς, ἀλλὰ τοῦ ἐπιπόνου
5 εἴδους, ὃ μισθῶν θ᾽ ἕνεκα καὶ εὐδοκιμήσεων διὰ δόξαν
ἐπιτηδευτέον, αὐτὸ δὲ δι᾽ αὑτὸ φευκτέον ὡς ὂν χαλεπόν.
Οἶδα, ἦν δ᾽ ἐγώ, ὅτι δοκεῖ οὕτω καὶ πάλαι ὑπὸ Θρασυμάχου ὡς τοιοῦτον ὂν ψέγεται, ἀδικία δ᾽ ἐπαινεῖται· ἀλλ᾽ ἐγώ
τις, ὡς ἔοικε, δυσμαθής.

358a8 ἀδικία δ᾽ ἐπαινεῖται DF: om.A

BOOK 2

357

Now when I had said this I thought I had been released from the discussion; but it was after all, apparently, only a prelude. For Glaucon, who always proves himself very bold in everything, on this occasion in particular did not accept Thrasymachus' withdrawal from the debate, but said: [a5] 'Socrates, do you want the appearance or the reality of persuading us that in every circumstance it is better to be just than unjust?' [b1]

'I would prefer the reality,' I replied, 'if it were up to me.'

'Well then,' he said, 'you are not doing what you want. For tell me, do you think there is a certain kind of good which we would gladly possess, not from desire of its consequences, [b5] but welcoming it for its own sake? For example, experiencing joy and such pleasures as are harmless which result in nothing afterwards beyond enjoying the experience?'

'Yes,' I said, 'I think there is that kind of good.'

[c1] 'Well, again, is there a kind which we love both for itself and for its consequences: to give examples, understanding, sight and health? For such things we welcome, surely, for both reasons.'

[c5] 'Yes,' I replied.

'But,' he went on, 'do you perceive a third class of good, in which I would include taking exercise and being treated when sick, practising one's profession as a doctor and making money generally? For we would say that these are burdensome, but that they benefit us, and we would not consent to have them for their own sake but for the financial rewards and other things which result from them.' [d1]

'Why yes,' I replied, 'there is this third class too. But what of it?'

'In which of the classes,' he said, 'do you place justice?'

358 'In my opinion,' I replied, 'in the finest class, which any person aiming at future happiness must love both for its own sake and for its consequences.'

'Well,' he said, 'that isn't what most people think; they place it in the burdensome class of things [a5] which must be practised for the sake of financial reward and a favourable position in popular esteem, but which in itself is to be avoided as being difficult.'

'I know,' I said, 'that that is how it is regarded, and has long been disparaged as such by Thrasymachus, who praises injustice instead; but, I'm rather a bad pupil, it seems.'

b Ἴθι δή, ἔφη, ἄκουσον καὶ ἐμοῦ, ἐάν σοι ἔτι δοκῇ ταὐτά.
Θρασύμαχος γάρ μοι φαίνεται πρωαίτερον τοῦ δέοντος ὑπὸ
σοῦ ὥσπερ ὄφις κηληθῆναι, ἐμοὶ δὲ οὔπω κατὰ νοῦν ἡ
ἀπόδειξις γέγονεν περὶ ἑκατέρου· ἐπιθυμῶ γὰρ ἀκοῦσαι τί
5 τ᾽ ἐστὶν ἑκάτερον καὶ τίνα ἔχει δύναμιν αὐτὸ καθ᾽ αὑτὸ ἐνὸν ἐν
τῇ ψυχῇ, τοὺς δὲ μισθοὺς καὶ τὰ γιγνόμενα ἀπ᾽ αὐτῶν ἐᾶσαι
χαίρειν.
Οὑτωσὶ οὖν ποιήσω, ἐὰν καὶ σοὶ δοκῇ· ἐπανανεώσομαι τὸν
c Θρασυμάχου λόγον, καὶ πρῶτον μὲν ἐρῶ δικαιοσύνην οἷον
εἶναί φασιν καὶ ὅθεν γεγονέναι, δεύτερον δὲ ὅτι πάντες αὐτὸ οἱ
ἐπιτηδεύοντες ἄκοντες ἐπιτηδεύουσιν ὡς ἀναγκαῖον ἀλλ᾽ οὐχ
ὡς ἀγαθόν, τρίτον δὲ ὅτι εἰκότως αὐτὸ δρῶσι· πολὺ γὰρ
5 ἀμείνων ἄρα ὁ τοῦ ἀδίκου ἢ ὁ τοῦ δικαίου βίος, ὡς λέγουσιν.
ἐπεὶ ἔμοιγε, ὦ Σώκρατες, οὔ τι δοκεῖ οὕτως· ἀπορῶ μέντοι
διατεθρυλημένος τὰ ὦτα ἀκούων Θρασυμάχου καὶ μυρίων
d ἄλλων, τὸν δὲ ὑπὲρ τῆς δικαιοσύνης λόγον, ὡς ἄμεινον
ἀδικίας, οὐδενός πω ἀκήκοα ὡς βούλομαι· βούλομαι δὲ
αὐτὸ καθ᾽ αὑτὸ ἐγκωμιαζόμενον ἀκοῦσαι, μάλιστα δ᾽ οἶμαι
ἂν σοῦ πυθέσθαι.
5 Διὸ κατατείνας ἐρῶ τὸν ἄδικον βίον ἐπαινῶν, εἰπὼν δὲ
ἐνδείξομαί σοι ὃν τρόπον αὖ βούλομαι καὶ σοῦ ἀκούειν
ἀδικίαν μὲν ψέγοντος, δικαιοσύνην δὲ ἐπαινοῦντος. ἀλλ᾽ ὅρα εἰ
σοι βουλομένῳ ἃ λέγω.
Πάντων μάλιστα, ἦν δ᾽ ἐγώ· περὶ γὰρ τίνος ἂν μᾶλλον
e πολλάκις τις νοῦν ἔχων χαίροι λέγων καὶ ἀκούων;
Κάλλιστα, ἔφη, λέγεις· καὶ ὃ πρῶτον ἔφην ἐρεῖν, περὶ
τούτου ἄκουε, οἷόν τ᾽ ἐ(στὶ) καὶ ὅθεν γέγονε δικαιοσύνη.
πεφυκέναι γὰρ δή φασιν τὸ μὲν ἀδικεῖν ἀγαθόν, τὸ δὲ
5 ἀδικεῖσθαι κακόν, πλέονι δὲ κακῷ ὑπερβάλλειν τὸ ἀδικεῖσθαι
ἢ ἀγαθῷ τὸ ἀδικεῖν· ὥστ᾽ ἐπειδὰν ἀλλήλους ἀδικῶσί τε καὶ
ἀδικῶνται καὶ ἀμφοτέρων γεύωνται, τοῖς μὴ δυναμένοις τὸ
359 μὲν ἐκφεύγειν τὸ δὲ αἱρεῖν δοκεῖ λυσιτελεῖν συνθέσθαι
ἀλλήλοις μήτ᾽ ἀδικεῖν μήτ᾽ ἀδικεῖσθαι. καὶ ἐντεῦθεν δὴ
ἄρξασθαι νόμους τίθεσθαι καὶ συνθήκας αὑτῶν, καὶ ὀνομάσαι
τὸ ὑπὸ τοῦ νόμου ἐπίταγμα νόμιμόν τε καὶ δίκαιον, καὶ εἶναι

358b1 δοκῇ ταὐτά F: ταὐτὰ δοκῇ AD
358e3 οἷον τ᾽ ἐστὶ Blass: οἷόν τε F: τί ὄν τε A: τί οἷόν τε D

358b1
[b1] 'Come then,' he said, 'hear also what I have to say, and see whether you can agree too. For Thrasymachus appears to me to have given in to you before he really needed to, like a snake you have charmed; but I am not yet satisfied in my mind about the proof for each of them, justice and injustice, for I want to hear what each of them is, and what power each has in and of itself, dwelling in the soul, [b5] and to leave aside the financial rewards and what comes from them.

'So this will be my procedure, if you agree: I shall revive Thrasymachus' argument [c1] and first state what people say about what justice is and how it arises. Secondly, I shall argue the point that all who practise it do so unwillingly, as a necessity and not as a good, and thirdly, that their action is reasonable, since the life of the unjust person is after all far better than that of the just, [c5] as people say. Though, Socrates, that's not at all how I see it myself. Yet I feel at a loss with my ears ringing, when I hear the arguments of Thrasymachus and of countless others, [d1] while I have never yet heard the case for justice being better than injustice stated as I wish by anybody. I want to hear it being praised in and of itself, and I think that is most likely to come from you.

[d5] Therefore I am going to exert myself and speak in praise of the unjust life, and in so doing I will be demonstrating to you the manner in which I want to hear you in your turn censure injustice and praise justice. But see whether you like my idea.'

'Nothing could suit me better,' I replied; for on what subject would anyone of sense be happier to talk and listen again and again?' [e1]

'Excellently put,' he replied. 'And now listen to what I said I would talk about first: what justice is and where it comes from.

'Now, you see, people say that to commit injustice is naturally good, while to be its victim is bad. Yet the excess of evil involved in being a victim of injustice is greater than the good involved in committing it, [e5] with the result that, whenever people wrong each other and are also victims of wrong and have a taste of both sides, those who are unable to avoid the one or achieve the other believe that it is in their interest to make an agreement with each other not to commit injustice nor suffer it. **359** From this basis, we are told, they begin to make laws and covenants with each other, and they give the terms legal and just to what is laid down by the

5 δὴ ταύτην γένεσίν τε καὶ οὐσίαν δικαιοσύνης, μεταξὺ οὖσαν
   τοῦ μὲν ἀρίστου ὄντος, ἐὰν ἀδικῶν μὴ διδῷ δίκην, τοῦ δὲ
   κακίστου, ἐὰν ἀδικούμενος τιμωρεῖσθαι ἀδύνατος ᾖ. τὸ δὲ
b δίκαιον ἐν μέσῳ ὂν τούτων ἀμφοτέρων ἀγαπᾶσθαι οὐχ ὡς
   ἀγαθόν, ἀλλ᾽ ὡς ἀρρωστίᾳ τοῦ ἀδικεῖν τιμώμενον· ἐπεὶ τὸν
   δυνάμενον αὐτὸ ποιεῖν καὶ ὡς ἀληθῶς ἄνδρα οὐδ᾽ ἂν ἑνί ποτε
   συνθέσθαι τὸ μήτε ἀδικεῖν μήτε ἀδικεῖσθαι· μαίνεσθαι γὰρ
5 ἄν.
   Ἡ μὲν οὖν δὴ φύσις δικαιοσύνης, ὦ Σώκρατες, αὕτη τε καὶ
   τοιαύτη, καὶ ἐξ ὧν πέφυκε τοιαῦτα, ὡς ὁ λόγος. ὡς δὲ καὶ οἱ
   ἐπιτηδεύοντες ἀδυναμίᾳ τοῦ ἀδικεῖν ἄκοντες αὐτὸ ἐπιτη-
   δεύουσι, μάλιστ᾽ ἂν αἰσθοίμεθα εἰ τοιόνδε ποιήσαιμεν τῇ
c διανοίᾳ· δόντες ἐξουσίαν ἑκατέρῳ ποιεῖν ὅτι ἂν βούληται,
   τῷ τε δικαίῳ καὶ τῷ ἀδίκῳ, εἶτ᾽ ἐπακολουθήσαιμεν θεώμενοι
   ποῖ ἡ ἐπιθυμία ἑκάτερον ἄξει. ἐπ᾽ αὐτοφώρῳ οὖν λάβοιμεν ἂν
   τὸν δίκαιον τῷ ἀδίκῳ εἰς ταὐτὸν ἰόντα διὰ τὴν πλεονεξίαν, ὃ
5 πᾶσα φύσις διώκειν πέφυκεν ὡς ἀγαθόν, νόμῳ δὲ βίᾳ
   παράγεται ἐπὶ τὴν τοῦ ἴσου τιμήν.
   Εἴη δ᾽ ἂν ἡ ἐξουσία ἣν λέγω τοιάδε μάλιστα, εἰ αὐτοῖς
d γένοιτο οἵαν ποτέ φασιν δύναμιν †τῷ Γύγου τοῦ Λυδοῦ
   προγόνῳ† γενέσθαι. εἶναι μὲν γὰρ αὐτὸν ποιμένα θητεύοντα
   παρὰ τῷ τότε Λυδίας ἄρχοντι· ὄμβρου δὲ πολλοῦ γενομένου
   καὶ σεισμοῦ ῥαγῆναί τι τῆς γῆς καὶ γενέσθαι χάσμα κατὰ τὸν
5 τόπον ᾗ ἔνεμεν. ἰδόντα δὲ καὶ θαυμάσαντα καταβῆναι καὶ
   ἰδεῖν ἄλλα τε δὴ μυθολογοῦσιν θαυμαστὰ καὶ ἵππον χαλκοῦν,
   κοῖλον, θυρίδας ἔχοντα, καθ᾽ ἃς ἐγκύψαντα ἰδεῖν ἐνόντα
   νεκρόν, ὡς φαίνεσθαι μείζω ἢ κατ᾽ ἄνθρωπον· τοῦτον δὲ
e ἄλλο μὲν ἔχειν οὐδέν, περὶ δὲ τῇ χειρὶ χρυσοῦν δακτύλιον,
   ὃν περιελόμενον ἐκβῆναι.
   Συλλόγου δὲ γενομένου τοῖς ποιμέσιν εἰωθότος, ἵν᾽ ἐξαγ-
   γέλλοιεν κατὰ μῆνα τῷ βασιλεῖ τὰ περὶ τὰ ποίμνια, ἀφικέ-
5 σθαι καὶ ἐκεῖνον ἔχοντα τὸν δακτύλιον. καθήμενον οὖν μετὰ
   τῶν ἄλλων τυχεῖν τὴν σφενδόνην τοῦ δακτυλίου περιαγα-
   γόντα πρὸς ἑαυτὸν εἰς τὸ εἴσω τῆς χειρός, τούτου δὲ

359d1–2 τῷ Γύγου ADF Proclus: Γύγου secl. Hermann: τῷ Γύγῃ Schol.: Γύγῃ τοῦ Κροίσου
Jowett-Campbell

359e1 ἔχειν om. A

359e2 ὂν ADF: secl. Winckelmann

law. This is indeed the origin and essence of justice, [a5] lying between what is best – to commit wrong with impunity, and what is worst, not being able to get revenge when wronged. So justice, being mid-way between these two, is welcomed not as a good thing, [b1] but valued through our being too weak to commit injustice. For anyone who had the power to do wrong and was a real man would never make a compact with anybody not to inflict or suffer injustice: he would be mad to do so. [b5] This, then, is the nature of justice, Socrates, the sort of thing it is and how it has evolved like this, as the argument goes.

'We would most effectively grasp the point that people who practise justice do so because they are unable to commit injustice if we were to explore the following idea. [c1] Imagine giving to each of them, the just and the unjust, the capacity to do whatever they wish and then following each of them, watching where their desire will lead. We should then catch the just person red-handed resorting to the same activities as the unjust, impelled by the greed which all nature naturally pursues as a good thing, [c5] when not forcibly deflected by the law into respect for equality.

'The capacity I am talking about is particularly like the kind which would come from having the power which they say was once possessed by †the ancestor of Gyges the Lydian†. [d1] They say that he was a shepherd in the service of the then king of Lydia, and when a heavy shower of rain came on together with an earthquake, the ground opened up, creating a chasm in the place where he was tending his flock. Amazed at the sight he climbed down [d5] and among the marvels there, so the story goes, he saw a bronze horse which was hollow and fitted with openings. Peeping in, he saw a corpse inside which appeared to be of more than human size, wearing nothing else, but with a gold ring on its finger, which he took off and then climbed out. [e1] When the time came for the shepherds' regular meeting to make their monthly report to the king about the flocks, he attended also, wearing the ring. [e5] Now while seated with the others he happened to twist the setting of the ring towards himself, to the inside of his hand; at this he became invisible to those sitting by him and they spoke about

360 γενομένου ἀφανῆ αὐτὸν γενέσθαι τοῖς παρακαθημένοις, καὶ
διαλέγεσθαι ὡς περὶ οἰχομένου. καὶ τὸν θαυμάζειν τε καὶ
πάλιν ἐπιψηλαφῶντα τὸν δακτύλιον στρέψαι ἔξω τὴν σφενδόνην, καὶ στρέψαντα φανερὸν γενέσθαι, καὶ τοῦτο ἐννοή-
5 σαντα ἀποπειρᾶσθαι τοῦ δακτυλίου εἰ ταύτην ἔχοι τὴν
δύναμιν, καὶ αὐτῷ οὕτω συμβαίνειν, στρέφοντι μὲν εἴσω
τὴν σφενδόνην ἀδήλῳ γίγνεσθαι, ἔξω δὲ δήλῳ. αἰσθόμενον
δὲ εὐθὺς διαπράξασθαι τῶν ἀγγέλων γενέσθαι τῶν παρὰ τὸν
b βασιλέα, ἐλθόντα δὲ καὶ τὴν γυναῖκα αὐτοῦ μοιχεύσαντα, μετ᾽
ἐκείνης ἐπιθέμενον τῷ βασιλεῖ ἀποκτεῖναι καὶ τὴν ἀρχὴν
κατασχεῖν.
Εἰ οὖν δύο τοιούτω δακτυλίω γενοίσθην, καὶ τὸν μὲν ὁ
5 δίκαιος περιθεῖτο, τὸν δὲ ὁ ἄδικος, οὐδεὶς ἂν γένοιτο, ὡς
δόξειεν, οὕτως ἀδαμάντινος, ὃς ἂν μείνειεν ἐν τῇ δικαιοσύνῃ
καὶ τολμήσειεν ἀπέχεσθαι τῶν ἀλλοτρίων καὶ μὴ ἅπτεσθαι,
ἐξὸν αὐτῷ καὶ ἐκ τῆς ἀγορᾶς ἀδεῶς ὅτι βούλοιτο λαμβάνειν,
c καὶ εἰσιόντι εἰς τὰς οἰκίας συγγίγνεσθαι ὅτῳ βούλοιτο, καὶ
ἀποκτεινύναι καὶ ἐκ δεσμῶν λύειν οὕστινας βούλοιτο, καὶ
τἆλλα πράττειν ἐν τοῖς ἀνθρώποις ἰσόθεον ὄντα. οὕτω δὲ
δρῶν οὐδὲν ἂν διάφορον τοῦ ἑτέρου ποιοῖ, ἀλλ᾽ ἐπὶ ταὐτὸν
5 ἴοιεν ἀμφότεροι.
Καίτοι μέγα τοῦτο τεκμήριον ἂν φαίη τις ὅτι οὐδεὶς ἑκὼν
δίκαιος ἀλλ᾽ ἀναγκαζόμενος, ὡς οὐκ ἀγαθοῦ ἰδίᾳ ὄντος, ἐπεὶ
ὅπου γ᾽ ἂν οἴηται ἕκαστος οἷός τε ἔσεσθαι ἀδικεῖν, ἀδικεῖν.
d λυσιτελεῖν γὰρ δὴ οἴεται πᾶς ἀνὴρ πολὺ μᾶλλον ἰδίᾳ τὴν
ἀδικίαν τῆς δικαιοσύνης, ἀληθῆ οἰόμενος, ὡς φήσει ὁ περὶ τοῦ
τοιούτου λόγου λέγων· ἐπεὶ εἴ τις τοιαύτης ἐξουσίας ἐπιλα-
βόμενος μηδέν ποτε ἐθέλοι ἀδικῆσαι μηδὲ ἅψαιτο τῶν
5 ἀλλοτρίων, ἀθλιώτατος μὲν ἂν δόξειεν εἶναι τοῖς αἰσθανομέ-
νοις καὶ ἀνοητότατος, ἐπαινοῖεν δ᾽ ἂν αὐτὸν ἀλλήλων ἐναντίον
ἐξαπατῶντες ἀλλήλους διὰ τὸν τοῦ ἀδικεῖσθαι φόβον.
Ταῦτα μὲν οὖν δὴ οὕτω. τὴν δὲ κρίσιν αὐτὴν τοῦ βίου πέρι
e ὧν λέγομεν, ἐὰν διαστησώμεθα τόν τε δικαιότατον καὶ τὸν
ἀδικώτατον, οἷοί τ᾽ ἐσόμεθα κρῖναι ὀρθῶς· εἰ δὲ μή, οὔ. τίς
οὖν δὴ ἡ διάστασις; ἥδε. μηδὲν ἀφαιρῶμεν μήτε τοῦ ἀδίκου
ἀπὸ τῆς ἀδικίας, μήτε τοῦ δικαίου ἀπὸ τῆς δικαιοσύνης, ἀλλὰ
5 τέλεον ἑκάτερον εἰς τὸ ἑαυτοῦ ἐπιτήδευμα τιθῶμεν. πρῶτον
μὲν οὖν ὁ ἄδικος ὥσπερ οἱ δεινοὶ δημιουργοὶ ποιείτω, οἷον
κυβερνήτης ἄκρος ἢ ἰατρὸς τά τε ἀδύνατα ἐν τῇ τέχνῃ καὶ τὰ
361 δυνατὰ διαισθάνεται, καὶ τοῖς μὲν ἐπιχειρεῖ, τὰ δὲ ἐᾷ· ἔτι δὲ

360a1

him as if he had gone away. **360** He was amazed and, feeling the ring again, he turned the setting outwards and became visible. He pondered this and experimented with the ring to see if it actually had this power, [a5] and he found that this was the case: if he turned the setting inwards he became invisible, if outwards, he became visible again. As soon as he became aware of this, he immediately arranged to become one of the messengers who went to the king, and when he got there he seduced his wife [b1] and with her help attacked the king, killed him and took possession of his kingdom.

'Now if there should exist two such rings, and the just person were to put on one and the unjust person the other, [b5] nobody, it could be supposed, could have such an iron will as to stick to justice and have the strength to resist taking other peoples' property, while at the same time being capable of taking from the market-place whatever he wanted with impunity. [c1] He could go into houses and seduce anyone he pleased, killing and releasing from prison whoever he liked, and in all other matters behaving like a god among humans. In acting thus, the behaviour of neither (the just and the unjust) would differ in any way from the other. Both would take the same course. [c5]

'And indeed, one would say that this is firm evidence that no-one is voluntarily just but only under compulsion: justice is thought to give no personal benefit, since in any circumstances where an individual thinks he will be able to get away with being unjust, he is so. [d1] That there is far more personal profit in injustice than in justice is what every man believes, and rightly so, as the person putting forward this sort of argument will maintain; because if a person who had this sort of opportunity within his grasp should be unwilling ever to behave unjustly or seize the possessions of another person, he would be regarded as most miserable and foolish by observers, [d5] though in front of each other they would commend him, deceiving one another for fear of being treated unjustly themselves. So this covers that point.

[e1] 'But to come now to our judgement on the life we are talking about, if we distinguish the extremes of just and unjust we will be able to make a correct decision, but if not, then we shall not. In what, then, lies the distinction? It's this: let us take away nothing from the injustice of the unjust person, nor from the justice of the just person, but take each to be perfect in his own way of life. [e5] First, then, the unjust person: let him operate as clever skilled professionals do – for example, as a first-rate navigator or doctor, who clearly distinguish what is and is not possible in their skill, and attempt the former but leave the latter alone.

361 'Then, too, if they ever do make any mistake, they are equal to correcting

ἐὰν ἄρα πῃ σφαλῇ, ἱκανὸς ἐπανορθοῦσθαι. οὕτω καὶ ὁ ἄδικος
ἐπιχειρῶν ὀρθῶς τοῖς ἀδικήμασιν λανθανέτω, εἰ μέλλει
σφόδρα ἄδικος εἶναι. τὸν ἁλισκόμενον δὲ φαῦλον ἡγητέον·
5 ἐσχάτη γὰρ ἀδικία δοκεῖν δίκαιον εἶναι μὴ ὄντα.

Δοτέον οὖν τῷ τελέως ἀδίκῳ τὴν τελεωτάτην ἀδικίαν, καὶ
οὐκ ἀφαιρετέον ἀλλ᾽ ἐατέον τὰ μέγιστα ἀδικοῦντα τὴν
b μεγίστην δόξαν αὑτῷ παρεσκευακέναι εἰς δικαιοσύνην, καὶ
ἐὰν ἄρα σφάλληταί τι, ἐπανορθοῦσθαι δυνατῷ εἶναι, λέγειν τε
ἱκανῷ ὄντι πρὸς τὸ πείθειν, ἐάν τι μηνύηται τῶν ἀδικημάτων,
καὶ βιάσασθαι ὅσα ἂν βίας δέηται, διά τε ἀνδρείαν καὶ ῥώμην
5 καὶ διὰ παρασκευὴν φίλων καὶ οὐσίας. τοῦτον δὲ τοιοῦτον
θέντες τὸν δίκαιον παρ᾽ αὐτὸν ἱστῶμεν τῷ λόγῳ, ἄνδρα
ἁπλοῦν καὶ γενναῖον, κατ᾽ Αἰσχύλον οὐ δοκεῖν ἀλλ᾽
εἶναι ἀγαθὸν ἐθέλοντα.

c   Ἀφαιρετέον δὴ τὸ δοκεῖν· εἰ γὰρ δόξει δίκαιος εἶναι,
ἔσονται αὐτῷ τιμαὶ καὶ δωρεαὶ δοκοῦντι τοιούτῳ εἶναι.
ἄδηλον οὖν εἴτε τοῦ δικαίου εἴτε τῶν δωρεῶν τε καὶ τιμῶν
ἕνεκα τοιοῦτος εἴη. γυμνωτέος δὴ πάντων πλὴν δικαιοσύνης
5 καὶ ποιητέος ἐναντίως διακείμενος τῷ προτέρῳ· μηδὲν γὰρ
ἀδικῶν δόξαν ἐχέτω τὴν μεγίστην ἀδικίας, ἵνα ᾖ βεβασανι-
σμένος εἰς δικαιοσύνην τῷ μὴ τέγγεσθαι ὑπὸ κακοδοξίας καὶ
τῶν ἀπ᾽ αὐτῆς γιγνομένων. ἀλλὰ ἴτω ἀμετάστατος μέχρι
d θανάτου, δοκῶν μὲν εἶναι ἄδικος διὰ βίου, ὢν δὲ δίκαιος, ἵνα
ἀμφότεροι εἰς τὸ ἔσχατον ἐληλυθότες, ὁ μὲν δικαιοσύνης, ὁ δὲ
ἀδικίας, κρίνωνται ὁπότερος αὐτοῖν εὐδαιμονέστερος.

Βαβαῖ, ἦν δ᾽ ἐγώ, ὦ φίλε Γλαύκων, ὡς ἐρρωμένως
5 ἑκάτερον ὥσπερ ἀνδριάντα εἰς τὴν κρίσιν ἐκκαθαίρεις τοῖν
ἀνδροῖν.

Ὡς μάλιστ᾽, ἔφη, δύναμαι. ὄντοιν δὲ τοιούτοιν, οὐδὲν ἔτι,
ὡς ἐγᾦμαι, χαλεπὸν ἐπεξελθεῖν τῷ λόγῳ οἷος ἑκάτερος βίος
e ἐπιμένει. λεκτέον οὖν· καὶ δὴ κἂν ἀγροικοτέρως λέγηται, μὴ
ἐμὲ οἴου λέγειν, ὦ Σώκρατες, ἀλλὰ τοὺς ἐπαινοῦντας πρὸ
δικαιοσύνης ἀδικίαν.

Ἐροῦσι δὲ τάδε, ὅτι οὕτω διακείμενος ὁ δίκαιος μαστιγώ-
5 σεται, στρεβλώσεται, δεδήσεται, ἐκκαυθήσεται τὠφθαλμώ,
362 τελευτῶν πάντα κακὰ παθὼν ἀνασχινδυλευθήσεται, καὶ
γνώσεται ὅτι οὐκ εἶναι δίκαιον ἀλλὰ δοκεῖν δεῖ ἐθέλειν. τὸ
δὲ τοῦ Αἰσχύλου πολὺ ἦν ἄρα ὀρθότερον λέγειν κατὰ τοῦ
ἀδίκου. τῷ ὄντι γὰρ φήσουσι τὸν ἄδικον, ἅτε ἐπιτηδεύοντα
5 πρᾶγμα ἀληθείας ἐχόμενον καὶ οὐ πρὸς δόξαν ζῶντα, οὐ

361a2

it. Similarly, let the unjust person going about his wrongdoing in a faultless way escape detection for his wrongdoing, if he is going to be thoroughly unjust. The person who is caught must be considered a bungler, for the height of injustice is to seem just when you are not. [a5]

So we must grant the completely unjust person the most complete injustice, and not deprive him of any of it, but allow the greatest wrongdoer to obtain for himself the greatest reputation for justice, [b1] and if he should slip up at all, to be capable of correcting his error and to be capable of arguing to persuade people, if any of his injustices come to light; to use force when force is needed, through his courage, strength and the backing of friends and material resources. [b5]

Having set the unjust person up as this sort of character, let us in turn place the just person by his side in the argument: a straightforward and noble man who, to quote Aeschylus, "wants not to seem, but to be" good. Now we must deprive him of the appearance of justice; for if he is going to be reputed just, [c1] he will have the honours and gifts this sort of reputation bestows on him, and then it will be unclear whether he has such a character for justice's sake or because of his gifts and honours. He must indeed be stripped of everything except his justice and made exactly opposite to the unjust person we imagined before; [c5] although doing no wrong, let him have a reputation for the greatest injustice so that he may be tested for his justice by his not weakening in the face of ill-repute and all that goes with it. But let him hold an unalterable course until death; [d1] while really just, let him be regarded as unjust throughout his life, so that, when both have pursued their life to its extreme, the one of justice and the other of injustice, we may judge which of them is the happier.'

'Bless me, my dear Glaucon', I said, 'how vigorously you're scouring your two men clean as if each was a sculpture entered for a competition!' [d5]

'To the best of my ability,' he replied. 'If their two natures are as I have described them, there will not, I think, be any further difficulty in going through the story of the sort of life that awaits each of them. [e1] So, it must be told; moreover if my account is delivered in a somewhat vulgar manner, don't suppose that I am the one speaking, Socrates, but those who commend injustice over justice. What they will say is that, such being his character, the just person will be whipped, stretched on the rack and imprisoned; **362** his eyes will be burnt out and finally, after suffering every evil, he will be impaled on a stake, and come to realise that not to be, but to seem just is what one must aim for. So the saying I quoted from Aeschylus would be more correctly applied to the unjust person. For in reality, they will say, the unjust person, [a5] inasmuch as what he does in his life relates to truth and does

δοκεῖν ἄδικον ἀλλ' εἶναι ἐθέλειν,

βαθεῖαν ἄλοκα διὰ φρενὸς καρπούμενον,
b ἐξ ἧς τὰ κεδνὰ βλαστάνει βουλεύματα,

πρῶτον μὲν ἄρχειν ἐν τῇ πόλει δοκοῦντι δικαίῳ εἶναι, ἔπειτα
γαμεῖν ὁπόθεν ἂν βούληται, ἐκδιδόναι εἰς οὓς ἂν βούληται,
συμβάλλειν [κοινωνεῖν] οἷς ἂν ἐθέλῃ, καὶ παρὰ ταῦτα πάντα
5 ὠφελεῖσθαι κερδαίνοντα τῷ μὴ δυσχεραίνειν τὸ ἀδικεῖν· εἰς
ἀγῶνας τοίνυν ἰόντα καὶ ἰδίᾳ καὶ δημοσίᾳ περιγίγνεσθαι καὶ
πλεονεκτεῖν τῶν ἐχθρῶν, πλεονεκτοῦντα δὲ πλουτεῖν καὶ τούς
c τε φίλους εὖ ποιεῖν καὶ τοὺς ἐχθροὺς βλάπτειν, καὶ θεοῖς
θυσίας καὶ ἀναθήματα ἱκανῶς καὶ μεγαλοπρεπῶς θύειν τε καὶ
ἀνατιθέναι, καὶ θεραπεύειν τοῦ δικαίου πολὺ ἄμεινον τοὺς
θεοὺς καὶ τῶν ἀνθρώπων οὓς ἂν βούληται, ὥστε καὶ
5 θεοφιλέστερον αὐτὸν εἶναι μᾶλλον προσήκειν ἐκ τῶν εἰκότων
ἢ τὸν δίκαιον.

Οὕτω φασίν, ὦ Σώκρατες, παρὰ θεῶν καὶ παρ' ἀνθρώπων
τῷ ἀδίκῳ παρεσκευάσθαι τὸν βίον ἄμεινον ἢ τῷ δικαίῳ.

d Ταῦτ' εἰπόντος τοῦ Γλαύκωνος ἐγὼ μὲν ἐν νῷ εἶχόν τι
λέγειν πρὸς ταῦτα, ὁ δὲ ἀδελφὸς αὐτοῦ Ἀδείμαντος, Οὔ τί
που οἴει, ἔφη, ὦ Σώκρατες, ἱκανῶς εἰρῆσθαι περὶ τοῦ λόγου;
Ἀλλὰ τί μήν; εἶπον.
5 Αὐτό, ἦ δ' ὅς, οὐκ εἴρηται ὃ μάλιστα ἔδει ῥηθῆναι.

Οὐκοῦν, ἦν δ' ἐγώ, τὸ λεγόμενον, ἀδελφὸς ἀνδρὶ παρείη·
ὥστε καὶ σύ, εἴ τι ὅδε ἐλλείπει, ἐπάμυνε. καίτοι ἐμέγε ἱκανὰ
καὶ τὰ ὑπὸ τούτου ῥηθέντα καταπαλαῖσαι καὶ ἀδύνατον
e ποιῆσαι βοηθεῖν δικαιοσύνῃ.

Καὶ ὅς, Οὐδέν, ἔφη, λέγεις· ἀλλ' ἔτι καὶ τάδε ἄκουε. δεῖ
γὰρ διελθεῖν ἡμᾶς καὶ τοὺς ἐναντίους λόγους ὧν ὅδε εἶπεν, οἳ
δικαιοσύνην μὲν ἐπαινοῦσιν, ἀδικίαν δὲ ψέγουσιν, ἵν' ᾖ σαφέ-
5 στερον ὅ μοι δοκεῖ βούλεσθαι Γλαύκων.

Λέγουσι δέ που καὶ παρακελεύονται πατέρες τε ὑέσιν, καὶ
363 πάντες οἱ τινῶν κηδόμενοι, ὡς χρὴ δίκαιον εἶναι, οὐκ αὐτὸ
δικαιοσύνην ἐπαινοῦντες ἀλλὰ τὰς ἀπ' αὐτῆς εὐδοκιμήσεις,
ἵνα δοκοῦντι δικαίῳ εἶναι γίγνηται ἀπὸ τῆς δόξης ἀρχαί τε
καὶ γάμοι καὶ ὅσαπερ Γλαύκων διῆλθεν ἄρτι, ἀπὸ τοῦ

362b4 κοινωνεῖν secl. Cobet
362d1 μὲν AD: μὲν αὖ F

not accord with his reputation, does not want to seem unjust but to be so:

harvesting the deep furrow of his thought,

from which spring valuable counsels, [b1]

first, by holding office in the city because he is thought to be just, secondly by marrying into any family he wishes, marrying off his children to whomever he wishes, joining up in business with anyone he likes; and in all this he is helped to gain advantage by the fact that he does not have any scruples about committing injustice. [b5] And so, engaging in lawsuits, private and public, he wins and gets the better of his enemies, and this enables him to become rich and do good to his friends and harm to his enemies. [c1] He will make sacrifices and dedicate votive offerings to the gods on an appropriately magnificent scale, and do service to the gods and any humans he wishes far more effectively than the just person, so that it is reasonable to suppose that he is also more loved by the gods than the just person. [c5] Thus they say, Socrates, that a better life is provided by gods and men for the unjust than for the just person.' [d1]

When Glaucon had finished this speech I had it in mind to make some reply, but his brother Adeimantus interposed: 'Surely, Socrates, you don't think that the topic has been sufficiently aired, do you?'

'Well yes, why not?' I replied.

[d5] 'The most vital point,' he said, 'has not been stated.'

'Then,' I replied, 'let brother stand by brother, as the saying goes; so, if this fellow here has fallen short in any way, you too come to his aid. And yet, as far as I'm concerned, what he has already said is quite sufficient to floor me and make me incapable of coming to the aid of justice.' [e1]

'You're talking nonsense,' he answered; 'but just listen to this further point. We should also go through the arguments contrary to what he said, those which commend justice and censure injustice, so that what I suppose to be Glaucon's meaning may become clearer. [e5]

'Fathers surely talk to their sons, as do all those who have anybody in their charge, and urge that one should be just, **363** commending justice not as something in itself, but for the good reputation it brings. This is in order that the person with the reputation of justice may acquire from this reputation offices and marriage alliances, and all that Glaucon has just enumerated – rewards which come to the just person

5 εὐδοκιμεῖν ὄντα τῷ δικαίῳ. Ἐπὶ πλέον δὲ οὗτοι τὰ τῶν δοξῶν λέγουσιν. τὰς γὰρ παρὰ θεῶν εὐδοκιμήσεις ἐμβάλλοντες ἄφθονα ἔχουσι λέγειν ἀγαθὰ τοῖς ὁσίοις, ἅ φασι θεοὺς διδόναι· ὥσπερ ὁ γενναῖος Ἡσίοδός
b τε καὶ Ὅμηρός φασιν, ὁ μὲν τὰς δρῦς τοῖς δικαίοις τοὺς θεοὺς ποιεῖν ἄκρας μέν τε φέρειν βαλάνους, μέσσας δὲ μελίσσας· εἰροπόκοι δ᾽ ὄιες, φησίν, μαλλοῖς καταβεβρίθασι, καὶ ἄλλα δὴ πολλὰ ἀγαθὰ τούτων
5 ἐχόμενα. παραπλήσια δὲ καὶ ὁ ἕτερος· ὥς τέ τευ γάρ φησιν

ἢ βασιλῆος ἀμύμονος ὅς τε θεουδὴς
c εὐδικίας ἀνέχῃσι, φέρῃσι δὲ γαῖα μέλαινα
πυροὺς καὶ κριθάς, βρίθῃσι δὲ δένδρεα καρπῷ,
τίκτῃ δ᾽ ἔμπεδα μῆλα, θάλασσα δὲ παρέχῃ ἰχθῦς.

Μουσαῖος δὲ τούτων νεανικώτερα τἀγαθὰ καὶ ὁ ὑὸς αὐτοῦ
5 παρὰ θεῶν διδόασιν τοῖς δικαίοις· εἰς Ἅιδου γὰρ ἀγαγόντες τῷ λόγῳ καὶ κατακλίναντες καὶ συμπόσιον τῶν ὁσίων
d κατασκευάσαντες ἐστεφανωμένους ποιοῦσιν τὸν ἅπαντα χρό- νον ἤδη διάγειν μεθύοντας, ἡγησάμενοι κάλλιστον ἀρετῆς μισθὸν μέθην αἰώνιον. οἱ δ᾽ ἔτι τούτων μακροτέρους ἀποτεί- νουσιν μισθοὺς παρὰ θεῶν· παῖδας γὰρ παίδων φασὶ καὶ γένος
5 κατόπισθεν λείπεσθαι τοῦ ὁσίου καὶ εὐόρκου.
Ταῦτα δὴ καὶ ἄλλα τοιαῦτα ἐγκωμιάζουσιν δικαιοσύνην· τοὺς δὲ ἀνοσίους αὖ καὶ ἀδίκους εἰς πηλόν τινα κατορύττουσιν ἐν Ἅιδου καὶ κοσκίνῳ ὕδωρ ἀναγκάζουσι φέρειν, ἔτι τε
e ζῶντας εἰς κακὰς δόξας ἄγοντες, ἅπερ Γλαύκων περὶ τῶν δικαίων δοξαζομένων δὲ ἀδίκων διῆλθε τιμωρήματα, ταῦτα περὶ τῶν ἀδίκων λέγουσιν, ἄλλα δὲ οὐκ ἔχουσιν.
Ὁ μὲν οὖν ἔπαινος καὶ ὁ ψόγος οὗτος ἑκατέρων. πρὸς δὲ
5 τούτοις σκέψαι, ὦ Σώκρατες, ἄλλο αὖ εἶδος λόγων περὶ δικαιοσύνης τε καὶ ἀδικίας ἰδίᾳ τε λεγόμενον καὶ ὑπὸ
364 ποιητῶν. πάντες γὰρ ἐξ ἑνὸς στόματος ὑμνοῦσιν ὡς καλὸν μὲν ἡ σωφροσύνη τε καὶ δικαιοσύνη, χαλεπὸν μέντοι καὶ ἐπίπονον, ἀκολασία δὲ καὶ ἀδικία ἡδὺ μὲν καὶ εὐπετὲς κτήσασθαι, δόξῃ δὲ μόνον καὶ νόμῳ αἰσχρόν. λυσιτελέστερα
5 δὲ τῶν δικαίων τὰ ἄδικα ὡς ἐπὶ τὸ πλῆθος λέγουσι, καὶ πονηροὺς πλουσίους καὶ ἄλλας δυνάμεις ἔχοντας εὐδαιμονί- ζειν καὶ τιμᾶν εὐχερῶς ἐθέλουσιν δημοσίᾳ τε καὶ ἰδίᾳ· τοὺς δὲ
b ἀτιμάζειν καὶ ὑπερορᾶν, οἳ ἄν πῃ ἀσθενεῖς τε καὶ πένητες

363a4
from being well thought-of. [a5] But these people enlarge still further on the fruits of a good reputation. For, throwing in good standing with the gods, they are able to list good things without stint which they say the gods give to the pious, as the noble Hesiod and Homer record. Hesiod says that for the just the gods make oaks bear "acorns at the top, [b1] bees in the middle;" he adds "the woolly sheep are weighed down by their fleeces" and many other benefits like these. And Homer speaks similarly: for he says, "like someone": [b5]

a noble king who, god-fearing,

upholds good government, and the black earth bears

[c1] *wheat and barley, and the trees are weighed down with fruit,*

the sheep continually bear young, and the sea teems with fish.

But Musaeus and his son sing of still more exhilarating rewards that the just can expect from the gods; for the story goes that when they have conducted them down to Hades [c5] they sit them down to a wine party of the pious that they have laid on, and have them pass the whole time in drinking with garlands on their heads, [d1] in the belief that the finest reward of virtue is to be drunk for all eternity. But others extend the rewards bestowed by the gods to a still greater length; they say that those who are pious and keep to their oaths leave behind children's children and an unfailing posterity. [d5] So with these and similar recommendations they praise justice; but the impious and unjust, on the other hand, they bury in some sort of mud in Hades and force them to carry water in a sieve, and while they are still alive they bring them into evil repute, and all the punishments which Glaucon [e1] described as falling on the just people who appeared wicked, these they allot in their poems to the unjust; they have no others to record. Such is the praise and censure of the just and unjust.

[e5] 'But consider further, Socrates, another line of argument again about justice and injustice found in ordinary conversation and in the poets. **364** For all with one voice hymn moderation and justice as fine things, but hard and laborious,while licentiousness and injustice are pleasant and easily acquired and regarded as shameful only in opinion and by convention. They say that unjust deeds are for the most part [a5] more profitable than just, and they are quite ready and willing to call the wicked happy and honour them in public and private, provided that they are wealthy or have other sources of power, [b1] whereas those in any way weak

ὦσιν, ὁμολογοῦντες αὐτοὺς ἀμείνους εἶναι τῶν ἑτέρων.

Τούτων δὲ πάντων οἱ περὶ θεῶν τε λόγοι καὶ ἀρετῆς
θαυμασιώτατοι λέγονται, ὡς ἄρα καὶ θεοὶ πολλοῖς μὲν
5 ἀγαθοῖς δυστυχίας τε καὶ βίον κακὸν ἔνειμαν, τοῖς δ' ἐναντίοις
ἐναντίαν μοῖραν. ἀγύρται δὲ καὶ μάντεις ἐπὶ πλουσίων θύρας
ἰόντες πείθουσιν ὡς ἔστι παρὰ σφίσι δύναμις ἐκ θεῶν
ποριζομένη θυσίαις τε καὶ ἐπῳδαῖς, εἴτε τι ἀδίκημά του
c γέγονεν αὐτοῦ ἢ προγόνων, ἀκεῖσθαι μεθ' ἡδονῶν τε καὶ
ἑορτῶν, ἐάντε τινὰ ἐχθρὸν πημῆναι ἐθέλῃ, μετὰ σμικρῶν
δαπανῶν ὁμοίως δίκαιον ἀδίκῳ βλάψει ἐπαγωγαῖς τισιν καὶ
καταδέσμοις, τοὺς θεούς, ὥς φασιν, πείθοντες σφίσιν ὑπηρε-
5 τεῖν.

Τούτοις δὲ πᾶσιν τοῖς λόγοις μάρτυρας ποιητὰς ἐπάγονται
οἱ μὲν κακίας πέρι, εὐπετείας διδόντες, ὡς

d τὴν μὲν κακότητα καὶ ἰλαδὸν ἔστιν ἑλέσθαι
ῥηϊδίως· λείη μὲν ὁδός, μάλα δ' ἐγγύθι ναίει·
τῆς δ' ἀρετῆς ἱδρῶτα θεοὶ προπάροιθεν ἔθηκαν,

καί τινα ὁδὸν μακράν τε καὶ τραχεῖαν καὶ ἀνάντη. οἱ δὲ τῆς
τῶν θεῶν ὑπ' ἀνθρώπων παραγωγῆς τὸν Ὅμηρον μαρτύ-
5 ρονται, ὅτι καὶ ἐκεῖνος εἶπεν

λιστοὶ δέ τε καὶ θεοὶ αὐτοί,
καὶ τοὺς μὲν θυσίαισι καὶ εὐχωλαῖς ἀγαναῖσιν
e λοιβῇ τε κνίσῃ τε παρατρωπῶσ' ἄνθρωποι
λισσόμενοι, ὅτε κέν τις ὑπερβήῃ καὶ ἁμάρτῃ.

βίβλων δὲ ὅμαδον παρέχονται Μουσαίου καὶ Ὀρφέως,
Σελήνης τε καὶ Μουσῶν ἐκγόνων ὥς φασι, καθ' ἃς θυηπο-
5 λοῦσιν, πείθοντες οὐ μόνον ἰδιώτας ἀλλὰ καὶ πόλεις, ὡς ἄρα
λύσεις τε καὶ καθαρμοὶ ἀδικημάτων διὰ θυσιῶν καὶ παιδιᾶς
365 ἡδονῶν εἰσι μὲν ἔτι ζῶσιν, εἰσὶ δὲ καὶ τελευτήσασιν, ἃς δὴ
τελετὰς καλοῦσιν, αἳ τῶν ἐκεῖ κακῶν ἀπολύουσιν ἡμᾶς, μὴ
θύσαντας δὲ δεινὰ περιμένει.

Ταῦτα πάντα, ἔφη, ὦ φίλε Σώκρατες, τοιαῦτα καὶ
5 τοσαῦτα λεγόμενα ἀρετῆς πέρι καὶ κακίας, ὡς ἄνθρωποι
καὶ θεοὶ περὶ αὐτὰ ἔχουσι τιμῆς, τί οἰόμεθα ἀκουούσας

364c7 διδόντες ADF: ᾄδοντες Muretus

364b2
and poor they dishonour and disregard, even while admitting that they are better
than the others. But strangest of all these are the stories that are told about the gods
and virtue, how the gods, too, have assigned to many good people misfortunes and
a miserable life, but to their opposites a reverse fate. [b5] Wandering priests and
prophets approaching the doors of the wealthy persuade them that there is a power
from the gods conveyed through sacrifices and incantations, and any wrongdoing
committed either by an individual or his ancestors can be expiated with charms
and feasts. [c1] Or if he wishes to injure any enemy of his, for a small outlay he
will be able to harm just and unjust alike with certain spells and enchantments
through which they can persuade the gods, they say, to serve their ends. [c5] For
all these stories they call on the poets as support. Some, on the ease of acquiring
vice, quote as follows:

Evil can be obtained in abundance,

[d1] *And easily; smooth is the way, and it lives close by.*

But the gods have placed sweat in the path of virtue,

and a long, hard and uphill road. Others bring in Homer as a witness for the
beguiling of gods by men, [d5] since he also said:

The gods themselves can be moved by supplication;

And humans, with sacrifices and soothing prayers

[e1] *With libations and sacrifices, turn their wills*

By prayer, when anyone has overstepped the mark and offended.

And they produce a babble of books by Musaeus and Orpheus, descendants, as
they claim, of Selene and the Muses, and using these books for their rituals they
sacrifice, and persuaded [e5] not only individuals but cities that they really can
have remissions and purification for their wrongdoing through sacrifices **365** and
playful delights, while they are still alive and, equally, after death. These they
actually call initiations, which free us from evils in the next world, while terrible
things await those who neglect to sacrifice.

'How, my dear Socrates,' he continued, 'do we imagine the souls of young men
will react on hearing all this and such a lot of other talk like it [a5] about virtue
and vice, and in what esteem they are held by men and gods? I mean those young

νέων ψυχὰς ποιεῖν, ὅσοι εὐφυεῖς καὶ ἱκανοὶ ἐπὶ πάντα τὰ
λεγόμενα ὥσπερ ἐπιπτόμενοι συλλογίσασθαι ἐξ αὐτῶν ποῖός
b τις ἂν ὢν καὶ πῇ πορευθεὶς τὸν βίον ὡς ἄριστα διέλθοι; λέγοι
γὰρ ἂν ἐκ τῶν εἰκότων πρὸς αὐτὸν κατὰ Πίνδαρον ἐκεῖνο τὸ
Πότερον δίκᾳ τεῖχος ὕψιον ἢ σκολιαῖς ἀπάταις
ἀναβὰς καὶ ἐμαυτὸν οὕτω περιφράξας διαβιῶ; τὰ μὲν
5 γὰρ λεγόμενα δικαίῳ μὲν ὄντι μοι, ἐὰν μὴ καὶ δοκῶ ὄφελος
οὐδέν φασιν εἶναι, πόνους δὲ καὶ ζημίας φανεράς· ἀδίκῳ δὲ
δόξαν δικαιοσύνης παρασκευασαμένῳ θεσπέσιος βίος λέγε-
c ται. οὐκοῦν, ἐπειδὴ τὸ δοκεῖν, ὡς δηλοῦσί μοι οἱ σοφοί,
καὶ τὰν ἀλαθείαν βιᾶται καὶ κύριον εὐδαιμονίας, ἐπὶ
τοῦτο δὴ τρεπτέον ὅλως· πρόθυρα μὲν καὶ σχῆμα κύκλῳ περὶ
ἐμαυτὸν σκιαγραφίαν ἀρετῆς περιγραπτέον, τὴν δὲ τοῦ
5 σοφωτάτου Ἀρχιλόχου ἀλώπεκα ἑλκτέον ἐξόπισθεν κερδα-
λέαν καὶ ποικίλην.
"Ἀλλὰ γάρ, φησί τις, οὐ ῥᾴδιον ἀεὶ λανθάνειν κακὸν ὄντα."
Οὐδὲ γὰρ ἄλλο οὐδὲν εὐπετές, φήσομεν, τῶν μεγάλων· ἀλλ'
d ὅμως, εἰ μέλλομεν εὐδαιμονήσειν, ταύτῃ ἰτέον, ὡς τὰ ἴχνη
τῶν λόγων φέρει. ἐπὶ γὰρ τὸ λανθάνειν συνωμοσίας τε καὶ
ἑταιρίας συνάξομεν, εἰσίν τε πειθοῦς διδάσκαλοι χρημάτων
σοφίαν δημηγορικήν τε καὶ δικανικὴν διδόντες, ἐξ ὧν τὰ μὲν
5 πείσομεν, τὰ δὲ βιασόμεθα, ὡς πλεονεκτοῦντες δίκην μὴ
διδόναι.
"Ἀλλὰ δὴ θεοὺς οὔτε λανθάνειν οὔτε βιάσασθαι δυνατόν."
Οὐκοῦν, εἰ μὲν μή εἰσιν ἢ μηδὲν αὐτοῖς τῶν ἀνθρωπίνων
μέλει, τί καὶ ἡμῖν μελητέον τοῦ λανθάνειν; εἰ δὲ εἰσί τε καὶ
e ἐπιμελοῦνται, οὐκ ἄλλοθέν τοι αὐτοὺς ἴσμεν ἢ ἀκηκόαμεν ἢ
ἔκ τε τῶν νόμων καὶ τῶν γενεαλογησάντων ποιητῶν; οἱ δὲ
αὐτοὶ οὗτοι λέγουσιν ὡς εἰσὶν οἷοι θυσίαις τε καὶ εὐχωλαῖς
ἀγανῇσιν καὶ ἀναθήμασιν παράγεσθαι ἀναπειθόμενοι, οἷς ἢ
5 ἀμφότερα ἢ οὐδέτερα πειστέον. εἰ δ' οὖν πειστέον, ἀδικητέον
366 καὶ θυτέον ἀπὸ τῶν ἀδικημάτων. δίκαιοι μὲν γὰρ ὄντες
ἀζήμιοι μόνον ὑπὸ θεῶν ἐσόμεθα, τὰ δ' ἐξ ἀδικίας κέρδη
ἀπωσόμεθα· ἄδικοι δὲ κερδανοῦμέν τε καὶ λισσόμενοι ὑπερ-
βαίνοντες καὶ ἁμαρτάνοντες, πείθοντες αὐτοὺς ἀζήμιοι ἀπαλ-
5 λάξομεν.
"Ἀλλὰ γὰρ ἐν Ἅιδου δίκην δώσομεν ὧν ἂν ἐνθάδε

365d3 χρημάτων F: om. AD

365e2 νόμων F: λόγων AD Cyrillus

men who are naturally gifted and capable of flitting around all these sayings, as it were, and gathering from them what sort of character they should have, and what path through life they should take in order to live it as well as possible. [b1] Because such a person might reasonably ask himself, in the words of Pindar: "Is it by justice I should ascend the higher tower, or by crooked deceit?" and thus "live out my life securely fenced around?" For if I am just, these sayings, unless I also seem just, will, they say, be of no use; [b5] they will involve suffering and public penalties. But for the unjust person who has cultivated a reputation for justice a life fit for the gods is predicted. Therefore, since, as the wise men reveal to me, [c1] "appearance even overmasters truth" and governs our happiness, I must devote myself entirely to appearance; as a front and façade I must sketch out around myself a painted illusion of virtue, but drag on a lead behind me that "cunning" and wily fox, from the poetry of most wise Archilochus. [c5]

"But," someone may object, "it is not easy to be wicked and always escape detection." Yes," we will reply, "but neither is any other major undertaking easy; [d1] yet all the same, if we aim to be happy we must take the path to which the steps of our argument point. For with a view to lying hidden we will organise conspiratorial gatherings and clubs, and there are teachers of persuasion who, for a fee, can pass on the arts of the assembly and the court-room, where, by persuading some and forcing others, [d5] we will outdo them without having to pay a penalty.

"But surely against the gods neither subterfuge nor force can be attempted". But, if the gods do not exist, or if human affairs are of no concern to them, why should it be a concern to us to escape their attention? But even if they do exist and do care about us, [e1] our knowledge of them comes from nowhere other than from what we have heard or from the laws and the poets who provide genealogies. Yet these are those very authorities who tell us that the gods can be persuaded and diverted by sacrifices, "soothing prayers" and dedications; [e5] they should carry conviction in both aspects or neither. Now, if they are to carry conviction one should do wrong and make sacrifice from the proceeds of wrongdoing. **366** For if we are just we will merely escape punishment from the gods, but at the same time we will be rejecting the profit which would come from injustice. But if we are unjust we will profit, and, provided we accompany our transgressions and wrongdoing with supplication, will be able to use persuasion on them to get off unpunished. [a5]

"Not so, for we will pay in Hades for the misdeeds done in this world – either we

ἀδικήσωμεν, ἢ αὐτοὶ ἢ παῖδες παίδων." Ἀλλ', ὦ φίλε, φήσει
λογιζόμενος, αἱ τελεταὶ αὖ μέγα δύνανται καὶ οἱ λύσιοι θεοί,
b ὡς αἱ μέγισται πόλεις λέγουσι καὶ οἱ θεῶν παῖδες ποιηταὶ καὶ
προφῆται τῶν θεῶν γενόμενοι, οἳ ταῦτα οὕτως ἔχειν
μηνύουσι.

Κατὰ τίνα οὖν ἔτι λόγον δικαιοσύνην [ἂν] πρὸ μεγίστης
5 ἀδικίας αἱροίμεθ' ἄν, ἣν ἐὰν μετ' εὐσχημοσύνης κιβδήλου
κτησώμεθα, καὶ παρὰ θεοῖς καὶ παρ' ἀνθρώποις πράξομεν
κατὰ νοῦν ζῶντές τε καὶ τελευτήσαντες, ὡς ὁ τῶν πολλῶν τε
καὶ ἄκρων λεγόμενος λόγος; ἐκ δὴ πάντων τῶν εἰρημένων τίς
c μηχανή, ὦ Σώκρατες, δικαιοσύνην τιμᾶν ἐθέλειν ᾧ τις
δύναμις ὑπάρχει ψυχῆς ἢ σώματος ἢ χρημάτων ἢ γένους,
ἀλλὰ μὴ γελᾶν ἐπαινουμένης ἀκούοντα; ὡς δή τοι εἴ τις ἔχει
ψευδῆ μὲν ἀποφῆναι ἃ εἰρήκαμεν, ἱκανῶς δὲ ἔγνωκεν ὅτι
5 ἄριστον δικαιοσύνη, πολλήν που συγγνώμην ἔχει καὶ οὐκ
ὀργίζεται τοῖς ἀδίκοις, ἀλλ' οἶδεν ὅτι πλὴν εἴ τις θείᾳ φύσει
δυσχεραίνων τὸ ἀδικεῖν ἢ ἐπιστήμην λαβὼν ἀπέχεται αὐτοῦ,
d τῶν γε ἄλλων οὐδεὶς ἑκὼν δίκαιος, ἀλλ' ὑπὸ ἀνανδρίας ἢ
γήρως ἤ τινος ἄλλης ἀσθενείας ψέγει τὸ ἀδικεῖν, ἀδυνατῶν
αὐτὸ δρᾶν. ὡς δέ, δῆλον· ὁ γὰρ πρῶτος τῶν τοιούτων εἰς
δύναμιν ἐλθὼν πρῶτος ἀδικεῖ, καθ' ὅσον ἂν οἷός τ' ᾖ.

5 Καὶ τούτων ἁπάντων οὐδὲν ἄλλο αἴτιον ἢ ἐκεῖνο, ὅθενπερ
ἅπας ὁ λόγος οὗτος ὥρμησεν καὶ τῷδε καὶ ἐμοὶ πρὸς σέ, ὦ
Σώκρατες, εἰπεῖν, ὅτι "Ὦ θαυμάσιε, πάντων ὑμῶν, ὅσοι
e ἐπαινέται φατὲ δικαιοσύνης εἶναι, ἀπὸ τῶν ἐξ ἀρχῆς ἡρώων
ἀρξάμενοι, ὅσων λόγοι λελειμμένοι, μέχρι τῶν νῦν ἀνθρώπων
οὐδεὶς πώποτε ἔψεξεν ἀδικίαν οὐδ' ἐπήνεσεν δικαιοσύνην
ἄλλως ἢ δόξας τε καὶ τιμὰς καὶ δωρεὰς τὰς ἀπ' αὐτῶν
5 γιγνομένας· αὐτὸ δ' ἑκάτερον τῇ αὑτοῦ δυνάμει ἐν τῇ τοῦ
ἔχοντος ψυχῇ ἐνόν, καὶ λανθάνον θεούς τε καὶ ἀνθρώπους,
οὐδεὶς πώποτε οὔτ' ἐν ποιήσει οὔτ' ἐν ἰδίοις λόγοις ἐπεξῆλθεν
ἱκανῶς τῷ λόγῳ, ὡς τὸ μὲν μέγιστον κακῶν ὅσα ἴσχει ψυχὴ
367 ἐν αὑτῇ, δικαιοσύνη δὲ μέγιστον ἀγαθόν. εἰ γὰρ οὕτως
ἐλέγετο ἐξ ἀρχῆς ὑπὸ πάντων ὑμῶν καὶ ἐκ νέων ἡμᾶς
ἐπείθετε, οὐκ ἂν ἀλλήλους ἐφυλάττομεν μὴ ἀδικεῖν, ἀλλ'
αὐτὸς αὑτοῦ ἦν ἕκαστος ἄριστος φύλαξ, δεδιὼς μὴ ἀδικῶν
5 τῷ μεγίστῳ κακῷ σύνοικος ᾖ."

366b4 ἂν secl. Slings
366c2 ἢ σώματος ἢ χρημάτων F: ἢ χρημάτων ἢ σώματος AD

366a7
ourselves or our children's children." "But, my friend," will come the considered
reply, "again, initiation rites and gods who give absolution are very powerful, as
the greatest cities affirm [b1] and the children of gods who have become poets and
prophets for the gods reveal that these things are so."

'Well then, what argument might still remain for us to prefer justice above the
greatest injustice, which, if we possess it with a counterfeit elegance, [b5] we will
be able to practise as we like among gods and men, in this world and the next, as
the argument of the majority and the acutest minds declare? Indeed, from all that
has been said, what strategy is there, Socrates, [c1] for someone of any distinction
of mind or body or wealth or family, to wish to honour justice and not laugh when
he hears it being praised? I'm telling you, if there is anybody able to prove what
we have said is false and has come to be sufficiently aware that justice is best,
[c5] he surely feels much sympathy and not anger for the unjust, knowing that
unless there is a person who by his godlike nature disdains injustice or acquires
the knowledge to refrain from it, none of the rest are voluntarily just, [d1] but they
censure injustice from cowardice or old age or some other weakness which prevents
them from being able to commit it. It is obvious that this is so; for the first of such
people into power is the first to commit injustice, as far as he is able.

[d5] 'And the root cause of all this is none other than the point from which the whole
of this argument of Glaucon here and myself with you, Socrates, started out, when
we said: "My friend, of all of you who claim to praise justice, [e1] starting from
the heroes of old, whose words survive right up to the present day, none has ever
censured injustice or praised justice otherwise than for the reputation and honour
and gifts which flow from them. [e5] But what each of these qualities does through
its own innate power when it is within the soul which possesses it, escaping the
observation of gods and men, nobody, either poet or prose writer, has ever argued
through adequately, setting out the proof that injustice is the greatest of evils which
the soul contains within itself, while justice is the greatest good. **367** For if it had
been set out thus by all of you from the beginning and you had persuaded us from
our youth up, we would not be on our guard against each others' wrong-doing, but
each person would be his own best guardian, in fear that in doing wrong he would
be sharing his house with the greatest evil." [a5]

Ταῦτα, ὦ Σώκρατες, ἴσως δὲ καὶ ἔτι τούτων πλείω
Θρασύμαχός τε καὶ ἄλλος πού τις ὑπὲρ δικαιοσύνης τε καὶ
ἀδικίας λέγοιεν ἄν, μεταστρέφοντες αὐτοῖν τὴν δύναμιν
b φορτικῶς, ὥς γέ μοι δοκεῖ. ἀλλ᾽ ἐγώ, οὐδὲν γάρ σε δέομαι
ἀποκρύπτεσθαι, σοῦ ἐπιθυμῶν ἀκοῦσαι τἀναντία, ὡς δύναμαι
μάλιστα κατατείνας λέγω. μὴ οὖν ἡμῖν μόνον ἐνδείξῃ τῷ
λόγῳ ὅτι δικαιοσύνη ἀδικίας κρεῖττον, ἀλλὰ τί ποιοῦσα
5 ἑκατέρα τὸν ἔχοντα αὐτὴ δι᾽ αὑτὴν ἡ μὲν κακόν, ἡ δὲ ἀγαθόν
ἐστιν· τὰς δὲ δόξας ἀφαίρει, ὥσπερ Γλαύκων διεκελεύσατο.
εἰ γὰρ μὴ ἀφαιρήσεις ἑκατέρωθεν τὰς ἀληθεῖς, τὰς δὲ ψευδεῖς
προσθήσεις, οὐ τὸ δίκαιον φήσομεν ἐπαινεῖν σε ἀλλὰ τὸ
c δοκεῖν, οὐδὲ τὸ ἄδικον εἶναι ψέγειν ἀλλὰ τὸ δοκεῖν, καὶ
παρακελεύεσθαι ἄδικον ὄντα λανθάνειν, καὶ ὁμολογεῖν Θρασυμάχῳ ὅτι τὸ μὲν δίκαιον ἀλλότριον ἀγαθόν, συμφέρον τοῦ
κρείττονος, τὸ δὲ ἄδικον αὐτῷ μὲν συμφέρον καὶ λυσιτελοῦν,
5 τῷ δὲ ἥττονι ἀσύμφορον.
Ἐπειδὴ οὖν ὡμολόγησας τῶν μεγίστων ἀγαθῶν εἶναι
δικαιοσύνην, ἃ τῶν τε ἀποβαινόντων ἀπ᾽ αὐτῶν ἕνεκα ἄξια
κεκτῆσθαι, πολὺ δὲ μᾶλλον αὐτὰ αὑτῶν, οἷον ὁρᾶν, ἀκούειν,
φρονεῖν, καὶ ὑγιαίνειν δή, καὶ ὅσ᾽ ἄλλα ἀγαθὰ γόνιμα τῇ
d αὑτῶν φύσει ἀλλ᾽ οὐ δόξῃ ἐστίν, τοῦτ᾽ οὖν αὐτὸ ἐπαίνεσον
δικαιοσύνης, ὃ αὐτὴ δι᾽ αὑτὴν τὸν ἔχοντα ὀνίνησιν καὶ ἀδικία
βλάπτει, μισθοὺς δὲ καὶ δόξας πάρες ἄλλοις ἐπαινεῖν· ὡς ἐγὼ
τῶν μὲν ἄλλων ἀποδεχοίμην ἂν οὕτως ἐπαινούντων δικαιο-
5 σύνην καὶ ψεγόντων ἀδικίαν, δόξας τε περὶ αὐτῶν καὶ
μισθοὺς ἐγκωμιαζόντων καὶ λοιδορούντων, σοῦ δὲ οὐκ ἄν,
εἰ μὴ σὺ κελεύοις, διότι πάντα τὸν βίον οὐδὲν ἄλλο σκοπῶν
e διελήλυθας ἢ τοῦτο. μὴ οὖν ἡμῖν ἐνδείξῃ μόνον τῷ λόγῳ ὅτι
δικαιοσύνη ἀδικίας κρεῖττον, ἀλλὰ καὶ τί ποιοῦσα ἑκατέρα
τὸν ἔχοντα αὐτὴ δι᾽ αὑτήν, ἐάντε λανθάνῃ ἐάντε μὴ θεούς τε
καὶ ἀνθρώπους, ἡ μὲν ἀγαθόν, ἡ δὲ κακόν ἐστι.
5 Καὶ ἐγὼ ἀκούσας ἀεὶ μὲν δὴ τὴν φύσιν τοῦ τε Γλαύκωνος
καὶ τοῦ Ἀδειμάντου ἠγάμην, ἀτὰρ οὖν καὶ τότε πάνυ ἥσθην
368 καὶ εἶπον· Οὐ κακῶς εἰς ὑμᾶς, ὦ παῖδες ἐκείνου τοῦ ἀνδρός,
τὴν ἀρχὴν τῶν ἐλεγείων ἐποίησεν ὁ Γλαύκωνος ἐραστής,
εὐδοκιμήσαντας περὶ τὴν Μεγαροῖ μάχην, εἰπών

παῖδες Ἀρίστωνος, κλεινοῦ θεῖον γένος ἀνδρός.

5 τοῦτό μοι, ὦ φίλοι, εὖ δοκεῖ ἔχειν· πάνυ γὰρ θεῖον πεπόνθατε,
εἰ μὴ πέπεισθε ἀδικίαν δικαιοσύνης ἄμεινον εἶναι, οὕτω

367a6
'This, Socrates, and perhaps still more than this Thrasymachus and maybe someone else would say about justice and injustice, inverting their true potential, crudely, in my view. [b1] But as I do not need to hide anything from you, I put my case, having exerted myself as much as I can because I want to hear you refute it. So, don't merely demonstrate by your argument to us that justice is superior to injustice, but show what each does in and of itself to the person who possesses it – the one doing harm and the other good; [b5] but, as Glaucon urged, take away their reputations. For if you don't remove from each of them their true reputation and add on the false, we shall say that you are praising not justice, but its reputation, nor censuring the reality of injustice but the pretence, [c1] and that you are advising someone to do wrong in secret, and that you agree with Thrasymachus that justice is the good of someone else, the interest of the stronger, but injustice is what is in the interest and to the profit of oneself and to the disadvantage of the weaker. [c5]

Now, you have admitted that justice is among the greatest goods, those which are worth possessing for their consequences, but far more for their own sake, for example sight, hearing, intelligence, and health too of course, and all other good things which are inherently so by their very nature and not just by repute. [d1] So, praise that very aspect of justice, which entirely on its own benefits the person who has it, whereas injustice harms him, and leave it to others to commend the rewards and reputations. [d5] While I would put up with other people commending justice and censuring injustice by praising and disparaging the reputation and rewards which come from them, I could not take this from you unless you insisted, because you have passed your whole life considering nothing else but this subject. [e1] So do not demonstrate to us simply by argument that justice is superior to injustice, but also what each of them does to its possessor in and of itself, whether observed or not by gods and humans, whereby the one is good, the other evil.'

[e5] On hearing this, much as I had always admired the inborn abilities of Glaucon and Adeimantus, on this particular occasion I was especially pleased and said: 368 'Sons of that man, Glaucon's lover did not speak badly of you both, when he wrote at the beginning of the elegy, when you had distinguished yourselves in the battle of Megara:

Sons of Ariston, divine race, sprung from a famous man;

[a5] I think that sums it up well, my friends. For you really must have something god-like in your disposition if you are not convinced that injustice is better than

δυνάμενοι εἰπεῖν ὑπὲρ αὐτοῦ. δοκεῖτε δή μοι ὡς ἀληθῶς οὐ
b πεπεῖσθαι· τεκμαίρομαι δὲ ἐκ τοῦ ἄλλου τοῦ ὑμετέρου
τρόπου, ἐπεὶ κατά γε αὐτοὺς τοὺς λόγους ἠπίστουν ἂν ὑμῖν·
ὅσῳ δὲ μᾶλλον πιστεύω, τοσούτῳ μᾶλλον ἀπορῶ ὅτι
χρήσωμαι. οὔτε γὰρ ὅπως βοηθῶ ἔχω· δοκῶ γάρ μοι
5 ἀδύνατος εἶναι· σημεῖον δέ μοι, ὅτι ἃ πρὸς Θρασύμαχον
λέγων ᾤμην ἀποφαίνειν ὡς ἄμεινον δικαιοσύνη ἀδικίας, οὐκ
ἀπεδέξασθέ μου· οὔτ᾽ αὖ ὅπως μὴ βοηθήσω ἔχω· δέδοικα γὰρ
c μὴ οὐδ᾽ ὅσιον ᾖ παραγενόμενον δικαιοσύνῃ κακηγορουμένῃ
ἀπαγορεύειν, καὶ μὴ βοηθεῖν ἔτι ἐμπνέοντα καὶ δυνάμενον
φθέγγεσθαι. κράτιστον οὖν οὕτως ὅπως δύναμαι ἐπικουρεῖν
αὐτῇ.

368a7
justice, when you are able to plead its case like that. Of course, I believe that you are not really convinced: [b1] this I infer from your general character, since going by the speeches themselves I would disbelieve you; but the more I trust you, the more I am at a loss as to what I should do. And I don't know how I am to help you. I doubt my ability, [b5] the reason being that you did not accept from me the arguments I used when I thought I had demonstrated to Thrasymachus that justice was better than injustice. Nor, on the other hand, do I know how I can refuse to come to your aid, for I fear that it would be impious to stand by and renounce justice when it is being slandered, [c1] and not come to the rescue while I have breath and voice in me. So the best course for me is to support justice to the best of my ability.' [c4]

COMMENTARY

Title: *Republic* is the traditional, but somewhat misleading English translation, derived from Latin, of the Greek title *Politeia* (Πολιτεία), more accurately rendered 'The state', 'Citizenship' or 'Government' (the Greek word suggests both an institution and the activities of the people in it). The dialogue is cited by name by Aristotle at *Politics* 2. 1261a6. The subtitle 'or *On Justice*', found in a number of MSS. was probably added by the scholar and organiser of the Platonic corpus, Thrasyllus of Alexandria (d. A.D. 36).

BOOK 1

327a1–328d7

A deceptively casual introduction, in which the main activity of the dialogue is introduced, in lifelike fashion, as a chance diversion from S.'s original intention – of attending the festival of Bendis at the Piraeus and then going back home to Athens. He accepts an invitation to go to Polemarchus' house, ostensibly for dinner and subsequent public socialising at the festival, all of which gets forgotten as the dialogue proceeds. These involuntary changes of plan reflect, in miniature, the presentation of the whole dialogue as an unplanned and unexpected evolution, in both setting and argument, from commonplace beginnings (see Introduction, p. 28 and note on 328a7–9).

327a1   Yesterday I went down to the Piraeus with Glaucon the son of Ariston: a famously unassuming start to a massive and wide-ranging work. Dionysius of Halicarnassus, *De Compositione Verborum* 25 (see also Quintilian, *Institutio Oratoria* 8.6.64 and Diogenes Laertius 3.37), in order to illustrate the care Plato took over stylistic matters even into old age, tells the anecdote (from Euphorion (3rd century) and Panaetius (2nd century)) of the tablet found after his death containing this first sentence arranged in a variety of ways. 'I went down' (*katebēn*), the first word in Greek, was interpreted by the Neoplatonic commentator on Plato, Proclus (5th century A.D.) as representing a symbolic descent by Socrates from the ideal world of the philosopher down to the everyday, anticipating the *katabasis* (descent) required of philosophers into the shadow world of the Cave (*Republic* 7.520c), an allegorical interpretation which has modern adherents (see *e.g.* Burnyeat 6; Vegetti (1994) 93–104). However, more obviously, the choice of Piraeus, the port of Athens, as the place to which S. 'goes down' from the city strongly suggests an unaccustomed geographical and social displacement from the agora and gymnasia, venues beloved of the city-bound S. Although still nominally inside the city walls (the Long Walls, built in the mid-5th century as Athenian military defences linking the city proper to its ports) S. journeys to the commercial sea-port world of the non-citizen resident aliens (*metics*) represented by Cephalus and Polemarchus, in whose household the action of *Republic* takes place. The backdrop of this cosmopolitan melting-pot assists Plato in initially distancing his new enquiry from the traditional world of the Athenian citizen democracy and its values so that he can set out his entirely new conception of the state. On S. as narrator, see Introduction, p. 6; on Glaucon and his dramatic role, see Introduction, p. 10).

a2–4   ...to offer my prayers to the goddess...holding it: 'the goddess', without qualification, regularly denotes Athena (as at *Timaeus* 21a and 26e), but later, 354a10–11 makes it clear that the goddess whose festival is being celebrated in *Republic* is the Thracian Bendis; Plato's words here seem to imply that this is a formal introduction of the goddess into the Piraeus (although the name and cult were known in the mid-fifth century, and see further Introduction, p. 4). Allan suggests that a dual festival to Bendis and the associated Greek Artemis may be implied (both had temples in the Piraeus); hence the two processions, 'local' (a4) and Thracian (either resident or a special foreign delegation), see Allan n. *ad loc.* and further, Adam 62 (Appendix I to Book 1). The festival, as an opening dramatic context for the dialogue, both emphasises S.'s respectability as a dutiful observer of religious rites (see Xenophon, *Memorabilia* 1.3.1, 4.3.16 – very different from the S. of the indictment recorded in *Apology* 24b) and at the same time, by introducing a foreign deity, reinforces the idea of the detachment of the whole scene from the centre of Athenian civic life (see previous note).

b1–2   ...we started back to town: 'town' is *to astu,* the central area surrounded by defensive walls, as opposed to the *polis,* the whole of the territory of the Athenian city-state, including its ports.

b8   ...said Glaucon: ὅς used as a demonstrative pronoun for οὗτος, found mainly in Homer and Plato; especially in the phrase ἦ δ᾽ ὅς, 'he said' (cf. ἦν δ᾽ ἐγώ, 'I said'), see also 327c6 and *passim.*

c1–14   S. and Glaucon are prevented from returning to the city by *force majeure* once the festival is over; humour is generated by the sharp verbal exchanges couched in vivid conversational idiom. There is an expressed contrast between force, jokingly threatened by Polemarchus, and persuasion, equally humorously offered by S., which foreshadows S.'s later arguments with Thrasymachus in Book I and, more generally (c12), signals the weakness of the individual in not being able to persuade the many who refuse to listen (for the serious political sub-text of this passage, see Ober 216). For Polemarchus, his subsequent fate and that of his household, see Introduction, pp. 7–8.

c10–11   '...for us to persuade you that you ought to let us go: S.'s suggestion that he and Glaucon might be released introduces jokingly the motif of 'letting S. go' which recurs seriously as a denial of 'release' from the argument – a dramatic device to forward the discussion at later stages in the dialogue: at key points in the dialogue S.'s interlocutors will not 'release' him, *e.g.* Glaucon at the beginning of Book 2, see note below on 357a1. (There is a further instance of Polemarchus and Adeimantus not 'releasing' S. from further explanation of his argument at Book 5. 449b1–c1).

328a2   '...torch race on horseback...: this kind of relay-race, also in Herodotus (8.98), celebrated in honour of the god Hephaestus, gives further scope for Platonic metaphor, cf. *Laws* 6. 776b (of generations '...handing the torch of life to one another').

a7–9   'After dinner...converse: conversing with young men in public places featured prominently among S.'s activities (*Apology* 23c), though usually up in the city. On this occasion the eventual length of the discussion makes it clear that this after-dinner excursion never happens, which has been taken as a point in favour of seeing *Republic* I as planned originally as a separate dialogue, of a length to make Polemarchus' plan dramatically credible. But one might perhaps more plausibly take this detail as a dramatic device, a deliberately false anticipation of closure, in which none of the participants, including S., initially realise that the conversation is going to develop far beyond the conventional 'early dialogue' type of discussion (see S.'s remark at the beginning of Book 2 that at this point (357a1) he thought (wrongly) that '…I had been released from the discussion; but it was after all, apparently, only a prelude'). See further above, note on 327c10–11, and Introduction, pp. 4–5.

b4–8   **…and there we found Lysias…Cleitophon, son of Aristonymus:** Lysias the well-known speech-writer is silent in *Republic*, but, in his speech *Against Eratosthenes,* he is our main source for the later robbery and violence inflicted on his rich *metic* family, including the execution of his brother Polemarchus, at the hands of the Thirty Tyrants, the oligarchic junta which ruled Athens immediately following defeat in the Peloponnesian War in 404, and which badly needed money to pay for the Spartan garrison which supported their regime (see Lysias 12. 6–20). Plato may indeed have presented the peaceful, civilised atmosphere here as an intentionally ironic, even tragic contrast with what happened to this family subsequently (see Gifford 52–97). Notable in the gathering at Polemarchus' house is the social mix of: firstly, citizens, Glaucon and Adeimantus (Plato's brothers), Cleitophon and Socrates himself, and possibly also Niceratus, the son of the distinguished general Nicias, who is in the original group which encountered S. (327c1–2), and who also was killed by the Thirty Tyrants for his money (see Xenophon, *Hellenica* 2.3.38–9); secondly, *metics*, i.e. the family of Polemarchus; and finally foreigners, principally the sophist Thrasymachus from Chalcedon, a city on the Asiatic side of the Bosphorus. It may be significant that the argument of Book 1 is conducted by S. principally with the non-Athenians (Cephalus, Polemarchus and Thrasymachus), whereas in the positive dialectic of Books 2–10, S. converses almost entirely with the citizens (Glaucon and Adeimantus). For all these characters and their activities, see Introduction, pp. 7–8.

b8   **Polemarchus' father, Cephalus, was there too…:** Cephalus, the first interlocutor of *Republic*, was a wealthy Syracusan merchant who had come to Athens at the request of the Athenian leader Pericles, according to his son, Lysias (*Against Eratosthenes* 5). He was the owner of a large shield factory which was later confiscated by the Thirty (see previous note). He is presented as a genial purveyor of conventional wisdom and values, which form an effective launching-pad for S.s' more searching enquiries. There is considerable divergence of scholarly opinion over how sympathetically we are meant to view C.; see the views of *e.g.* Annas 181–23, Blondell 169–70, Gifford 52–69 as opposed to the more sympathetic position of Reeve (1988) 7–9, Beversluis 185–202 (and see further, Introduction pp. 14–15). The immediate picture at c1ff. lays emphasis on his central position in the household, his religious piety and familial contentment, reminiscent of the aged hero Nestor among his family in Homer *Odyssey* 3.31ff.

c6   **'You don't often come down to see us…':** the MSS οὐδὲ (read by Adam and Slings) may be a '(not easily analysed) colloquialism' (Denniston 198, following Adam): 'You don't often come down to see us either (i.e. as well as other faults I could mention)'. Other suggestions include Burnet's οὐ δὲ (following Jowett and Campbell) as some kind of adversative: '(You are welcome) but you don't…'). οὔτι ('You really don't often come…') supported by Allan (note *ad loc.*) and Gifford 62 n. 31, has much to recommend it, not least that it is almost a quotation from Homer, *e.g. Odyssey* 5. 88, of Calypso to Hermes: πάρος γε μὲν οὔ τι θαμίζεις ('Formerly you have not come often.'). Cf. also Homer, *Iliad* 18. 385. As the rest of his discourse demonstrates, C. likes to reflect the poets in his speeches; for the Homeric atmosphere of the scene, see the previous note.

C.'s sentiments in c5–d7 and the language used are also strikingly reminiscent of those of a similar situation in an earlier dialogue, *Laches* 181c1ff., where S. is also approvingly addressed by an elderly Lysimachus as a welcome acquaintance whose visit is long overdue. In both instances this detail adds to the presentation of S. as conventionally respectable (see also the religious observance above), in marked contrast to his *persona* as presented in such confrontational dialogues as *Gorgias*. The parallel with *Laches* extends to the dramatic structure: like Lysimachus, the elderly C. is very soon out of his depth and hands over the discussion to younger participants.

d3–5   **'...the more the pleasures of the body wither away, the more my desire for conversation and my pleasure in it increase:** this expresses a characteristically Platonic contrast between the ephemeral pleasures of the body and the enduring delights of the mind (see *e.g. Phaedrus* 258e). Annas' interpretation of C.'s 'tactless and insensitive' words as meaning that '[philosophy] is fine once you have nothing better to do.' (Annas 19), does not seem justified in view of the importance C. places in his discourse on his philosophy of life as a consolation in old age (for more detailed discussion of this issue, see Introduction, pp. 14–15). There is no doubt, though, that C.'s anticipation of some gentle moralising conversation is not what S. ultimately has in mind. For the idea of philosophical discussion as appropriate to a particular age-group, see Callicles in *Gorgias* 485bff., though, directly contrary to C., he would ideally confine it to the young (as C. shortly tacitly concedes by his abrupt departure at 331d10).

d6   **'...mix with these lads here...':** *neaniskos* = 'youth', 'lad', appropriate, perhaps, from C.s' elderly perspective; but Polemarchus and Lysias would be at least in their late 20's at the earliest possible dramatic date of *Republic,* and at 328b4 the house is said to belong to Polemarchus (see Introduction, p. 9).

328d8–331b7

S. introduces very informally one of the key topics of the dialogue: how one should live one's life, a subject to which old people like C. might be expected to make a particularly valuable contribution from their long experience. From a discussion of old age the conversation moves on to the subject of money and its relation to virtue, an issue of some resonance for a wealthy and prominent metic like C. (the question of wealth and virtue also surfaces later in the dialogue, cf. Republic 8. 550e4–8). They then return again to old age and the prospect of death and what part wealth plays in the individual's attitude to it, which leads C. back to the issue of the well-ordered life. The tripartite movement of the section is therefore a kind of mini ring-composition, in which the final section (on attitudes to old age and the importance of dying without consciousness of wrong-doing) returns the discussion to its starting-point, but enriched by the intervening theme of wealth and attitudes towards it. Underlying the leisurely pace of the narrative we can see outlined one of the basic issues of the dialogue: what constitutes living the good life? – a theme to which Glaucon and Adeimantus will return with more coherence and insight at the beginning of Book 2.

For a detailed discussion and assessment of dramatic and philosophical issues related to the episode between Socrates and Cephalus, see Introduction, pp. 13–15.

328d8 '**...I do enjoy talking to very old men:** not borne out by Plato at any rate; in the dialogues as a whole, and in the remainder of the *Republic* for that matter, Socrates' interlocutors tend to be young men (see Blondell 170). The compliment, however, serves its immediate dramatic purpose – to draw C. out and introduce one of the main themes of the dialogue, the life and afterlife of the just/unjust person, raised appropriately here with someone approaching death.

e3–4 '**...rough and difficult or easy and accommodating:** the 'difficult/easy' path of life is a traditional theme in Greek popular morality, and S.'s language here may be suggested by Hesiod, *Works and Days* 288, 290–2; cf. also the sophist Prodicus' story of the choice of Heracles between personified vice and virtue in Xenophon, *Memorabilia* 2.1.21–28. However Plato, while adapting the idea, changes the connotation: ultimately an 'easy' road, rather than suggesting a prospect of evil (as in Xenophon), is likely to result from adopting a virtuous life, the consequences of which C. outlines in the following speech – with what degree of underlying irony on Plato's part is a significant question (see Introduction, p. 14).

e6 '**..."on the threshold of old age":** this proverbial phrase occurs frequently *e.g.* in Homer (*Iliad* 22.60; *Odyssey* 15.246). The image is of life as a house with entrance and exit, each with a threshold; the further threshold (to death) consists of (*descriptive genitive*) old age (Adam) or old age itself as the house and C. at the threshold (Allan), the further extremity of it, one supposes, (but, on this interpretation, why not, equally plausibly, the *nearer* extremity?). In e7 the old person, being near to death, is characterised as an *exangelos,* like a messenger in Greek tragedy who 'gives a report' of what is happening behind the scenes (cf. life as a stage onto which one enters and from which one exits, as in a (probably spurious) Democritus fragment, DK B84 (*Die Fragmente der Vorsokratiker* vol. II. p.165.7–8).

329a3 '**...the old proverb:** it must be something like: 'birds of a feather' (so well-known that C. does not feel it necessary to quote it). See *Phaedrus* 240c ('like age delights in like.'), and the scholiast on 329a (Greene 189): 'jackdaw sits next to jackdaw' (ὁ κολοιὸς ποτὶ κολοιὸν ἱζάνει).

a4–5 '**...longing for the pleasures of youth:** bewailing the grimness of old age and expressing a longing for youth again are conventional sentiments, found in elegiac and lyric poets, *e.g.* Mimnermus fr. 1 Gerber; Simonides fr. 520 Campbell (vol. III); Sophocles, *Oedipus at Colonus* 1235ff., and frequently elsewhere.

b1 '**...the abuse shown to their advanced years by their families:** the Greek for 'abuse' (*propēlakisis*) has a strongly physical connotation, literally 'cover with mud'; (Waterfield (1993) aptly translates 'treat old age like dirt'). Respect for elderly relatives, which C.'s family situation seems to exemplify (see 328c1–4), was the Athenian ideal; penalties for the neglect or abuse of parents (*kakōsis goneōn)* were enshrined in Athenian law dating back to the statesman Solon in the sixth century. Athenian practical concern with conflict between parents and children is given prominence in fifth century comedy, *e.g.* Aristophanes, *Wasps* and *Clouds.*

c2–4 '"**Hush, man...savage master":** 'hush' (*euphēmei:* literally 'speak auspicious words') is a reply to avert the effect of a word of ill-omen. The anecdote supports the picture of Sophocles' personality as 'easy' or 'good natured', see Aristophanes, *Frogs* 82. (Sophocles would have been in his 70's at the dramatic date of *Republic*). For sexual desire as a burden, see extensively the lyric poets again, *e.g.* Ibycus, fr. 287 Campbell (vol. III); Anacreon, fr. 358 Campbell (vol. II).

d2–4 **'...there is just one thing to blame...human character:** 'character', which translates *tropos* ('disposition', 'habit', 'temper') is the key ethical term which lies at the heart of C's world-view, and moderates the somewhat fatalistic aspect of the popular tradition; he recommends a *tropos* which is 'easy' or 'contented' (*eukolos*), like his model, Sophocles (Aristophanes uses exactly that word of him: see ref. in the previous note); it is largely this *tropos*, and not external factors, which, C. claims, determines the individual's success on the path of life. How far C.'s *tropos* is really independent of external factors or how far its qualities are sufficient in all circumstances for living the good life, remains to be seen below (and see Introduction, pp.14–15).

d8 **And I was full of admiration for what he said:** an extravagantly favourable reaction by S. to a speech by one of his interlocutors, followed by a critical interrogation, is a dramatic sequence found elsewhere, *e.g. Protagoras* 328d, *Symposium* 198a. Here the actual (very short) interrogation (*elenchus*) does not occur until 331c, and our estimate of the degree of irony intended in S.'s description of his admiration must be closely related to an evaluation of Plato's presentation of C.'s contribution taken as a whole. Nevertheless, the challenging aspect of S.'s next speech is clearly indicated by his use of 'draw out' (*kinein* = 'rouse' e1), regularly of stimulating discussion with interlocutors.

e3–4 **'...you bear old age lightly not because of your character, but because of the great wealth you have acquired:** S., matching for the moment the pace and tone of C.'s leisurely moralising, here introduces a key 'external factor' (see above, note on d2) which might (but as is argued below, does not) prove fatal to the latter's reliance on the idea of *tropos*. For S.'s attitude to excessive concern for wealth as being detrimental to the good life, see *e.g. Apology* 29d2ff, 41e3ff.; but here, in keeping with the non-confrontational tone, he attributes a critical stance not to himself, but to 'most people' (*tous pollous*), and matches C. by himself introducing a 'saying' at e4–5.

e7–8 **'But Themistocles' retort is particularly apt here:** Herodotus tells the same anecdote (8.125), but with different details. Seriphos was an insignificant island in the Cyclades, here the equivalent of our 'Timbuktoo'.

330a4–6 **'an estimable man might not find old age entirely easy to bear...nor would an unworthy person ever find peace with himself...:** 'estimable', (*epieikēs*) would appear to fit well with the rest of C.'s rather generalised moral vocabulary, as describing the person of 'contented disposition'. But it also runs over into Platonic terminology, used by S. in *Apology* of more sensible or thoughtful individuals (*e.g.* 22a5) and, in its superlative form, is regularly used later in *Republic* to describe the ideal city's intellectual elite, the Guardians. Far from indignantly repudiating S.'s suggestion that wealth might play any part in his *tropos*, C. counters rather effectively by introducing into the discussion an important and quite subtle qualification – that external circumstances are influential but do not wholly determine the path of life, and are much less important than what sort of person encounters them. (see *e.g.* Beversluis 189–90).

b1 **'You want to know how much I made, Socrates?:** the repetition of the question may indicate surprise or a speech-habit of old age (Allan, note *ad loc.,* comically (and improbably) suggests that the repetition indicates that C. is rather deaf!). Jowett-Campell (note *ad loc.*) suggests that C.'s interrogative is in effect a wry admission of the small addition he has been able to make to the diminished fortune he inherited. But C.'s reiteration of the second alternative offered by Socrates (making rather than inheriting his wealth) rather indicates a defensive attitude of a *metic* towards his own wealth-creation in the face of the Athenian aristocratic contempt for 'trade'. It is notable that at b1–7, C. is careful to place himself financially between his grandfather and father, as someone engaged more or less in restoring the family fortunes, rather than making money for the sake of it.

c3–5   **'For just as poets love their own poems, and fathers their own children, so too, those who have made money take it seriously...**: For the parent/poet/money-maker comparison, see also Aristotle *Nichomachean Ethics* 4.1.20. S.'s response (b8–c8) reflects a conventional Athenian upper-class view of money-making which shows that C.'s resort to a defensive stance (see previous note) is fully justified in the circumstances.

d1–3   **'what do you believe is the greatest benefit you have enjoyed from the acquisition of all your wealth?**: S.'s question is designed to probe still further and, possibly, to force an admission from C. of his reliance on wealth as purely instrumental for living the good life, thereby fatally undermining his ethical stance. But C., on the interpretation advanced here, is not quite so naïve!

d7–8   **'The stories told about what goes on in Hades, how the wrong-doer here must suffer punishment there...**: an existence for the attenuated ghost of the individual in an afterlife in Hades, and punishments for certain notorious evil-doers in the mythological tradition, are attested in Homer (*Odyssey* 11. 576–600); the Mystery religions, such as that at Eleusis, promised happiness in the hereafter for the initiated (*e.g.* in Pindar, fr. 121 Bowra), and a close correlation between behaviour in this life and punishment/reward in the next is taken up by Plato in his major eschatological myths in *Gorgias, Phaedo* and most elaborately in the 'Myth of Er' at the end of the present dialogue. See also in visual art three white-ground cups by the Sotades Painter from mid-fifth century Athenian graves, which appear to depict the afterlife (see Osborne (1988). 'Wrong-doer' and 'suffer punishment' (*adikēsanta* and *didonai dikēn*) bring the discussion specifically onto the subject of *dikē* ('justice') which occupies the rest of the Book.

331a2   **'..."nourisher of old age"...**: the passage quoted in a5–8 is fr. 202 Bowra. Pindar's *gērotrophos* ('nurse of the elderly') takes up the idea of nurture whose absence is implied in the image just used, of the old waking up from sleep in fear of death, like (comfortless) children (330e6–7).

a9ff **'It is indeed for this that I take the acquisition of wealth to be of the most value, certainly not for everyone, but for the person of an estimable life**: Stobaeus adds 'well-ordered' (*kosmios*) at the end of the sentence, adopted by some editors, and see above 329d5). What instrumental role does wealth play for C. in this context? It enables the individual possessing it to avoid departing this world with certain injustices outstanding, such as owing money to fellow humans or sacrifices to gods. 'Cheating...unintentionally' and 'telling lies' (b1–2) surely refer to the person who, without enough resources to repay a debt, for example, has to resort to subterfuge to escape the consequences.

b5–7   **'...but taking one thing with another I would claim that for a man of sense... that is not the least important thing for which wealth is particularly useful:** (i.e. dying without fear). Plato characterises C. with a discursive style which verges on parody in this final speech and especially in the prolixity of the final sentence.

Evaluations of C.'s moral stance have been critical of his attitude here, accusing him of fixing on the moral rectitude which wealth allows as a mere expedient to avoid fear of retribution in the afterlife: in effect, bribing the gods. This ignores two points: 1. C. still emphasises 'disposition', saying explicitly (b1) that in these circumstances wealth is not of value for everyone (by implication, not for the person of 'unreasonable' disposition who simply uses his wealth instrumentally to earn remission in the afterlife). It remains merely a (useful) adjunct to the good life. 2. C.'s attitude towards the gods must not be taken out of the context of the 'ordinary Athenian': conventional Greek values regarded respect paid to the gods not as simply a 'bribe' given in return for favourable treatment by the gods, but part of normal civic life in which all individuals paid due attention to the gods, whose attitude to humans could be extremely arbitrary. 'One sacrificed: not because one was sinful, but because one was human; the ritual of sacrifice was a way of acknowledging one's limitations and thereby avoiding *hubris*.' (Beversluis 190 n. 19; see also Dover (1994) 75–81). Even Plato's S. (as well as, predictably, the more conventional S. of Xenophon, cf. *Memorabilia* 1.2.64) was assiduous in paying due respect to the gods, notably in his last request while dying, at the end of *Phaedo* (118a7–8), that his friend Crito should sacrifice a cock to the god Asclepius.

331c1–d10

In the final short section of the dialogue with C., Socrates changes the pace and tone of the conversation; he introduces a brief, but characteristic elenchus: taking what C. has said about justice as a definition (*horos*), he argues that it entails an unacceptable conclusion. Polemarchus comes to his father's defence and C. exits.

331 c1 **'Bravo, Cephalus':** as at 329d8, Plato presents S.'s admiration as a preface to further probing. *Pankalōs* ('excellent!') is often used in Plato with ironic overtones (*e.g. Euthyphro* 7a2).
c1–3 **'...this very thing, justice: are we to say that it is simply truthfulness without qualification and giving back whatever one may have taken from someone?:** S. seizes on C.'s references to justice and injustice in the previous speech and abruptly poses the question of what justice is. This is very similar to S.'s initial procedure in other, especially early, dialogues: the interlocutor is asked by S. to define a moral quality, *e.g.* virtue (*Meno*), courage (*Laches*) or holiness (*Euthyphro*), and replies with a definition, *e.g.* courage as 'not running away in battle' (*Laches* 190e5–6) or holiness as 'what the gods love' (*Euthyphro* 6e6), to which S. proceeds to provide a counter-example or examples which invalidate the original definition. Here, on the reasonable assumption that C. is not going to be up to the task of putting forward a definition himself, S. puts up his own (inadequate) definition as an 'Aunt Sally', promptly knocking it down himself with a counter-example which, by general agreement, does not fit the concept to be defined: it is, self-evidently, not justice to tell the truth or return his property to a madman who is a friend. The strict criterion for a Socratic definition (as he says here) is that the examples of it must fit the concept to be defined exactly (*'haplōs houtōs'* = 'simply and without qualification', i.e. with no exceptions, a criterion frequently required by S. elsewhere in the Platonic dialogues, *e.g. Protagoras* 351c7, *Gorgias*

468e3). Here, S.'s definition, if intended 'simply and without qualification', is invalidated by the 'qualification' of a single exception, and further enquiry is necessary. This is basically the Socratic *elenchus*, on the ramifications and controversies of which, see the definitive discussion by Vlastos (1983).

S. clearly indicates that for him justice (*dikaiosunē*) has substantial existence: (c1) 'this very thing' (*touto d'auto*), and the key issue is to define the boundaries of it. How far defining in this manner is philosophically useful, and whether S.'s criteria for a definition of a given concept are the right ones, is a major and disputed issue (see *e.g.* Cross & Woozley 6–10, Geach). However, accepting what S. appears to be aiming at, in this particular case one could still point out in C.'s defence that he was not giving, nor even asked to provide, any kind of definition, and, further, that in any case he was advancing a *general* rather than a *universal* moral rule, which a single and highly unusual exception does not necessarily invalidate. However, looking at the discussion from S.'s point of view, if the exchanges are to get beyond this gentle moralising the participants have to know more precisely what they are talking about. This is S.'s motivation for the sudden change of gear. Dramatically and philosophically, whatever the fairness or otherwise of S.'s question, C. has at this point reached the limits of his usefulness for the discussion.

d2 **'Then this is not a definition of justice...':** S.'s word here for definition, *horos* = 'boundary', suggests that the main aim of a definition is to indicate what it is precisely which separates (i.e. determines the boundary between) justice and other similar concepts.

d5 **'...if we should give any credence to Simonides:** thus far the poets have been quoted uncontroversially and with approval by C. to support his claims. The abrupt contradiction of S. by C.'s son Polemarchus is Plato's characteristically dramatic way of changing the speaker, tone and content of the discussion (cf. *Gorgias* 461b, 481b). A poem of Simonides (6th–5th century) is subjected to analysis also in *Protagoras* 339aff. The present saying is otherwise unknown, and therefore we have no way of establishing independently what Simonides actually said.

d8 **'So am I, Polemarchus,' he said, 'not heir to what is yours?':** attempts have been made to regularise the syntax here; one MS (F) reverses the order of ἔφη ἐγώ (Οὐκοῦν ἐγώ, ἔφη Π. κτλ: 'Am I not, said Polemarchus, heir to what is yours?') Allan (note *ad loc.*) translates, keeping the text and assuming displacement of words (a stylistic device called *hyperbaton*). The translation favoured here might seem 'rather affected' (Allan); but the rhetorical reference to self ('...I, Polemarchus...') well reflects P.'s dramatic and assertive character (n.b. his 'coercion' of S. at 327c7ff. above). The image of inheritance, prominent in S.'s initial questioning of C. (see above 330a7ff.), is taken up by Polemarchus from the previous line, where C.'s 'handover' (*paradidōmi*), also means 'bequeath' (see also S.'s ironic echo at e1, below). The argument is his property, 'inherited' by his eldest son, Polemarchus. The Greek, *tōn sōn*, literally '[heir] of your...,' without noun expressed, allows the reader to understand *logōn* (words or argument) as well as property.

d10 **'Certainly you are', replied Cephalus with a laugh, and he promptly went off to the sacrifice:** C.'s exit, like his entrance, emphasises his religious piety in observing sacrifices. His laughter might be interpreted as amusement at his son's assertiveness or possibly a reaction to the turn the discussion is taking towards *philologia* (Adam). A remark of the late Republic Roman writer and statesman Cicero is regularly quoted here (*Letters to Atticus*

4.16.3), to the effect that Plato did not think it appropriate to keep a man of C.'s age too long in conversation. It is also worth noting that any irony implicit in Plato's presentation of C.'s character appears to pass Cicero by: for him, C. is a *locupletem et festivum senem* ('a rich, genial old gentleman').

331e1–333e2

The continuation of the elenchus. Following his intervention in his father's dialogue, Polemarchus (with S.'s help) asserts the truth of a modified form of what he claims Simonides was saying: the addition, first of giving back 'what is owed' (e3–4), and then 'what is due to friends and enemies' (332a9–b5), to the original definition of justice. These two additions qualify S.'s original definition in such a way as to embrace the apparent exception (returning a weapon to a madman). S. then, in the first of four arguments with P., attempts to delimit the area in which justice operates by 'rendering what is due and appropriate'; he makes an assumption, which P. does not question, that justice is a skill (*technē*) by analogy with *e.g.* medicine, cookery, warfare, navigation. The conclusion is reached that, on this argument, justice cannot be very important, since in each case which can be thought of, its operation is more effectively carried out by the practice of other skills.

For detailed discussion and evaluation of dramatic and philosophic issues relevant to the episode between Socrates and Polemarchus, see Introduction, pp. 15–19.

331e3   'That it is just...to give back to every person what he is owed: the absence of the definite article before *dikaion* ('it is just...) indicates that P. intends this saying as an *instance* rather than a *definition* of justice (*to dikaion*), despite a moment ago (d4) objecting, against S., that Simonides' saying *was* a definition of justice. P.'s inconsistency probably suggests that at this point he did not discern the difference between a definition of justice and an instance of it (see Allan, note *ad loc.*). *Dikē, dikaiosunē* and *to dikaion* are translated as 'justice' here, with the proviso that the words often, as in *Republic,* have a wider reference in Greek ethics than the English words suggest, covering the whole range of relationships between persons in a social context, often translated as 'right' (see Introduction, p.2 and n.4, and Dover (1994) 184). On whether or not P. was attempting a definition, from the point of view of modern philosophical analysis, see Cross and Woozley, 4–11.

e5   'Well, it is certainly not easy to doubt Simonides: Σιμωνίδῃ γε mockingly echoes P.'s ἔμοιγε (e4): '[whatever we may think about your beliefs] we can't disbelieve Simonides...'; see Adam n. *ad loc.*

e6   '...for he was a wise and inspired man: S. regularly uses 'inspired' (*theios* = literally 'godlike') ironically (*e.g. Protagoras* 315e, *Meno* 99c), to imply that poets, like prophets, spoke under divine influence, but that their exact meaning was unclear. On Plato's critical attitude to the role of inspiration in poetry, see in general, *Ion.*

332a8   '...it is just to give back what is owed: S.'s formulation of Simonides' saying appears to follow that of Polemarchus, with the ambiguity of *dikaion* (definition or instance? – see note above on 331e3).

a9–10   '...friends owe it to friends to do them some good, nothing evil: according to P. 'what is due' is governed by traditional Greek morality: to do good to friends (*philoi*) and evil to enemies (*echthroi*) (see *e.g. Meno* 71e), the category of 'friends' being much wider than the translation implies, including household, family, more distant relations and political allies. See generally Dover (1994) 180–4.

b7–8   '…**what is appropriate from one enemy to another – something bad:** it should be noted that, on these criteria, in the original 'madman' example non-return of the weapon will only be what is due and appropriate to the man if he happens to be a friend, as in S.'s formulation (331c6). If he is an enemy, then one's duty is unclear: return of the weapon might cause him to kill himself (in which case he is, as an enemy, getting his due), but he might kill oneself or one's friends instead! For detailed philosophical analysis of the argument here, see Young 466ff.

c1   '…**Simonides…was defining the just in riddles, like a poet:** Plato classed poets with *e.g.* deliverers of oracles in hinting (*ainittomai*) rather than speaking their meaning clearly (see above note on 331e6).

c5–7   '…**what if someone were to ask him: "Simonides, what then gives medical skill its name – what does it render that is owed and appropriate, and to what things?":** hypothetical questioning of or by absent (or in this case, dead) individuals and personified entities is a common Platonic rhetorical device (used, notably, in *Crito* 50aff. by S. in imagining his own cross-examination by the personified Laws of Athens). Here, to give the discussion more immediacy, Polemarchus is required to imagine that he is answering for the dead Simonides. 'Skill' or 'craft' (*technē*), a key term in Plato, indicates a systematic body of knowledge which can be taught, contrasted (*e.g.* in *Gorgias* 462bff.) with 'a rule of thumb' or 'knack', i.e. something arising simply from experience. The activities of a craft are regularly used elsewhere in Plato (*e.g. Apology* 22cff.), as a paradigm of knowledge (*epistēmē*) as opposed to mere opinion (*doxa*). A particular criterion of a *technē* is relevant here: that it must have a product which is to somebody's or something's benefit. So, if justice is a *technē* it must meet the appropriate criteria (on S.'s use of the *technē* analogy, see Introduction, pp. 16–17).

c10–11   '**And what gives the skill of cookery its name…:** in the inclusion of cookery among the *technai* (plural of *technē*) Plato is not consistent between dialogues; in *Gorgias,* cookery is classed as an *empeiria* ('knack based on experience'), a pseudo-*technē* which pretends to care for the health of the body as opposed to medicine which, being a proper *technē,* really does. The discrepancy is explained by the difference in the contexts of the two comparisons: in *Gorgias,* S. is constructing a polar schema of *technai* and corresponding pseudo-*technai* (and putting emphasis on differences between the two) whereas here he is simply listing *technai* as a context in which to place (or rather, ultimately, fail to place) justice.

d2–3   '**So then, the skill of giving what and to whom could be called justice?:** note how S. introduces justice as a skill by analogy at this point and puts emphasis on what he presents as a natural progression ('So then') from medicine and cookery to justice (with the same Greek syntactical construction for each). This more or less forces on P. the more controversial assumption that justice is, like them, a *technē*. P. is not presented as bright enough to question this jump (which is the basis of their whole dialogue together, and on which it finally founders), but his reply in d4–5 ('If the answer has to be at all consistent with what we said before…') suggests some uneasiness with the analogy.

d7ff.   Having conceded that rendering what is 'appropriate' to friends and enemies (good and evil, respectively) describes the *technē* of justice, P. is faced with a sequence of argument in which S. argues that benefit and harm – what (they have just agreed) the *technē* of justice renders to its object – can in a variety of instances more effectively be delivered to friends and enemies by a series of other specialist skills, which leave no significant role for justice.

e2 **'A ship's captain:** the Greek *kubernētēs* combines the meanings of our 'ship's captain', 'helmsman' and 'navigator'; here 'captain' is the appropriate translation in view of the 'ruling' emphasis S. gives to the analogy later at 341c10.

e5 **'In making war and alliances, I would think:** although S. swiftly goes on to counter P. here (e6–11) by denigrating (not denying) this limited role for the just man, the discussion between them does contain what could be the basis of an answer to S.'s relentless exclusion of justice from consideration: if it is to be a skill, why not of a special, 'superordinate' kind (Irwin (1995) 60), which can decide more basic issues than those concerned with mere technical skill: for example, justice might be used in *e.g.* the military sphere to decide whether it is better, in a broader ethical sense, for alliances to be made, or, in other fields, *e.g.* medicine, whether it is better for individuals to be kept alive or allowed to die, issues which, it could be argued, are outside the province of particular military or medical expertise, but might, indeed, guide them. It is not, however, dramatically appropriate to expand this idea (which is touched upon in earlier dialogues, *e.g. Laches* 195c, *Gorgias* 511e, *Euthydemus* 289a7–b3) at this early stage of the *Republic*, since S.'s immediate purpose appears to be to force through a demonstration of the weakness of the concept of justice as a *technē* (or, at least, the kind of *technē* so far demonstrated).

e6 **'...but when someone is not ill...a doctor is useless:** Polemarchus loses an opportunity here; S. ignores the role of medicine in preserving health, about which Greek doctors were quite concerned, *e.g.* the Hippocratic *A Regimen for Health.*

333a1ff. S. continues the sequence by 'squeezing' justice out of a series of everyday activities: P. having suggested 'partnerships' as a likely area of operation for justice, S. lists partnerships where the collaboration of an 'expert' in a particular *technē* will be more useful than that of the just man. Justice is useful, then, as the 'skill' of keeping things safe, i.e. when they are not being used.

a14 **'By business contracts you mean partnerships...?:** by 'partnerships' (*koinōnēmata*) P. probably understands *e.g.* a contract between buyer and seller, where justice could be said to have a real, 'superordinate', role (see above, note on 332e5) over and above the business expertise of the partners to the contract, in ensuring fair dealing; in this activity justice would have an obvious and unique role to play. S., however, immediately (b1), and much more favourably to his argument, chooses to interpret a 'partner' as an associate in a *joint* venture, where a conventional 'expert' in *e.g.* draughts, building etc. has a much more obvious use, but justice a much less easily-defined role. P., in character, does not spot or question the shift of emphasis.

d9 **'...you turn to the skill of the hoplite...:** the Greek hoplite was a heavily armed foot-soldier, whose shield, in combination with others, formed a solid wall of defence against the weapons of the enemy; hence S.'s example.

d11–12 **'...justice is useless when each thing is being used, but useful when it is not?:** S. polishes off the argument with a polar expression in epigrammatic form: literally: '...in use useless, in uselessness useful' (*en men chrēsei achrēstos, en de achrēstiāi chrēsimos:*

n.b. the neatly balanced 'chiastic' ABBA form of the expression). S. carefully minimises the role of justice in safe guardianship by describing this activity as 'useless', playing on the ambiguity of *achrēstos* = 'useless' or, more appropriately here, 'unused'. The snappy, mannered epigram and paradoxical expression, reminiscent of the style of the sophist Gorgias, is perhaps intended by Plato to indicate the sophistic tendency of S.'s whole line of argument. P.'s 'It seems so' (d13) indicates his somewhat reluctant assent. For an overview of the argument, see Introduction, pp. 16–17.

333e2–334b9

S.'s second argument with P. hinges on the moral ambivalence of *technai*. The person who is skilled at effecting the consequences of a particular *technē* will also be skilled at bringing about their opposite. So, if the just man is skilled in using his *technē* to bring about certain consequences, he will also be skilled in bringing about their opposite.

333e3   '...isn't the person who is most formidable in striking blows...also the person who is best at guarding against them?: not obviously true, one might think, in battle or boxing, despite P.'s clear assent (defence and attack require different skills); but the two aspects have to be subsumed under the heading of a 'unitary' skill if the argument is going to work (Xenophon's S. assumes generalship involves skills of defence and attack: *Memorabilia* 3.1.6). The idea of a single body of knowledge which is as effective in subverting as in promoting an end is more plausible in S.'s subsequent examples: knowing the techniques of guarding something gives someone an advantage in countering them (to take a modern example, using reformed car thieves as those most likely to be skilled in combating car crime). Note how in e6ff. the conclusion of each example leads on to the next: 'guarding (against blows)' leads to 'guarding against disease' (*phulaxasthai*); 'introducing (disease) undetected' leads to 'stealing a march on the enemy'.
334a7   'If, then, the just person is skilful at guarding money he will also be skilful at stealing it: it has been agreed at 333c8 that guarding money is the skill of the just man; combining this with the current argument, S. engineers a *reductio ad absurdum* – effectively a contradiction: 'the just man is unjust'. As with the previous argument, this only follows if the analogy between justice and other skills holds (see above note on 332e5).
a10   'Then it appears that the just man is unveiled as some kind of thief...: this paradox is worked out at length by S. in *Lesser Hippias* (see esp. 375d–376b). Here the reference is to *Odyssey* 19.395. In a joking reference to Homeric authority, S. plays on the idea of Odysseus' grandfather Autolycus' supremacy in the skills of thieving and lying as some kind of justice. P. naturally objects; in a sequence familiar from other examples of the Socratic *elenchus,* reluctant assent to the steps of S.'s argument (a6, a9) has led to a bewildered denial of a conclusion which S. is clearly not serious in drawing, but which does follow from the idea of justice as a skill like others.
b7   '...but I no longer know what I did mean: S.'s capacity to bewilder his interlocutors in the *elenchus* is frequently described in the dialogues, *e.g. Euthyphro* 11b; *Laches* 194b; *Meno* 80a. True to his character, P. nevertheless sticks to his guns here, and forces S. to probe the 'friends/enemies' argument from a different angle.

334c1– 335b1

In the third argument S. draws the distinction between friends and enemies who seem, and those who really are, good or bad. If you misjudge your friends and enemies you may end up harming the good and helping the bad. If 'help friends – harm enemies' is to be retained as a definition of justice the skill must be practised on real and not mistaken friends/enemies.

c1 '...a person's friends are those who *seem* **worthy to each individual...**: *chrēstos* ('worthy') and *agathos* ('good') appear to be practically synonyms for purposes of this argument (and are treated as such by most translators); *chrēstos* is perhaps used in this section to emphasise subjective belief, i.e. people who seem *chrēstoi*, as opposed to those who actually are *agathoi*.

e5–6 'But let us change our ground; for it looks as if we didn't define the friend and the enemy correctly: unusually for the Socratic *elenchus* here it is the interlocutor (P.) and not S. who offers a modification of the definition (which, admittedly, has been pretty glaringly hinted at by S.).

335a8–9 '...it is just to do good to a friend if he is good, and harm to an enemy if he is bad?: Plato seems to be having S. string out this very simple argument to inordinate length; the reasons for this might be: 1. the significance of a potential weakness, from a philosophical point of view, in a fundamental tenet of popular morality: the circumstantial nature of friendship and enmity, involving simply family, relations, political allies and opponents – the people who happen to be on your side or against you (on the popular idea, see Dover (1994) 180ff.), as opposed to an assessment of their intrinsic worth, i.e. whether they really are good or bad; 2. the need to underline the point that, if justice is a skill, and we assume, for the sake of argument, that the Simonides definition is correct, then justice must be based on real and not mistaken knowledge.

335b2–336a10

The final argument with P., the most substantial, tackles the 'help friends, harm enemies' definition from the point of view of what S. claims is the innate function of a *technē*, to benefit the object on which it is practised. Therefore it cannot be the function of the *technē* of justice to harm people, if this involves making them worse.

c1 'But of humans..., when harmed, they become worse by the standard of human excellence?: *aretē* (excellence) is the ideal function of a wide range of things, from knives to animals to humans. Harming *e.g.* horses or dogs decreases their *aretē*, making them function worse as horses, dogs etc., and by analogy, S. argues, human *aretē* works in the same way; if justice is a human excellence (P. agrees at c5) then harming humans (which, S. claims the Simonides definition stipulates, is one of the functions of the *technē* of justice) makes them worse rather than better. But clearly, this is not what Polemarchus (Simonides) means by 'harming' enemies; the traditional aim of the 'just' person was to cause enemies pain and/or unhappiness (not make them worse enemies). Concealed in the argument appears to be an ambiguity in the meaning of 'harm' (*blaptein*): 1. to make worse; 2. to cause pain and/or unhappiness. S.'s analogies suggest that he is either not interested in the ambiguity or has not noticed it (for a detailed discussion of this issue, see Jeffrey (1979) and also Introduction p. 17).

c9 **'Well, are musicians through their musical skill able to make people unmusical?:** the *technē* of music provides a familiar Socratic analogy (see *e.g. Gorgias*, 460b). Having already established that 'harming' makes its object worse, S. goes on, with this analogy, to establish that the essence of a *technē* is the opposite – the *technē* of a musician or horseman must by definition benefit pupils, in order to legitimise their claim to be a musician or horseman.

d3 **'No, for it is not...the function of heat to cool things, but of its opposite:** hot, cold (and in d6, dry and wet) seen as powers, were standard opposites whose operation formed the basis of much scientific and medical theory in the 5th and 4th centuries. The attempt to suggest that these powers have a parallel function to that of a human *technē* (n.b. the slide from d6–d8, from physical powers to the good person) has a strongly sophistic feel. The appeal to these powers nevertheless implies that the beneficial operation of a *technē* is somehow fixed in nature, a claim which the argument of the remainder of *Republic* supports (on the effectiveness of the analogy to establish the beneficial function of justice as 'natural', see Lycos 104).

e5–6 **'it has become apparent to us that it is in no way just to harm anyone:** a distinction should probably be made between the conviction with which S. establishes this conclusion, fundamental to Plato's Socratic ethics generally (cf. *Crito,* 49b–c), and the quality of the specific arguments used here to reach it. It should be noted, moreover, that this conclusion directly contradicts that of argument 2 above (333e2–34b9), the argument that a *technē* can be used to harm as well as benefit its object.

e8–10 **'So you and I...will fight together against anyone who claims that this view was put forward by Simonides...or any other of the blessed sages:** S.'s suggestion that, rather than show Simonides to be wrong, they must deny that he, and other 'wise men' could actually be responsible for the exploded definition, must be more than a little tongue in cheek (*makarios,* 'blessed', and *sophos,* 'wise', clearly have ironical overtones here, though this passes P. by). In the Platonic dialogues S. is presented as having a consistently low opinion of the value of the 'wisdom' of the poets, notably in *Republic* 2 and 3, where he concludes that they are in general not fit to practise their profession in his ideal state because they do not deal in knowledge. The inclusion of Bias and Pittacus (sixth century statesmen and lawgivers, two of the traditional seven 'wise men') demonstrates that Plato shares the popular Greek view that poets should be a source of moral and social improvement (although he differed radically from popular opinion in his view that they were not). For Plato's view of the placing of poets in rank order of human wisdom, cf. *Phaedrus* 248d–e.

e11 **'Well...*I'm* ready enough to join in the fight:** another illustration of P's combative character (see above, notes on 327c1–14, 331d8).

336a5–6 '...Periander or Perdiccas or Xerxes or Ismenias of Thebes...: the first three were absolute rulers (of Corinth, Macedon and Persia respectively) whose despotic power makes them likely candidates, S. (surely only semi-seriously) suggests, for a false definition of justice (for the stark Platonic contrast between supposed power and real power, based on knowledge, see *Gorgias* 467aff.). Ismenias of Thebes' inclusion here derived from the scandal of his taking of bribes from Greece's enemy, Persia (Xenophon, *Hellenica* 3.5.1).

The reference to Ismenias' activities, dated after S.'s death to 395, is clearly anachronistic; Adam tentatively suggests that the inclusion of the Ismenias incident may indicate a date in the 390's for the composition of *Republic* 1, '...when the disgraceful affair was still fresh in men's minds.' (Adam note *ad loc.*), but this is hardly strong enough evidence on which to build a hypothesis of the separate composition of Book 1 (see Introduction, pp. 4–5).

a9   '...it has become apparent that neither justice nor the just consists in this...: for the distinction between *dikaiosunē* and *to dikaion,* see Introduction p. 2 and n. 4. The essentially negative presentation of the argument with P. is demonstrated by the fact that S. introduces the Platonically correct conclusion of the final argument with him – that the just man would never harm anybody – simply as a conclusion which renders the 'Simonides' definition incorrect and so leads to *aporia.*

336b1–338c1

This whole section is in formal terms an Interlude in the argument, which also serves as an introduction to the third and most important of S.'s encounters in Book I, that with Thrasymachus. In this 'sparring' prelude, T.'s overbearing personality and boorish behaviour are humorously and unflatteringly presented both in his own conversational style and in commentary (to unknown audience) by S. as narrator. The latter reacts to T.'s insults with typical 'irony', detected and commented upon unfavourably by T. (337a4). Nevertheless the increasing sophistication of the overall argument is heralded by the little 'spat' between S. and T. (336c5ff.) over what constitutes an acceptable form for a definition. (For discussion of the historical T. and his relation to Republic, see Introduction, p. 9, and see Quincy, White).

336b1   Now Thrasymachus, even while we were talking...: Plato typically uses the dramatic means afforded by S.'s role as internal narrator to 'overlap' the conversations with Polemarchus and Thrasymachus by presenting T.'s role as already in progress (see also a similar treatment of S.'s narrator-role in *Protagoras* 314eff.); T.'s attempts at intervention are in effect 'stage directions' by S., and T.'s final bursting into speech is presented as the result of a long build-up of frustration with the conduct of the argument, which is intended to reflect his character (cf. Polus and Callicles in *Gorgias* 461b3, 481b6). Note also that here S.'s narrator-role (largely abandoned after *Republic* 1) allows him to paint an unflattering picture of T. even before the latter speaks, and of his mode of speech when he finally succeeds. For S.'s appreciation of T.'s oratorical qualities elsewhere, see *Phaedrus* 267c–d. On T.'s character, see Quincy, 306.

b5–7   ...gathering himself up like a wild beast, he sprang on us...Polemarchus and I were panic stricken...: the image recalls the Homeric simile-type comparing Greeks fighting Trojans to wild animals attacking panicking sheep, *e.g. Iliad* 16. 352ff., explicit in b6 'wanting to tear in pieces', διαρπασόμενος, see *Iliad* 16. 355 διαρπάζουσιν; see also *Odyssey* 18.340: Odysseus terrifying the serving-women. S. exploits the simulated terror and mock heroic image to produce a narrative 'wink' at the reader/listener here (we will see later that T., for all his ferocity, is tamed). T. as a wild beast suggests a 'spirited' nature which may look forward to later books of *Republic* (*e.g.* T. as exhibiting the *thumos* characteristic of the second aspect of the tripartite soul in Book 4, 434d2ff.). On this see Wilson, White 307 n. 2.

c1–2 **'And why do you play the fool, deferring to each other like this?**: T.'s language here, shed of its boorish overtones, is sharply critical of the method of argument so far: 'play the fool' (*euēthisdomai*) recalls S. himself in *Charmides*, 175c8, describing the 'compliant' (*euēthikōn*) participants nevertheless unable to reach a solution to the argument. 'Deferring to each other' (*hypokataklinomenoi* = 'submitting, allowing oneself to be beaten' (of wrestling) or 'taking the lower place' at a banquet (see Jowett-Campell, note *ad loc.*)) is a telling, if uncharitable way of describing the role of Polemarchus in the *elenchus* T. has just witnessed. T. enlarges on his criticisms at c3–6: he believes S. is using the method to gain an unfair advantage by refuting Polemarchus without being required to produce his own definition. S. explains and justifies his procedure elsewhere, *e.g.* in *Theaetetus* 150c: he is the midwife who can himself bear no wisdom as 'offspring', but assists others to 'birth'. However, the combativeness lurking behind S.'s apparently supportive stance is detected by T. (cf. 'show off', c4) and well brought out by Blondell 122.

c5ff. **'So give an answer yourself...don't you be telling me that it is the obligatory or the beneficial or the advantageous or the profitable or the expedient, but make your definition clear and precise; for I won't take that sort of drivel from you:** καὶ ὅπως μοι μὴ ἐρεῖς 'don't you be telling me...' (c6–d1) is 'colloquial and abrupt, almost rude' (Adam, note *ad loc.*). In what sense could T. be justified in not regarding these suggested definitions as precise? Perhaps in the sense that they merely substitute synonyms without offering a context – *e.g.* what is the product of justice? This is a criticism which Cleitophon in the short dialogue of that name appears to be making of Socrates and his followers; the dialogue is of dubious authenticity and Plato (if it is by him and not by a student in the Academy) probably derives his list of the products of justice at *Cleitophon* 409c (nearly identical to the above) from *Republic*, rather than *vice-versa* (see Slings (1999) 182–4). It is not clear from the rest of Plato's dialogues why T. thinks that S. would produce such definitions, and anyway S. very effectively rebuts the *Cleitophon* criticism in the remainder of *Republic.* See further, Waterfield (1993) 468, note on *Cleitophon*, 409c.

d6–7 **...I believe that if I had not caught sight of him before he looked at me I would have been rendered speechless:** S. turns a traditional superstition into a joke: if a wolf looks at you before you catch sight of it, you are rendered dumb (Virgil *Eclogue* 9.53). S. as narrator continues to convey to us his simulated fear of T. as an uncontrolled beast, and great intellect, *e.g.* 'clever fellows like you' (337a2).

e2ff. **'Don't be harsh with us...:** the beginning of S.'s speech at e2 has the elevated tone of a formal supplication: μὴ χαλεπὸς ἡμῖν ἴσθι: 'be not harsh on us' (for μή + imperative in this context, see Sappho, fr. 1, 3–4: Campbell (vol. I): μή μ' ἄσαισι μηδ' ὀνίαισι δάμνα); Euripides, fr. 406 Nauck: μὴ σκυθρωπὸς ἴσθ' ἄγαν).Other rhetorical touches: μὴ γὰρ δὴ οἴου: 'for don't imagine', balanced by οἴου γε σύ: 'believe me...'; ἐλεεῖσθαι...ἡμᾶς: '[it is far more reasonable] to pity us'. In portraying himself as a helpless, supplicating victim S. is coming close to playing the fool here.

e4–7 **'...if we were looking for a piece of gold...yet in searching for justice, an objective more valuable than masses of gold...:** a form of *a fortiori* argument found elsewhere in *Republic* (*e.g.* 9.589e): here it means: 'gold is valuable: how much more valuable is justice'. For gold as wisdom, see Heraclitus, DK22 B22 (*Die Fragmente der Vorsokratiker*, vol. I. p.156.5–6).

337a3 **...he burst into loud sarcastic laughter:** 'sarcastic' translates *sardanion*, found in Homer, *Odyssey,* 20.302, of Odysseus' sinister smile at the violence of the suitors who are occupying his house. The derivation is possibly from *sairein* ('grin like an angry dog'), or, through popular etymology, from a bitter Sardinian herb which causes the eater to grimace before dying of its poison (see Adam, note *ad loc.*).

a4–5 **'Here we have that habitual ironic evasion of Socrates:** 'ironic evasion' = *eirōneia* 'irony', habitually attributed to S., especially with reference to his disclaimer of knowledge. T. is clearly using the word in its original sense of 'deliberate deceit' (this appears to be the basic meaning, first found *e.g.* in Aristophanes, *Wasps* 169–74, *Birds* 1208–11, *Clouds* 444–451) ; T. claims that S. wishes his pretence, 'shamming ignorance', to be believed (as opposed to the modern sense of 'irony', where the whole point is that the surface meaning of the statement is not to be believed, at least by a proportion of its hearers): on this passage in the context of a general discussion of Socratic/Platonic irony, see Vlastos (1991) 24. T. thinks he has seen through S.'s stance, but there is also a sense in which S. might aim to justify his claim of ignorance as sincere (see *e.g. Apology* 23a–b). In this particular instance, however, the heavy humour of narrator-S. strongly suggests that everybody, and not just T., is supposed to see through the Socratic pose, especially if already prompted in advance by T. (a5). See also the following note.

a8 **'That's because you're clever, Thrasymachus...:** *sophos* 'clever' or 'wise', can have a pejorative connotation in Greek (*e.g.* Euripides, *Bacchae* 395, and see above on Simonides and the 'blessed sages' note on 335e8–10). It is especially pointed here, taken in combination with 'clever fellows' (a2). The whole of S.'s language in reply to T. suggests that S. wishes his irony to be transparent to the present audience: see d6 below (T. to S.) '...you play the innocent...'.

c2 **'...how alike your example is to mine, to be sure!:** this is sarcastic; T.'s point is that such arithmetical definitions as Socrates has just offered are comprehensive and precise in a way which definitions of values are not. But S. also has a point at b6–9; if, hypothetically, he wishes to adopt one of the definitions at 336d1ff., T. would be wrong to exclude it in advance (and it was T. who was insisting on precision at 336d3).

d2 **'What penalty ought you to suffer?:** formula from Athenian court procedure: the defendant has the right to propose his own penalty (*e.g. Apology* 36b), cf. also d1 *apokrisis* = 'defence' as well as 'answer'.

d6 **'...along with the learning you must pay me some money too:** the proposal of an unconventional penalty by S. in d3–5 is similar to his equally unconventional proposal at his own trial of free maintenance by the state (*Apology* 36e). T. here caps the joke (which plays on the proverbial *pathein / mathein* 'suffering / learning' polarity); as well as 'learning', you must also 'suffer' (by parting with your money). *Philarguria* ('love of money'), with which Plato characterises the sophists, and T. in particular, is put into deliberate contrast with S.'s habitual indifference to money (unlike the sophists he does not charge pupils: see *e.g. Apology* 20a). On T.'s reputed love of money, see Quincy, 302–4.

d10 **'...we'll all chip in for Socrates:** for his friends' willingness to subsidise S. cf. *Apology* 38b. *Crito* 45b.

e1 **'...so that Socrates can do his usual trick...:** in this and the following exchanges both speakers maintain their ongoing stance of challenge (T.) and disclaimer (S.). S. is seen by T.

as deploying debating tactics essentially in the style of the sophists, the sole purpose being to win the argument.

338a5   It was clear that Thrasymachus was keen to speak in order to shine, since he believed he had a brilliant answer: narrator-S. has the advantage here; he can take the reader into his confidence in imputing unworthy and insincere motives to T., while his own, apart from what he chooses to tell us, remain unrevealed. *Pankalos* = 'brilliant' is often ironic in Plato (see S.'s use of the word on Cephalus' speech at 331c1).

The whole of this preliminary exchange between S. and T. is a kind of 'limbering up' before the main argument gets going. On one level it serves to discredit T. in terms of his personality and intellect, both through the direct exchanges and also in S.'s narrative asides. But T's hostile and unusually penetrating analysis of S.'s motives for his habitual disclaimer of knowledge has forced the latter into an exceptionally elaborate defence of the reasons for his method of argument. This leads us to expect an unusually closely-fought encounter.

338c2–341c4

The beginning of S.'s argument with T.: T.'s first definition of justice is 'what is advantageous to the stronger' (called here T1, see Introduction, p. 20ff.). In response to what he sees as S.'s unhelpful interpretation (c5ff.), T. then elaborates further, identifying justice with the advantage which the rulers ('the stronger') gain by passing laws according to their favoured political arrangements. The weaker (the ruled) are 'just' through their obedience to the laws which are made by the prevailing power. This leads on to an analysis of 'ruler' *via* an argument similar to one S. has introduced earlier with Polemarchus with regard to friends and enemies (334c6)): since rulers are not infallible and so liable to error, is the obedience of the ruled 'just', when the rulers make mistakes and consequently force the weaker to do what is to their (the rulers') disadvantage? In avoiding this trap, T. refines his definition: his 'stronger' only applies to the ruler who infallibly acts in his own interest.

338c2   'Hear this then...I say that justice is nothing other than what is advantageous to the stronger: 'Hear this then', a way of getting attention for an important statement (*e.g. Republic* 595c, *Protagoras* 353c, *Apology* 20d). In dramatic terms we can perhaps assume a pregnant pause after this statement, while T. impatiently waits for S.'s reaction. 'Justice... what is advantageous to the stronger' is the first expression of T's position (*T1*), and clearly states what T. considers a consistent underlying feature of justice: its close relation with power. It is just for the weaker to act in the interests of the stronger, or more powerful. On the much-discussed questions: 1. Is T. producing an actual definition here or simply producing an observation on how, in his opinion, justice invariably works? 2. Is *T1* consistent with T's later statement (343c3–4) that 'the just and justice are in reality someone else's good'? – see Introduction, pp. 23–4.

c7–9   'if Polydamas...it's to his advantage to eat beef to keep fit...: Polydamas was a Thessalian athlete who was a winner at the Olympic games in 408 (the *pancration* was a contest combining boxing and wrestling). For S.'s reduction of an opponent's statement to absurdity under the guise of clarification (which T. clearly recognises as an irritating debating manoeuvre here, d2–3), see *e.g. Gorgias* 490d.

d6–e2 '...some cities are governed by tyrannies, some by democracies and some by aristocracies...each ruling power passes laws with a view to its own advantage...: a very similar view of legislation is found in *Laws* 4.714b–d. The assumption that political constitutions are to be equated with factional power and self-interest reflects the late fifth-century political text falsely attributed to Xenophon, known as the 'Old Oligarch', probably contemporary with T.; see Pseudo-Xenophon, *Constitution of the Athenians* esp. Ch. 1. This is essentially T.'s second position (*T2*); see Introduction, pp. 22–3.

339b5–6 'That what is just is some kind of advantage is a thesis with which I too am in agreement...: common ground between S. and T. (as opposed to a Kantian idea of justice as a moral imperative irrespective of advantage). Plato's S. will nevertheless need to demonstrate that his notion of justice (as opposed to T.'s) is advantageous to the practitioner irrespective of practical consequences, which is in essence the challenge issued by Glaucon and Adeimantus in Book 2.

c1ff. **'Are the rulers in the various cities infallible or can they sometimes make mistakes?:** this question starts a long drawn-out sequence of argument, the point of which seems to be to make T. choose between 1. maintaining consistency with what he has just asserted (b9–10), by stating that justice is only doing what is *really* to the rulers' advantage, and 2. claiming that justice can also be what the stronger/rulers *believe* to be to their advantage, even if they are mistaken about what is actually to their advantage. Following the (over?)-elaborate exposition of the alternatives (Plato unusually brings in Polemarchus and Cleitophon to stage a mini-debate about it, 340a1–b9), at 340 c6, T. unhesitatingly chooses alternative 1.: that justice consists in doing only what is actually in the interests of the stronger; he justifies this by redefining 'ruler' more precisely as applicable only to rulers strictly understood, i.e. when they are not in error about their own interests. T. draws a (somewhat Socratic) analogy with professional skills: a doctor or mathematician can only, strictly speaking, be called a doctor or a mathematician when he is *correctly* exercising his skill (340d2ff., and see Reeve (1998) 13, for the idea of T. as an 'inverted Socratic'). Despite the Socratic trap into which this draws him (see next section below), T.'s choice is obviously the only sensible one for him in the circumstances here; if T. were to admit the alternative – that rulers capable of error still merit the name, and, more pertinently, that what they *erroneously* think is in their interest is justice – this, besides leading him into contradiction, as S. points out (339d1), would also lose him the link between justice and power which is absolutely vital for the credibility of his whole position (Lycos 57ff.).

c10 **'But whatever they legislate must be acted on by their subjects, and that is justice?:** the idea of justice as simply obedience to the laws which happen to be laid down by a government recalls Antiphon the Sophist DK87B44 (*Die Fragmente der Vorsokratiker* vol. II. p.346): 'Justice therefore is conforming to the rules and regulations of the community of which you are a citizen.' tr. *The First Philosophers*, 264–6). T. at this point in the dialogue appears to be recommending a 'reductive' or 'conventionalist' view of justice, i.e. the position, like that of Antiphon (above), that justice is nothing over and above obedience to the laws which happen to be laid down by the rulers in any given city and at any given time, whatever they may be. T.'s support for this view should not be taken very seriously however, since he is merely giving an over-hasty affirmative answer to a question by Socrates and he is shortly forced to repudiate it when he denies the name of 'ruler' to anyone mistaking his own interest; in that instance it would not be just for the subject to obey the law because it would not be to the ruler's advantage, as T. soon realises (see 340c6 below), and the idea of justice as simply obedience to the laws is tacitly dropped. On the whole issue see Kerferd (1947) 21ff., Annas 36, Everson 111ff. and Introduction, p. 23–4. For what it is worth, the historical T. seems to have believed in the substantial existence of justice, to judge from DK85B8 (*Die Fragmente der Vorsokratiker* vol. II. p. 328; tr. *The First Philosophers,* 274), in which he deplores the gods' apparent neglect of it.

e5   '...O most clever Thrasymachus...: on the pejorative connotation of *sophos* ('wise'), see above n. on 337a8. S.'s sarcastic epithet immediately precedes what he conceives to be a classic conclusion of the *elenchus,* the exposure to the interlocutor of the contradictory conclusions implied by his original position. And S., for all his ironic politeness, clearly returns T's dislike.

340a1 '...nothing could be more obvious: In their little exchange (340a1–b9) Polemarchus is made to perceive the horns of T.'s dilemma (as outlined above in the note on 339c1ff.) more clearly than the partisan and rather less perceptive Cleitophon.

a3   'Of course...if you are his witness: in addressing Polemarchus, Cleitophon is clearly being sarcastic (possibly reflecting P.'s capitulation to S.'s *elenchus* in the previous section?).

d2   'That's because you browbeat people in arguments, Socrates: 'browbeat' is used here to translate (as a verb) the noun *sukophantēs* (origin obscure), the name given to a person in the Athenian courts who made a living out of malicious prosecutions, whose aim was to extort money from defendants or reward prosecutors. The meaning of the Greek word, very different from the modern 'sycophant', implies both bullying and sharp practice. The implication here is of someone who argues with the deliberate intention of forcing his opponent into submission (that this is the sense in which the word is taken by both S. and T. is clear from 341a5ff.). On sycophancy in Classical Athens, see Osborne (1990).

e2–3   '...no skilled professional makes a mistake: 'skilled professional' translates *dēmiourgos,* literally 'worker for the people (*dēmos*)'. The word denotes skilled workers of all kinds, including doctors, handicraft workers and other people possessing a practical skill; in Plato the element of mastery of a particular craft or body of knowledge makes the equivalence to a modern 'professional' appropriate here.

341b1–2 '...you won't harm me by stealth, nor...by force: stealth/force is a commonplace polarity in Homer (*e.g. Odyssey* 9.406) and Tragedy (*e.g.* Aeschylus, *Prometheus,* 212, *Libation Bearers* 556–7). T. continues to emphasise the confrontational nature of the encounter, which S., on the surface at least (see his answer at b3) wishes to disguise.

c2   '...so mad as to attempt to shave a lion...: as the scholiast comments, 'to dare the impossible', as in the modern English proverb: 'to beard the lion'.

c4   '...though you were no good even then: literally: 'though in that respect also [i.e. when you tried just now] you were worthless'.

c5   'Enough of that sort of talk...: S. brings the sequence to an abrupt halt; T.'s redefinition of 'ruler' (341a) has enabled him to avoid contradiction (see note on 339c1ff., above), which forces S. to try another tack.

341c5–342e11

The very argument by which T. has extricated himself from the previous elenchus now plays into S.'s hands; the strict definition of 'ruler' (enlarged on by T. with 'Socratic' analogies) enables S. to make profitable use of the familiar Socratic idea of 'expertise' and its implications. S.'s purpose in this section, largely successful in formal terms at least, is to get T. to concede that the skill (*technē*) of the expert is always directed towards the benefit of its object and not of itself; so the expert ruler (as T. himself has defined him, at 340d2ff.) will always seek the interest of his subjects and not his own. T.'s main contention, that 'justice is to the advantage of the stronger/ruler', appears to have been refuted.

341c5–7 '…this precisely-defined doctor…is he a man of business or a carer of the sick?: S. uses the requirement of 'precision' to tie T. down to two things: 1. the doctor must be so by virtue of the correct exercise of his skill, as agreed at 340d2ff.; 2. what S. argues are the incidental features of *e.g.* doctoring, i.e. the fact that the doctor receives money for his services (is a 'man of business'), must be distinguished from the essential activity, care of those who are ill. The issue of 'the *technē* of earning wages' is discussed in more detail by S. and T. later (see below, 346b1ff.). Here it is introduced by S. simply as one of a number of examples designed to get at what he sees as the essential, as opposed to the incidental concerns of the expert.

d6 'Then, do these people each have something to their advantage?: T.'s immediate agreement to this at d7 shows that he hasn't yet seen the full implications of S.'s interpretation of 'advantage', which the latter begins to develop at d11ff., and which T. later strongly opposes (343b1ff.).

e1 'What do you mean by that?: the insertion of this kind of question by the interlocutor is a common Platonic device to allow the more careful explanation of an initially obscure idea: a *technē* aiming at 'being as perfect as possible' is rather obscure, to us as well as T. S. explains by taking a negative example: the body is not self-sufficient; it needs a *technē* which provides for its interests, i.e. medicine, in order to cure its ills.

e4 '…the skill of medicine has now been invented…: i.e. 'now', in our advanced stage of civilisation, as opposed to in more primitive times when the body had to fend for itself.

342a2–3 '…does any other skill need any excellence to perfect it – just as the eyes need sight…': S. uses here the conventional sense of *aretē*, 'excellence', as the end for which something, for example a sense, exists, *e.g.* sight is what eyes are for, for hearing, ears etc. *Technai* have no such need or defect. This is what S. means, then, by describing them as aiming at their own 'perfection'.

b4–5 '…nor does it belong to its nature to seek the advantage of anything else other than its own subject matter: 'its own subject matter', *literally* 'that of which it is the *technē*', i.e. that on which the *technē* is practiced. The 'eyes/sight' analogy (342a3) does its work for S., and enables him to make the logical move from *technē* to object of the *technē*, whose interests the *technē* watches over and provides for (a5).

b6–7 'Consider this in that precise sense of yours…: in the above argument S. has exploited T.'s insistence on ruler in the precise sense (340e1ff.), and T., although unhappy with the direction of the argument, is unable to counter it at this point (n.b. his less than enthusiastic responses at b8 and c6).

c7–8   '…skills surely also rule and hold sway over that of which they are the skills: S. is here, from our point of view, fudging the distinction between 'caring for' and 'ruling over' in order to enable his *technē* analogy to refute T's position, and the move from the analogy of doctor (d5) to that of captain in d10, i.e. from a 'caring' to a 'ruling' profession, helps S.'s move here (he even gives the doctor a 'ruling' verb, *epitattei* ('orders') at d6). As with the earlier arguments with Polemarchus, the success of S.'s argument here depends on acceptance of dubious analogies.

c10–d2   'So no body of knowledge considers or regulates the advantage of the stronger, but that of the weaker subjected to it': this is the position to which S.'s whole argument has been moving – the direct contradiction of T.'s original assertion, that justice (as a *technē*) is the advantage of the stronger.

d3–4   He finally agreed to this, too, though he tried to make a fight of it: an example of S.'s narrative control; we are not given any insight here or at e6 ('he assented reluctantly'), into the exact nature of T.'s resistance (see Blondell 43 and n.126).

343a1–344c9

Having been forced into a grudging assent to S.'s previous argument, T. now reformulates his original definition. Rulers do not rule for the advantage of the ruled but for their own. Justice is someone else's advantage, injustice is the interest of oneself (T3, see Introduction, pp. 21–3); this is the case in all social and political activities, where, because of his justice, the just person gains no profit, and the unjust person prospers, particularly when the injustice is perpetrated on a large scale, *e.g.* in a tyranny.

343a7–8 '…she's turning a blind eye at your snivelling nose: T., backed into a corner, resorts to childish abuse. A 'runny nose' was popularly thought to indicate stupidity (Lucian, *Alexander* 20). S. is allegedly stupid because he can't see how wrong he is.
       '..who can't even get you to recognise…: αὐτῇ: 'the dative implies that Socrates' ignorance is to [the nurse's] discredit' (Allan, note *ad loc.*).
b1ff. Having been unable to refute S.'s *technē*-analogy thesis in the previous *elenchus,* T. here resorts to a medium which he finds much more comfortable and effective, the sophistic *epideixis* or 'display speech'. His argument here that justice is someone else's good, and that injustice is the interest of the stronger (*T3*) is only superficially inconsistent with his first position (*T1*) – that justice is the interest of the stronger (see 338c2–3). T. is not shifting his ground here, but setting out his thesis in its clearest form, as he explains at the end (344c5–9): the profit for the 'stronger or ruler' (T. makes no distinction between simple power and government here) comes from the obedience of the weaker (so 'justice is the interest of the stronger' is seen from the *weaker's* point of view); from the *stronger's* point of view, *in*justice is more profitable. Why then did T. initially set out his thesis in an apparently misleading way at 338c2? Surely because this is the form in which S. posed the question: what is justice? '…what else can anyone suggest that it is?' at 336a10 (he didn't ask 'what is injustice?'). On T.'s consistency, see *e.g.* Kerferd (1947), Annas 45–6. See further, Introduction, pp. 23–4.
b1   '…you imagine that shepherds or herdsmen are considering the good of their flocks or herds…: an effective debating point against S.'s analogy of *technē* as care of its object; if

you follow through to the ultimate end of the *technē*, initial care of sheep is directed towards the object for which it is undertaken, 'what they are being reared for' (οὗ ἕνεκα τρέφονται), as Xenophon's S. says in *Memorabilia* 3.2.1, i.e. shearing or slaughter (see Reeve (1985) 260 n.28). For Plato's ideal philosopher, *e.g.* in *Theaetetus* 174d, T.'s analogy describes the typical tyrant, whom the philosopher sees as squeezing as much as he can out of the citizens nominally under his care.

c1   'And you are so far out in understanding...: so most translators, see LSJ πόρρω B II; or alternatively, as both Adam and Allan believe (notes *ad loc.*), heavily sarcastic: '...you are so far advanced (πόρρω εἶ) in understanding...that you are ignorant...'

c3–4 '...justice and the just are in reality someone else's good...: 'in reality' (τῷ ὄντι) emphasises the 'one-way concept' of another's good; acting justly for another's good will be to one's own disadvantage (see Boter 276).

c5–6 '...injustice...rules over those who are truly simple-minded...they serve the advantage of the one who is the stronger, and by serving him they promote his happiness...: 'happiness' = *eudaimonia*. This reversal of Socratic ethics, giving the most desirable end, 'happiness', to the unjust, reflects an emphasis on amoral 'realism' frequently found in the remains of the fifth-century sophists, *e.g.* Antiphon (see *The First Philosophers* 264–7); the clearest reversal of the connotations of *eudaimonia* is put into the mouth of Callicles in Plato's *Gorgias* (482cff.). T.'s general view of justice and power in *Republic* (not found in his surviving fragments) is very closely paralleled by the position given to the Athenians in their dialogue with the Melians by the historian Thucydides: '..it is a general and necessary law of nature to rule whatever one can.' (Thucydides 5.105), on which, see Guthrie (1969) 84–8.

d2   '...my most simple-minded Socrates...: *euēthēs* (= 'simple', 'silly') is frequently used to describe the apparent naivety of S.'s interlocutors (*e.g.* 336c1–2), here turned by T. on S. It has the same root as the word just used by T. for the 'simple-minded' (*euēthikon*) but just victims of the unjust person (c6), and by implication for S. and all those who think like him.

d4   '...business relations: this recalls the argument with Polemarchus (333a10ff), where the *technē* of justice appeared to have no place alongside the specialist skills of those who use it for specific purposes. Here, T. claims that justice is actually a disadvantage in business (almost an 'anti-*technē*', as it were).

d7–e1 '...when there are taxes to be paid...and when there are handouts...: *eisphorai* = special taxes levied from time to time on citizens in respect of their property; T.'s point is that the unjust person will minimise his wealth in order to escape a just assessment. *lēpseis* 'handouts' = exceptional distributions of land or money, or the rewards of an official position, T.'s point being, presumably, that the unjust person will grab more than his fair share.

e3–4 '...his private affairs becoming comparatively worse through neglect...: the neglect of private affairs by those engaged in public office is a Greek commonplace (see *e.g.* Herodotus 1.97), utilised later by S. against T., as part of the argument (346d1ff.) that rulers, strictly defined, are not acting in their own interest.

344a3 '...ἢ τὸ δίκαιον: = ἢ τὸ δίκαιον εἶναι. δίκαιον is masculine here: translate 'how much more he is personally benefited by being unjust than being just [brings benefit to the just person]'. See Adam note *ad loc.*

a7 'I'm talking about tyranny, which secretly and by force appropriates others'

possessions, sacred and secular, private and public…: *hiera kai hosia* ('sacred and secular') indicate a contrast between things which are reserved for the gods (*hiera*) and those which may be used by humans (*hosia* – not 'secular' in a modern sense; on the distinction, see Dover (1994) 248). On 'secretly and by force', see above note on 341b1–2. Obsession with the excesses of the *tyrannos* (see *e.g. Gorgias,* 469ff.) is found in the fifth century generally, see *e.g.* Thucydides 1.122.3 on Athens as a 'tyrannical city' (*polin tyrannon*), as seen through the eyes of its enemies. Tyranny's pejorative connotations would have made T.'s warm approval counter-intuitive to conventional Athenian sentiment as well as that of Plato. The rhetorical antitheses of T.'s language at this point and to the end of the section (see esp. c3–4) reflect the sophistic tendency to give stylistic emphasis to the peroration of a speech.

b7–8 **'…such people are called happy and fortunate:** the famed 'happiness' of the all-powerful tyrant is a commonplace of S.'s adversarial interlocutors (see *e.g.* Polus in *Gorgias* 470d–e, and also Euripides, *Phoenician Women* 549–50).

344d1–348a6

S., having emphasised the importance of T. staying to defend a thesis with, in his (S.'s) opinion, vital relevance to how one lives one's life, goes to work to refute T.'s argument that injustice is the profit and interest of oneself. S.'s main argument is a reiteration of the one he used immediately before T.'s *epideixis*: that the shepherd's *technē* is to rule his flocks in their, and not his, best interest (there are similarities with Argument (4) with Polemarchus, see Introduction p. 17). This is demonstrated by the fact that rulers require payment (because no other advantage to them accrues from ruling); moreover, since each *technē* has a distinct function, wage-earning is distinct from the *technē* in respect of which it is earned, and incidental to it; so no *technē,* strictly speaking, aims at the advantage of the operator. Hence rulers must be paid for ruling; good rulers do not aim at the ' advantages' of honour or wealth, but take up office as a 'necessary evil' to avoid being ruled by somebody worse than themselves.

d1–3 **…having, like a bath-attendant, emptied over our ears an incessant and copious flood of words:** a deliberately 'low' comic image; the *balaneus,* 'bath man', is coupled with prostitutes in Aristophanes (*Knights* 1403); likewise 'empty over', 'drench', of words (Aristophanes, *Wasps* 483). With varying degrees of irony S. claims in the dialogues to dislike and mistrust long speeches, as opposed to his preferred method of discussion, the *elenchus,* though he makes a long speech himself a little further on (347b5). Here he wishes to present to us T's rhetorically-constructed speech as a 'drenching', rather than a reasoned argument, and, likewise, T. is presented as not having the temperament (sincere commitment?) to stay and argue his case.

d6–7 **'…surely you don't intend to launch such an argument at us and then go away…:** a change of metaphor; Scythian archers proverbially shot their arrows at the enemy and then rode away (cf. Herodotus 4.128ff). For the metaphor, see Euripides, *Alcestis,* 679–80).

d7–e3 **'Do you think it's a minor matter… and not the course of a life which each of**

us should follow in order to live it most profitably?: the alternative textual reading of F here, ὅλου (A and D have ἀλλ' οὐ, translated here), gives a slightly different meaning; '...a minor matter...the course of a whole life...?

Whichever reading one takes, the basic meaning here is the importance of one's personal conduct of life right up to death. This is a theme to which Socrates obsessively returns in the dialogues (for detailed discussion, see below, n. on 352d6–7). Here, the addition of 'most profitably' puts the phrase in tune with T.'s recent argument, and, incidentally, reminds us that S. is arguing in *Republic* for the strong thesis that justice is not only right, but *profitable* for its practitioners. T. (in e4) strongly protests his agreement with the idea of profitability, but not, of course, with *justice* as the profitable activity.

345a1   '...won't be a bad investment: in the metaphor from finance S. is extracting humour at T.'s expense: for T. to stay and try to convince S. and the others and so benefit them will be profitable for him, i.e. in his interest (possibly a covert dig at his *philarguria* ('love of money') – see above, n. on 337d6).

b6–7   'Must I take the argument and implant it in your soul?: T., like most sophists, is portrayed as relying on the rhetorical force of his arguments leading to passive assimilation by the recipients rather than critical examination. The metaphor is from nurses feeding children (see Aristophanes, *Knights* 716f.). Hence S.'s strongly negative reply in b8: 'Socrates shudders at the prospect of having Thrasymachus for his intellectual nurse.' (Adam note *ad loc.*).

b9   '...if you shift your ground...: presumably, according to S., not adhering to the 'precision' of defining shepherd etc. in the strict sense of being concerned for the interests of the sheep. But we need to remember that T. only assented very reluctantly to S.'s other examples (of the doctor and ship's captain, 342d3ff.), and, for objections to S.'s definition as applying to sheep and shepherd, see above note on 343b1). S.'s argument, repeated below at c2ff., relies on an artificially narrow definition of the *technē* of the shepherd as unconcerned with commercial considerations – a position much harder to maintain than in his doctor/patient analogy, where an outcome unconcerned with commerce is much easier to maintain: a doctor might quite plausibly assert that his only concern was his patient's recovery (see further, Introduction, p. 21).

d3–5   '...since, I imagine, it has sufficiently provided what concerns itself with a view to its being at its best, as long as it in no way falls short of being the shepherd's skill: this is a difficult sentence both to translate and to interpret: ἐκπεπόρισται can be either Middle or Passive; most translators take it as Passive (Lee, Reeve, Shorey, Waterfield): '[the shepherding skill]...has been sufficiently provided for...'. I have taken it as Middle here (with Jowett-Campbell), with ἡ ποιμενική as subject, since at 342b1–2 in a passage which the present one more or less reiterates, S. emphasises the *active* role of the *technē* in seeking its own perfection. S. is here in essence recapping what he has already said at 342a2ff.: a skill's advantage must come from nothing other than the best possible practice of itself (and hence, S. would say, the advantage of its objects).

e7   '...no benefit from their rule will come to themselves but to those ruled?: Aristotle, *Nichomachean Ethics* 5.6.6–7 echoes this argument in describing justice as 'another's good' (from the point-of-view of the *rulers* on this occasion), so that rulers have to be recompensed with honour and dignity.

346a3 '**...don't answer contrary to your real belief...**: on S.'s 'sincerity requirement' of his interlocutors, see below note on 349a6.

b1 '**So doesn't the skill of wage-earning give us wages?**: S. wishes to eliminate the argument that a *technē* benefits its practitioner through the receipt of pay for services rendered, by demonstrating that wages are not an intrinsic part of the practice of the *technē* of doctoring, being a ship's captain etc. S. does successfully demonstrate that the practice of an art or skill is logically separate from the financial recompense received for practising it; a person can be an effective doctor, and his patient cured, without receipt of pay (346e1), and *vice versa*: obviously he may receive the financial reward despite failing to practise the *technē* properly. But S., in his effort to separate the practice of the skill from the financial reward, vitiates his argument, seemingly unnecessarily, by introducing the notion of the 'skill of wage-earning'; there are two obvious and damaging objections to this idea: 1. 'wage-earning' cannot really be called a *technē* – it's not an art or skill like medicine etc., but an incidental accompaniment to the skill; S.'s pursuit of the 'skill of wage-earning' seems positively perverse here. 2. if wage-earning were shown to be a *technē*, it would actually *contradict* the Socratic assertion that no *technē* benefits its practitioner, since 'wage earning' would certainly confer benefit on the recipient. T., while apparently conceding S.'s main point, remains fairly unimpressed with the idea of the 'skill of wage-earning' (see c12).

e8 '**...I made a point of saying...that nobody willingly chooses to govern...**: μηδένα ἐθέλειν ἑκόντα ἄρχειν...: μή + infinitive after verbs of saying tends to be used in sentences expressing emphatic denial.

347a5 '**...or incur a penalty if they refuse:** Glaucon's immediate request for clarification of this phrase (a6) follows a common Socratic pattern of introducing a new and unusual idea (see above n. on 341e1). Glaucon's unexpected intervention and the fact that it is he who makes the request here is significant: the idea S. is about to develop (b6ff.) appears to look forward to a key idea in the later books of the *Republic* in which Glaucon and his brother Adeimantus (as opposed to T.) are closely involved – the obligation on the philosopher to leave his contemplation of ideal truth and reason and reluctantly take office to avoid the job going to those less fitted (the penalty of refusal), see *Republic* 7.520aff., 540d–41a.

b6ff. An unusually long speech for S., the form and content of which constitutes strong evidence that Plato intended Book 1 as an integral part of *Republic* as a whole (see Introduction, pp. 4–5). In form it is really a digression from the main argument, but in fact represents a 'flagging' of one of the main themes of *Republic* as a whole – the reluctance, but nevertheless the necessity, of rule by those most fitted for it, namely the philosophers (here not yet distinguished as such; they are simply the 'best' or 'the estimable'). Strictly in terms of the present argument, it begs the question of whether the ruler really 'does not naturally consider his own interest' (d5), which has not yet been finally agreed with T.

b10 '**...for they are not ambitious...**: literally: '...not lovers of honour (*philotimoi*)'. S. here denies one of the key Greek values, honour (*timē*), as a goal for rulers' aspiration – a highly counter-intuitive move, which goes unchallenged by any of his interlocutors, doubtless because of the digressionary nature of the speech in its immediate context (Plato does not want S. to go down that route yet). The full justification of what S. is saying here lies in the argument of the later *Republic*.

d2–3 '**...a city of good men, were it to exist...**: a clear allusion to later construction of the 'Eutopia' of *Republic* as a whole.

d8–e2 '...I totally disagree with Thrasymachus when he claims that justice is the advantage of the stronger:** the fact that S. uses T.'s original formulation (*T1*) (338c2–3) rather than the reformulation at 343b1ff. (*T3*), is strong evidence (see also note on 343b1ff.) that Plato does not intend us to regard T. as having changed his position between *T1* and *T3*, since S. clearly regards the two positions as essentially the same.

e2–4 '...of much greater significance ...is what Thrasymachus was saying just now, when he asserted that the life of the unjust person is better than that of the just:** i.e. at 343d2ff. This assertion flows naturally from T.'s *T1–3*; S.'s move here to examination of the lives of the just and unjust persons signals a shift in emphasis which heralds the further reformulation of T.'s argument by Glaucon in Book 2.

e7 '**I say that the life of the just person is more profitable:** Glaucon is here much more unequivocally supportive of S.'s thesis than at the beginning of Book 2, doubtless because dramatically at this point it makes sense to resume the argument with T. rather than pursue the digression. But exactly why Glaucon supports S. so unequivocally at this point is never made entirely clear by Plato, given that at the beginning of Book 2 Glaucon says that actually he has not been convinced by S.'s Book 1 arguments. This is perhaps a dramatic weakness on Plato's part; Glaucon may instinctively feel that Socrates is right, but really the only arguments which are going to convince him and Adeimantus are yet to come.

348a7–350c11

A short interlude, marked (typically) by some brief discussion of the way the argument should be conducted and an agreement to continue with S.'s preferred method of *elenchus*, inaugurates the second part of his encounter with T. Previously, T. has set out his basic thesis that justice is the interest of the stronger and that injustice is more profitable than justice, and is unconvinced by S.'s attempts to counter his position. An exchange which establishes that T., in a reversal of the conventional value polarity, regards injustice as not only profitable (a position he has already maintained) but good and wise, leads to an argument which turns on the concept of 'one person outdoing, or having more than (*pleon echein*) another'. Socrates resorts to a sequence of argument involving his tried and tested analogies between skills such as music/medicine and justice which leads him to the conclusion that, like other skilled persons, the individual skilled in justice will not want to outdo another just person and so it is the just person who is 'good and wise, the unjust ignorant and bad' (350c10).

348a7–b3 '...if we set out our argument directly counter to his, enumerating all the good things to come from justice...But if we carry on the enquiry by mutual agreement...':** Socrates mentions a popular debating procedure, with successive speeches advancing contrasted or opposed positions, as *e.g.* in Athenian legal debate, the dramatic *agon* and some moral or political philosophising (*e.g.* Herodotus 8.83 on the ideal constitution). He contrasts this with the Socratic method of question and answer. Explicit contrast of these methods can be found at *e.g. Protagoras* 329a, 334–5, *Gorgias* 461–2 and *Laches* 184dff. In this last instance the requirement to appoint some judge or arbiter in the case of the former method is also emphasised, whereas S. points out that, using the latter method, the debaters can themselves be simultaneously judges and advocates. It is notable that at this point in *Republic* the respondent, Glaucon, goes for the latter method, and it is assumed that T., who is not consulted, will go along with this, which he does, up to a point.

b9 'You claim that perfect injustice is more profitable than justice in its perfect state?': this is the position previously developed by T. at 343b1–344c8. 'Perfect injustice' takes up T.'s insistence that profit comes from large-scale wrong-doing and not petty crime, i.e. injustice imperfectly managed, because in this latter case advantage is cancelled out by the strong likelihood of disgrace and punishment.

c10 'The opposite', he replied: by exploiting the polar connotations of justice/injustice as virtue (excellence)/vice (*aretē/kakia*) S. is trying to manoeuvre T. into the counter-intuitive position of reversing them, i.e. to move from his position that injustice is more profitable than justice to that of claiming, improbably, that, if injustice is a virtue, justice must actually be a vice (*kakia*). T., however, cannot bring himself to go this far against popular sentiment (see Stokes 82) and so S. only partially succeeds here. Having implied just that – that justice is a vice – in his reply at c10, T. draws back from going the whole hog, as it were, and characterises justice as 'a most noble good nature' (*panu gennaian euētheian*). Socrates seizes on this clearly ironically-intended definition (*euētheia* commonly = 'simplicity', 'silliness', see LSJ εὐήθεια, 2. and Thucydides 3.83.1; see above note on 343d2) and again attempts to corner T. (d1) by reversing the literal meaning and asking him if injustice might then be its opposite, i.e. 'bad nature' (*kakoētheia*). In again avoiding S.'s semantic trap, T. instead brings in the idea of 'good judgement' (*euboulia*) as a characteristic of injustice, which moves the argument away from linking justice to *aretē* (dangerous for T.) and away from this semi-sophistic sparring. (For a similar bold reversal of the conventional connotations of Greek value terms, see Callicles in *Gorgias* 492c., and, in a practical political/moral context, Thucydides 3.83.1).

e5 'That takes us on to a much stiffer proposition...and it's no longer easy to produce a reply: 'stiffer' because T.'s assertion that injustice is a virtue appears to leave S. and T. no common ground from which to '...discuss the matter along generally accepted lines.' (e8–9).

349a6 '...as long as I can take it for granted that you are saying what you think: sincerity in respondents appears to be an essential requirement of the Socratic *elenchus*, since Socrates claims that the questioning process is not an adversarial contest but a mutual exploration which ought to effect a change in how the participants spend their lives (see *Gorgias* 495a8–9 and Vlastos (1983) 35–6). The extreme nature of T.'s thesis here has led to S.'s doubts as to his sincerity (see 346a3–4 above). 349a4–8 suggests that S. wants to believe that he is serious, but T. is not prepared to enlighten him in a9–10. What is highly unusual here is S.'s admission (b1) that T.'s sincerity doesn't matter to him (see also 351c4–7). Is S. being ironical here (Vlastos (1983) 35 n. 24)? Or does S.'s admission suggest the rather artificial nature of the debate between S. and T.? (See further, Introduction, pp. 27–8).

b2–3 '...do you think that a just person would wish to outdo another just person?': *pleonexia* 'greediness', 'taking more than one's fair share' (the verbal form = *pleon echein* 'outdo') is the characteristic of T.'s unjust person (see also Callicles in *Gorgias* 483cff. – but for Callicles, such behaviour, characteristic of absolute monarchs like the Persian kings, is not injustice but natural justice; this is the chief difference between him and T.).

b6 'And would he go beyond the just action?: a rather obscure phrase: Waterfield(1993) renders, plausibly '...would he want to set himself up as superior to moral behaviour'.

b8–9   'But what of the unjust person – would the just consider outdoing him and think it right to do so, or not?**: the translation of *pleonektein* here as 'outdo' strongly suggests a false move in the argument; the fact that S. and T. go on to accept it, i.e. agree that the just person would think it right to be in a state of *pleoneoxia* over the unjust (as it stands, virtually a contradiction in terms), results from the ambiguity in the meaning of *pleonektein*, which can mean 'to take unfair advantage of', 'get more than one's fair share' or 'surpass', 'do better than', the latter being clearly how S. understands it here. T. probably cynically thinks that the just person would want to outdo (i.e. gain the upper hand over) the unjust if he could; S. must, if not involved in the contradiction, clearly intend the 'advantage' aimed at by the just man over the unjust to lie elsewhere than in mere competitive edge (*e.g.* to surpass the unjust in goodness, fairness etc.).

d4–5   'Yet the unjust is intelligent and good, and the just neither?**: T. is bound to agree to this formulation of his position as he has already done so at 348d5. In agreeing that he would describe the unjust as 'good' (*agathos*) T. is falling back on the sense which the word has in popular thought from Homer onwards, as indicating political/social success or pre-eminence, as related to *aretē* ('excellence').

e1–350c11 In attempting to refute T., S. has recourse here, as frequently, to a sequence of argument from analogy with professional skills (*technai*), the key stages of which are:

1. Those possessing skills, *e.g.* musicians, doctors, are intelligent, those without them are not (e4–5).
2. Those with these skills are good in respect of the things about which they are intelligent, and bad in respect of those where they lack intelligence (e6).
3. No professional, *e.g.* a musician tuning a lyre, would want to compete with or outdo (*pleonektein*) a fellow-professional ('one cannot tune a lyre which is in tune', Allan note *ad loc.*), nor would a doctor prescribing food and drink; but they would both want to outdo a non-professional (e10–350a10).
4. But the person without such knowledge would want to outdo both the knowledgeable and the ignorant (a11–b1).
5. The knowledgeable person (i.e. the person with the requisite skills) is wise and good (b3–6, from 2., above).
6. So (from 3+5) no wise and good person would want to outdo another wise and good person but only his opposite, the bad and ignorant (b7–8), whereas (from 4) the bad and ignorant would want to outdo both those like and those unlike him (b10).
7. The unjust person (i.e. the person without the 'skill' of justice) would (from 4) want to outdo both his like and his unlike (b12–13, and T. has already admitted this in 349b1–c9, as S. reminds him (b13)).
8. The just person is like the wise and good, the unjust like the bad and ignorant (c4–5).
9. Each of them is of the same kind as that which he is like (c7–8, previously agreed at 349d10).
10. So, the just person is wise and good, the unjust bad and ignorant (c10–11).

This sequence very effectively demonstrates the strengths and weaknesses of Socratic *elenchus*. By assimilating justice to *technē* S. can relate it to the specialist knowledge and aims which the musician and doctor have by virtue of their specific professional skill. His aim here is to show the falsity of T.'s claim that the unjust person is the wise person, and he attempts to do so by separating out the two ideas – of injustice and wisdom – by showing that, unlike the musician etc., the unjust person does not partake of the skills by virtue of which he could be called wise.

However, the argument has serious weaknesses, which a more percipient opponent might have exposed. Most obvious is S.'s exploitation (or unawareness) of the ambiguity of *pleonektein*, which, in the case of musicians/doctors etc., might be translated 'outdo' (the ignorant person does not know the parameters of the activity, and in his ignorance competes by tuning the strings of the lyre wrongly or prescribing inappropriate remedies). But even here there appears to be a sense in which professionals might be said to be competing and 'outdoing' one another (as well as those ignorant of their craft) within the rules of their specialist activity – n.b. the Greek proverb in *e.g.* Hesiod, *Works and Days* 25: '...and potter strives with potter and craftsman with craftsman'. Vlastos (1991) 269 n. 101 thinks that S. could claim that, when engaged in the activity of outdoing one another, musicians/doctors are not actually functioning as experts; but the Hesiod example above and many others one could think of (modern musical competitions for piano, singing etc.) contradict this, since it is perfectly possible in practice for experts in music and other skills to compete in their capacity as skilled experts.

However that may be, there is a more fundamental problem with S.'s argument here: there is no reason to suppose, as does S., that the unjust person's *pleonexia* is necessarily simply an ignorance of the 'professional' parameters of the just person's skill, as implied in the argument (stage 4 above). The unjust person may be playing a different game altogether: he may not aim to 'outdo' other people in the professional sense, but to 'get the better' of them, have 'more than his fair share' (another meaning of *pleonektein*); i.e. exercise greater power.

Underlying this unsatisfactory argument is S.'s assumption that justice and injustice can be treated as *technai* ('skills') – the 'craft analogy' – and that the just person shows greater wisdom in the skill of justice than the unjust. However, the weakness of arguing that justice is a *technē* has already been exposed by S. in the dialogue with Polemarchus (331e1–336a10), and it is therefore unclear how much weight Plato intends the argument to bear here (despite the absence of specific reference to *technē,* the 'craft analogy' is clearly, albeit implicitly, operating).

The general absence of objection to the stages of the argument, especially stages 6 and 7, from the otherwise combative T. may relate to an underlying unwillingness by the celebrated sophist to object to a line of reasoning which is, on the face of it, congenial to him in apparently emphasising the wisdom of professionals; T. does not realise the danger of this line of argument for his case until too late (with some doubt possibly indicated in his less than enthusiastic assent to some of S.'s questions, *e.g.* 350b9, b12, c6). Alternatively, T.'s agreement may relate to an increasing lack of serious engagement with S. indicated in the preliminaries to the argument at 349a4–b1 (see note on 349a5, and immediately below, 350d9–e4). On analysis and assessment of the argument see Cross & Woozley 51–3; Irwin (1995) 177–8; Annas 50–2; Beversluis 237–9.

350c12–352d2

T.'s agreement to the above argument is barely established (see the 'two versions' of the argument sequence referred to at 350c12 and note), and in the course of another interlude he and S. engage in a discussion of the conduct of the argument paralleling that with Glaucon at 348a7f. T.'s reluctance to cooperate seriously with S. is apparent, while S.'s appeal to the 'sincerity' factor (e.g.350 e5ff.) is even more half-hearted than usual. S. then embarks on a totally different line of argument focussing on T.'s assertion that injustice is more powerful than justice (stated at the end of T.'s key speech at 344c4–8). S. advances a counter-argument that, in order to have any power – to the limited extent of achieving objectives – unjust cities, armies or any other group must have justice within their society in order to achieve basic mutual cooperation. This principle extends to relationships between two persons and even, to avoid disharmony, within the single individual. So justice is more powerful than injustice.

350c12   Now Thrasymachus' agreement to all this did not come easily...: It is striking that S.'s statement here in his narrator role seems to indicate two versions of the conduct of the recent argument, the one indicating T.'s general agreement he narrates, presumably, for the sake of clarity, and the other in which S. informs us afterwards that T. put up some kind of resistance, though we cannot know whether this was intended by Plato to indicate merely prevarication or (more unlikely) to include any of the objections noted in the analysis of the argument above, note on 349e1–350c11.

d3   Thrasymachus blushing: an indication of shame at the social humiliation of being worsted in what the sophist perceives as a competitive situation (cf. *Euthydemus* 297a), rather than a reaction to climactic conditions. But T.'s following reply does not sound like an admission of defeat. The marked emphasis on T.'s physical and emotional reaction at this point seems almost designed to make the reader forget the patent (and perhaps deliberate?) weakness of the preceding argument.

d9–e1   'I know very well you would accuse me of ranting: S.'s opponents regularly protest at being compelled to adopt S.'s preferred method of discussion (arranged on this occasion by S. and Glaucon over T.'s head, see n. on 348a7–b3 above) rather than being allowed to debate in their preferred manner of making a speech at length (*makrologia*), as T. did earlier at 343b–344c, cf. *Protagoras* 335a. 'Ranting' (*dēmēgorein:* literally, 'acting like a demagogue') imports the pejorative connotations which Plato regularly gives to the word, with its implications of popular persuasive oratory by unofficial leaders in the democratic Assembly. On Athenian demagogues, see Finley.

e1–4   'So either allow me to say as much as I want...nod and shake my head: T's withdrawal from genuine involvement in S.'s *elenchus* is similar to that of Callicles, S.'s other major opponent, in *Gorgias* 501c7–8; here the comparison with 'old wives' tales' makes it more marked, and completely undercuts S.'s subsequent half-hearted request for sincerity (S.'s e8–9 effectively amounts to 'Have it your own way'). This exchange marks the final breakdown in cooperation between them, which S.'s subsequent ironic compliments on T's answers (351c2–6, d6) only serve to emphasise.

e6   'Yes, I will', he replied, 'to please you...: T.'s response is clearly asserting, against S.'s request, that he will speak against his own belief, since S.'s method of discussion gives him no choice ('to please you' is heavily sarcastic). See Guthrie (1969) 90 n. 4 (and note that Lee (1987) has noted a revision in his translation (2nd ed.) in response to Guthrie's interpretation).

351b1 '...would you say that a city is unjust to try to enslave other cities unjustly...?: this inaugurates a new, and in many ways more promising, line of argument by switching from micro- to macro- level, which anticipates S.'s procedure in the development of the positive discussion of the ideal *polis* in Book 2.368cff.

c3   'I really admire you...: it is hard not to see sarcasm here, and in c6 below '...well done you!' (and also d7).

d3   '...for injustice surely breeds dissension, hatreds and fighting among each other, whereas justice brings concord and friendship...: there is an unstated assumption behind this whole argument, namely that effective action among *e.g.* criminals must depend on justice; but fear of a leader or mutual dependence to avoid capture are equally plausible candidates for social cohesion of a gang in the perpetration of injustice on others outside their organisation (see *e.g.* Cross and Woozley 56). This argument also ignores the point that T. has been making all along – the effectiveness of the individual unjust person, the all-powerful tyrant (unless we anticipate the argument of the later *Republic* and give weight to the application of injustice to the parts of the individual person – but see below note on e7). There is also a further and more fundamental problem with S.'s argument: an unacknowledged 'slide' from discussion of the action of the group taken as a whole to the behaviour of individual members of the group towards each other (351d4ff.), and the assumption that 'the attributes of a group are...grounded in the attributes of the members of that group' (Inwood 101), which makes the argument with T. appear to work and also reflects a deeper problem in *Republic* as a whole (see esp. Book 4.444a–e). See further, Introduction p. 22).

d8–9   '...among free or slave...: we should not read too much here into S.'s inclusion of slaves in the argument; this is simply a conventional polar expression to emphasise universality of reference (cf. 'gods and men').

e7   '...what if injustice arises within one person...?: this instance is clearly not susceptible to the objections stated above, note on d3, but it only makes sense as part of a theory of internal harmony in the individual person, which does not enter the discussion until Book 4. In *Crito* Socrates claims that injustice harms the soul and in *Gorgias* Plato identifies justice with order in the soul, but at this stage in *Republic* S. has not yet mentioned the soul and, since he has not argued either for the individual as a multiplicity of parts, this argument can only be described as 'unconvincing rhetoric' (Annas 53). S. does have an answer to T., but not yet. However, one could read this argument 'proleptically', i.e. as an anticipation of subsequent argument in *Republic* Book 4 (as does *e.g.* Allan note *ad loc.* and Kahn (1993) 138–9). It should be noted, however, that the 'macro-micro' analogy continues to be a stumbling-block for S. in the later *Republic* (see Inwood 98ff., Williams).

352a11 '...the gods too are just?: it is not clear what, if anything, this adds to the argument; denial of the gods' moral status, or even of their existence, was a common sophistic position (see Kerferd (1981) 163ff.). One might have expected a straight denial from T. (the historical T. may well have argued that the gods are not concerned with justice (DK85B8; for full ref. see the end of the note above on 339c10). Here Plato is clearly not willing to interrupt the argument at this point to go down *that* side-alley; the morally equivocal status of the gods is argued by Adeimantus in Book 2 (see below 362eff.), but S. only really deals with the theological argument in the 'Myth of Er' in Book 10, 614bff. Here, T. simply maintains a marked neutrality in his answers at b1 and b4–5.

b4 '...feast on your argument with good cheer...': T. reintroduces the feast imagery (cf. the setting of the dialogue, 327a-328b) in order to emphasise the purely formal nature of his agreement with S.'s argument, and perhaps also to signify that he at least wants to wrap things up. The image of S. as the self-indulgent diner is reintroduced by S. himself, against himself, at the end of Book 1 (354b1ff.).

b7 'The fact is that the just...: in the Greek the first word of the sentence, ὅτι ('that'), has no main verb, and the straggling sentence effectively goes on until d1, resumed with ταῦτα μὲν οὖν...('Now this [i.e. all that has gone before since b7] is how I understand...').

c4 'But it is clear that there was some justice in them...: S. is arguing here for a minimal idea of justice even among evil groups as a kind of cohesive force, which must exist in some form within all organised bodies of people to enable them to function at all; but, besides the objections mentioned above (notes on 351d3 and e7), such an idea is not really strong enough on its own to support S.'s continual association of justice with wisdom and goodness.

352d2–354c3

Assuming that, despite T.'s minimal cooperation, he has by now established that the just are wise and good, S. goes on to ask whether they have a better life – reiterating the often repeated Socratic imperative (*e.g. Apology, Gorgias*), that the discussion is about a matter of the highest importance: how one ought to live. He uses an argument from function (*ergon*): everything, animal, part of the body, activity, has a function by means of which it can do what it is designed to do better than by means of anything else. Each of the things for which there is a particular function can also be said to have an excellence (*aretē*), which enables it to perform its function as well as possible. Like other things the human soul has a function (living) and an excellence, which is justice. The just person, therefore, lives well and is happy (*eudaimōn*), the unjust the reverse. Since it pays to be happy rather than miserable, it pays to be just. T.'s automatic responses do not impede this argument, but his final sarcastic comment at 354a10 does elicit S.'s admission that, like a greedy diner at the feast, he has been over-hasty in reaching his conclusions. The Book appears to end in a manner characteristic of the earlier Socratic dialogues, i.e. impasse (*aporia*).

352d2–4 '...whether the just have a better life than the unjust and are happier: *eudaimōn* ('happy') in Greek has a more objective connotation than the psychological state implied by the English translation (see Introduction, p. 3 n.5 ; for S. the 'happiness' of individuals is intimately connected with the way they choose to live their lives (see following note).

d6–7 'For the discussion is not about an incidental matter, but about the way we ought to live: this marks the move from considering the general effects of justice/injustice to a more specific argument about their nature and operation. The urgent expression of concern about how one should live is almost formulaic in Plato (cf. *Apology* 38a, *Crito* 48b *Republic* 344e2–3) and S.'s use of the phrase 'the way we ought to live' (*hontina tropon chrē zdēn*) heralds in *Gorgias* 500c3–4 (with virtually identical wording) an increasingly serious moral tone in the discussion with Callicles, leading to a theological climax in a myth which reveals that what happens to the individual after death is commensurate with behaviour during life; the comparable 'climax' of *Republic* is, of course, much further off (in Book 10), and any anticipation, in the phrase, of an approaching 'closure' within Book 1 is a (deliberately?) false signal to the reader.

d9–354a9 S.'s concluding argument of Book 1 uses two key concepts: *ergon* ('function') and *aretē* ('excellence') and makes characteristically broad analogies between different types of things which possess an *ergon* and *aretē*: senses, implements, the soul. The *ergon* is the activity for which there is a best or only instrument, and the *aretē* the best realisation of this *ergon* (the idea was briefly aired in *Meno* 72a by Meno in reply to S.'s request for a definition of *aretē*). Socrates' argument here can be expressed in tabular form thus:

organ /implement	function (*ergon*)	excellence (*aretē*) / defect (*kakia*)
eyes	sight	seeing well/badly (being blind)
ears	hearing	hearing well/badly (being deaf)
pruning knife	cutting a vine shoot	doing the job well/badly
soul	living (caring, ruling, deliberating)	justice /injustice

The validity of these analogies might be challenged immediately on the grounds that the human soul does not have an agreed and clearly-defined function in the sense that eyes and pruning-knives do. But S. is clearly assuming that it does (for Plato *ergon* is broader than 'function' – it is simply what the given thing does best), and from this flows his argument that the excellence (good performance) in the function of the human soul is justice.

The analogy between the function of objects/organs, where the excellence consists uncontroversially in the most efficient performance of activities, and human function, allows S. to avoid debating at this stage of *Republic* whether the soul actually does behave like these other instances and in fact has, as its excellence, justice. S. claims at 353e7–8 that he and T. have previously agreed this, but at no point has this been the case, unless S. is referring to 350c10, where S. 'proves' that the just person is good and wise – by no means the same thing – and S.'s report of this at 350 d4–5 '...we did reach agreement that justice is excellence and wisdom....' is not in the actual argument. A more acute or involved T. might have countered at 353e9 by questioning this vital step, without which S.'s argument fails; T. might have staged a comeback by asserting that it is equally plausible to argue that the 'excellence' of the function of living is (as he earlier implied) injustice, in the sense that the wholly unjust person can most efficiently attain his version of 'living well', i.e. prosperous wickedness (see Cross and Woozley, 58).

S. and T. both agree on certain basic positions (which were very deeply embedded in Greek ethics): that a choice of how to live should be profitable to the chooser, and that it is profitable to attain 'happiness' (*eudaimonia*) – as T. says at 354a7, in answer to S.'s statement (a6) that '...it does not pay to be miserable but happy (*eudaimōn*)', 'Of course'. Where they fundamentally disagree is over the nature of the life which produces this profit and leads to this *eudaimonia*. T.'s withdrawal from serious discussion possibly reflects Plato's awareness of the impossibility of a meaningful solution of this disagreement by following the Socratic method of the *elenchus*. At this point S. and T. have little more to say to each other. A radical change of argumentative method is required.

353d3 '...take the soul – does it have a function which you could perform with nothing else in the world...?: The Greeks regarded the *psuche* as that part of the human being which contained the life-force, which left the body at death to exist in a ghost-like state in the Underworld. For Plato, however, the soul was much more; it represented the essence of the person, his/her moral value, that part which was affected by the way in which the life of the individual was conducted (see above note to 351e7). S.'s move to the soul (*psuche*) is here depicted casually, although it is actually the whole point of the argument from analogy; the assumptions S. brings with the word guarantee the success of his demonstration: the soul is the part of the person that matters, and for 'living well' (in the Socratic sense) the soul is not only the best but the only instrument.

e12 '...according to your argument: S. is in the habit of using this phrase to force 'ownership' of the conclusions of the *elenchus* on his interlocutors. Here T. turns the tables, and clearly indicates his dissociation from S.'s conclusions.

354a10 'Well, let these conclusions be your feast...at the festival of Bendis: by sarcastically reintroducing the theme of the feast which has framed this final argument of S. (see 352b4 above), T. confirms, despite his apparent agreement, his dissatisfaction with S.'s arguments and implies that S.'s dialectic is distinguished chiefly by its entertainment value – S. has given everybody a 'holiday treat' (Lycos 41). Mention of the festival during which the conversation is taking place, and which the company is ostensibly planning to attend after dinner (see above 358a7–8), also serves to give Book 1 a false indication of approaching closure.

a12–b1 'Provided by you, Thrasymachus...now that you have become gentler...I have not feasted well, however...: completion of an interlocutor's syntax in order to cap his remark is common in Platonic dialogue, and typical of an element of one-upmanship often lurking in the discussion. Here, S. turns the tables on T. yet again by urbanely adding to T's remarks the rider that the 'feast' of arguments to which T. has given such reluctant assent are in fact T.'s own (and not S.'s, as T. asserted above at 353e12). The falsity of S.'s assertion is surely on this occasion particularly, and intentionally, transparent in view of T.'s passive role, especially in the latter part of his discussion with S. ('gentler' is heavily ironic). But S. then turns the 'feasting' jibe on himself by presenting himself as a greedy diner, while simultaneously suggesting, again with a degree of irony, that he has not sufficiently savoured the meal provided by T. Ownership of the arguments is passed back and forth between them like a tennis ball, each trying to attribute them to the other.

b3–6 '...before discovering what we were first investigating, what justice is, I let that subject drop in my rush to consider whether it is badness and ignorance or wisdom and excellence: as the discussion has progressed there has been a blurring of the distinction between saying what justice is (*e.g.* 'giving back to someone what is owed' 331c1ff.) and discussion of examples/properties of it (for Polemarchus' probable confusion between the two, see above note on 331e3). From S.'s request at the breakdown of the *elenchus* with Polemarchus at 336a10 ('...what else can anyone suggest that [justice] is?') we move to Socrates' statements: from 347eff. ('the life of the just person is more profitable'), to 350dff. ('justice is strong'), to 354a8–9 ('justice is more profitable than injustice'). This tendency to move from essence to properties is inherent in the *elenchus* method, partly arising from the ambiguity of 'is' in saying 'X is Y' (essence or property?). Underlying what S. says here about his own shortcomings is Plato's conviction that they are going to get no further in studying the essence of justice and the just by using this method; progress is only to be made by attempting a completely different approach to the subject.

* * * * * * * * * * * * * *

The multi-layered irony at the beginning of this final speech of S. underlines the unsatisfactory nature of the discussion. S.'s conclusion of *aporia* and his confession of failure is very similar to the conclusion of many of the earlier dialogues (*e.g. Charmides* 175b–76a), but the present instance is distinguished by S.'s unusually frank analysis of his own shortcomings and his conclusion: '...the current outcome of our enquiry is that I don't know anything' (b9–c1). Here there is an element of truth underlying S.'s customary *eirōneia*; he has not enjoyed the encounter with T. because he is conscious that he has not dealt adequately with the latter's case for injustice (hence the reluctance of either of them to 'own' the later arguments). T., a much more forceful and convincing opponent than any S. has previously met, has only conceded a formal defeat. S.'s transition from the optimistic conclusion of the apparently successful *elenchus* to self-confessed failure is abrupt and surely a deliberate strain on our credulity – we are meant to be uneasy at the paradox implied in such an inadequate closure (see further, Introduction p. 25).

But Plato clearly intends another angle on the discussion: the final arguments advanced by S. against T. (351b1–54a9), while, as we have seen, questionable in the immediate context, also look forward in a larger perspective, with the discussion of the *aretē* of the soul (353d3–e10), to the positive dialectic of remainder of *Republic,* a binding-in, as it were, of Book I with the remainder of the dialogue. The transition from Book 1 to the rest of *Republic* is further supplied by the more sustained and reasoned attack on S.'s position from Glaucon and his brother Adeimantus which follows in the first part of Book 2 to which we now turn.

BOOK 2

357a1–358e3

The discussion unexpectedly resumes: Glaucon has hitherto been largely silent with the exception of the single passage for him as interlocutor at 347a6–e7, when he agreed with S. that the just life is more profitable than the unjust. Nevertheless he now professes himself dissatisfied with S.'s victory over Thrasymachus. If S. wishes to persuade (as opposed to seeming to do so) that it is better to be just than unjust he needs to bring more convincing arguments to bear. G. outlines three categories of good, and gives examples of each: 1. things good for their own sake; 2. things good for their own sake and for their consequences; 3. things good only for their consequences. S. puts justice as a good in category 2.; G. retorts that most people would place it in 3., i.e. as not good in itself but good only for its consequences. Thrasymachus, according to G., has been too easily 'charmed' into submission. In order to hear justice being praised 'in and for itself' G. will act as devil's advocate and exert himself to oppose S. by reviving Thrasymachus' argument by praising the unjust life: stating first what it is and how it arises, secondly, that the just life is practised unwillingly, and thirdly, that this is reasonable, since the life of the unjust person is better than the just (that is to say, in the recent Book 1 discussion Thrasymachus was right and S. wrong). This procedure is agreed.

357a1   ...I thought I had been released from the discussion: for the recurring theme of S.'s 'release from argument' as marking key movements in the structure of the dialogue, see above note on 327c10–11.

a1–2   ...but it was after all, apparently, only a prelude: S. as narrator expresses dramatically the unpremeditated nature of the continuation (see above note on 328a7–9). *Prooimion* ('prelude') is used of a formal introduction to a larger work, a musical prelude or introduction to a lyric poem, or the exordium of a prose speech. Plato here begins to reveal the formal position of Book 1 in the structure of the whole *Republic.*

a2–3   ...Glaucon, who always proves himself very bold in everything...: he has already intervened uninvited at 347a6; his characterisation here as 'very bold' reflects the major and, in the dramatic structure of the Platonic dialogues, unprecedented role he is about to play in the immediate continuation, where, followed by his brother Adeimantus, he temporarily takes the initiative away from S. in mounting a comprehensive attack on S.'s position concerning justice. G.'s assertive and ambitious nature (*philonikia*) is alluded to by his brother at *Republic* 548d9, and, for evidence of this and his strong political ambitions, see Xenophon, *Memorabilia* 3.6.

a4–b2   'Socrates, do you want the appearance or the reality...?: the introduction of this dichotomy is a negative comment on the ostensibly successful conclusion of the Book 1 *elenchus,* which is, by implication, G.'s target here. As G. goes on to imply, it is not so much the conclusions of Book 1 but rather the method itself which is under suspicion: it produces only *seeming* truths. The 'truth/seeming' (*alētheia / doxa*) polarity, hitherto not explicit in the discussion, assumes a prominent role in this section, foreshadowing its cardinal importance in the remainder of *Republic.*

b4ff.   *The three classes of good.* The tripartite classification outlined here by G. is unparalleled in Plato, and, on the face of it, poses a problem for modern philosophers, who in moral argument are accustomed to working, roughly speaking, with variations on a two-fold classification: 1. a belief that one has a moral obligation to choose the good for its own sake irrespective of consequences (normally called 'deontological', associated with the eighteenth century German philosopher Kant), and, contrary to this, 2. a belief that a moral choice should be guided by its consequences (Utilitarianism, associated with the eighteenth –nineteenth century English thinkers Jeremy Bentham and John Stuart Mill). Problematic is G.'s second category, which initially seems to straddle these contradictory alternatives, in suggesting that certain types of good should be loved both for themselves *and* for their consequences (see Annas 60ff.). One way out of the dilemma has been suggested by Terence Irwin (Irwin (1999) 166–7): by describing justice as having happiness as a consequence, Plato was not implying a purely 'efficient-causal relation' between justice and happiness; rather, justice was to be seen as a *component* of happiness rather than an *instrumental means* to it (167), and this kind of consequence would not logically exclude the idea of a good 'in and of itself'.

It is notable that Socrates, when asked where he would place justice, immediately, and without hesitation, chooses the whole of this second category: he asserts that justice is a good both in itself *and* for the future happiness of the individual (358a1–3). This points forward to the development of his theory of justice later in *Republic,* culminating in the account of the fate of just/unjust souls in the afterlife in the 'Myth of Er' (614b2ff.). S., however, throughout the bulk of *Republic,* concentrates on defending the desirability of justice in and for itself, which is precisely what Glaucon claims S. has not addressed adequately in Book 1. So both Glaucon and Adeimantus, in order to provoke S. into a proper reply, wish to put the strongest possible 'devil's advocate' case for justice as a category 3. good, i.e. good not in itself but *only for its consequences*, which, they claim, is 'what most people think' about justice (358a4).

c7   '...practising one's profession as a doctor and making money generally...we would not consent to have them for their own sake but for the financial rewards and other things which result from them: S. has already argued in the previous Book (341c5) that, on the contrary, doctors and other professionals practise not for the sake of money or other reward, but for the object of their skill, patients etc. Thrasymachus did not accept his arguments then (343b1ff.), and here, apparently, neither does G., since he puts doctoring into category 3. and not into 2.

358a8–9 '...I'm rather a bad pupil...: this is S.'s familiar stance, with varying degrees of irony, of someone who knows little or nothing and who therefore needs to learn from his interlocutors; this occurs as a motif throughout the dialogue, *e.g.* 337d4, to Thrasymachus (there, clearly ironic) and notably at the end of Book 1 where the tone is more equivocal (see 354a12–b1, and note). Here it prepares us naturally for G.'s speech in which S. is uncharacteristically a listener (though the tone of S.'s interjections is significant – see below notes on 361d4–6, 368a1ff.).

b1   'Come then...hear also what I have to say...: this degree of formality marks a prelude to what amounts to an *epideixis* ('display oration': compare Thrasymachus' prelude at 338c2). G. shows an assertiveness and authoritative manner which is rare in the dialogues among S.'s interlocutors, and marks G. (and shortly his brother Adeimantus) out for a special role in this transitional part of *Republic.* (It is notable that, following their speeches, G. and A., though remaining prominent, are returned by Plato to a largely conventional 'Socratic interlocutor' role, not without some assertive interjections, for the rest of *Republic.*)

b2–3   'For Thrasymachus appears to me to have given in to you before he really needed to, like a snake you have charmed: on Thrasymachus' grudging assent to S.'s arguments in Book 1, see above note on 350e1–4; none of the participants, including S., seems to believe that this capitulation was genuine or even necessary. S.'s ability to persuade his interlocutors at a non-rational level is frequently alluded to by Plato, and criticised, using a number of images from nature (cf. *Meno* 80aff. – S. as the 'sting-ray fish' who numbs his opponents into agreement). His ability to use words to charm (*kēlein*), as musicians use instruments, is expounded by Alcibiades in *Symposium* 215c.

b4–6   '...for I want to hear what each of them is, and what power it has in and of itself, dwelling in the soul, and to leave aside the financial rewards and what comes from them : the first part of G.'s category 2.; justice as the kind of good we love for itself is what G. wants defended here, and in practice what S. argues for throughout most of the rest of the dialogue, cf. esp. the discussion of justice as the harmony of the individual soul (*psuchē*) in Book 4. The power (*dunamis*) of justice and injustice is what each possesses innately, irrespective of social ('artificial') consequences, such as prestige, money etc. The discussion of the good (natural) consequences of justice (the second part of G.'s category 2. is effectively postponed until the end of the dialogue, and the fate of the souls of humans in the afterlife (612bff.).

b8ff. **'This will be my procedure…first…Secondly…thirdly:** G. begins by formally outlining the plan of his *epideixis*, (a structure to which he faithfully adheres throughout his speech). This continuous exposition on a given topic proposed by G. (a hallmark of the sophists which S. regularly makes fun of in the dialogues, *e.g.* Protagoras in *Protagoras* 320c-329b), stands in stark contrast to S.'s conversational method in the previous Book.

c5–6 **'…as people say. Though, Socrates, that's not at all how I see it myself:** G., though, as we shall see, taking much of his case from known sophistic expositions of the topic, roots his argument in 'what people say' (common opinion). This arguing against his personal conviction makes it clear that G., like many of the sophists themselves, is simply 'putting a case' (for the sophistic penchant and ability to argue on either side of a case, see the anonymous sophistic treatise *Double Arguments, in The First Philosophers*, 285ff.). For G.'s earlier (unargued) support for S.'s position against Thrasymachus, see above note on 347e7.

c6–d1 **'Yet I feel at a loss with my ears ringing, when I hear the arguments of Thrasymachus and of countless others…:** another image for the non-rational effect of argument (see above n. on b2–3). This is reminiscent of the image of the arguments of the Laws of Athens against S.'s escape from prison ringing in Crito's ears and excluding all others, at the conclusion of *Crito* (54d). Note, however, that on this occasion it is Thrasymachus' and not (as in b2–3) S.'s arguments which have this effect on G., and T. is backed up by 'countless others' (c7–d1). A clear indication that, whatever his personal conviction, G. thinks there is a serious case to answer.

d5 **'Therefore I am going to exert myself and speak in praise of the unjust life…:** for 'praise' and 'blame' as a traditional form of sophistic advocacy, and its generic transformation by Plato, see Nightingale 93–132 (esp.132 n. 100); Ausland 125.

d9 **'Nothing could suit me better…:** G.'s assertive but non-confrontational approach elicits an equally conciliatory response from S., especially since G. has taken the trouble to dissociate himself personally from the position he is arguing for – people's egos are not on the line here as they were in Book 1 with Thrasymachus. It is notable, however, how easily S. abandons the *elenchus* method and appears to accept his part in the proposal for paired oppositional speeches – though, of course, his 'censuring of injustice and praise of justice' from section 368 onwards is something quite different from what any of the participants can envisage at this stage.

358e4–360d8

G. tackles the first part of his proposed argument: what justice is and how it arises. The popular view is that justice is a compromise between the best outcome, committing injustice, and the worst, suffering the effects of others' unjust acts. Laws are nothing more than compacts made between people who are not powerful enough to do injustice with impunity and correspondingly wish to avoid the effects on themselves of others' injustice. Justice is therefore not good in itself, since no-one with sufficient power to commit injustice with impunity would choose the option of being just. The story of the 'ancestor of Gyges the Lydian' demonstrates this point.

358e4   '**Now, you see, people say that to commit injustice is naturally good…:** in relating injustice to nature G. , in best lecture-room style, puts his discourse firmly in the fifth/fourth century sophistic tradition of opposing *physis* (nature) to *nomos* (law, or convention), notable in the statements of Antiphon the Sophist in the late 5th century (*The First Philosophers*, p. 284), broadened out by G. so that he is effectively representing Thrasymachus' argument as general opinion (n.b. his continual reminder that this is not his personal view, but 'what people say', *e.g.* at 359a3, b7). So S., when his turn comes to reply to G., will face a double challenge: he will have to attack a position which is allegedly held by most people *and* tackle it on their terms, i.e. he will have to show that justice, and not injustice, is good *by nature*.

e5–6   '**…the excess of evil involved in being a victim of injustice is greater than the good involved in committing it…:** the balance of antithetical clauses in this initial part of G.'s speech, mirroring the polarity of the victim/aggressor, is particularly marked in the Greek: πλέονι δὲ κακῷ ὑπερβάλλειν τὸ ἀδικεῖσθαι ἢ ἀγαθῷ τὸ ἀδικεῖν etc. Style matches content, suggesting a light parody of the forced oppositions in the rhetorical style of the sophist Gorgias (*e.g. Encomium of Helen,* in *The First Philosophers* p. 228ff., *e.g.* 'For there is no difference between…criticizing the praiseworthy and praising the blameworthy…').

359a2–3 '**From this basis…they begin to make laws and covenants with each other…:** there is a clear reference to the sophistic version of the 'social contract' theory of the origins of civilisation, implicit in *e.g.* Protagoras (*The First Philosophers,* pp. 217–19). G. here puts himself, for the sake of the argument, on the side of those who wish to emphasise the artificiality of justice as arising from *nomos* (law); he presents it simply as covenants (*sunthēkas,* a3) between those too weak to follow nature (*physis*) and exercise unlimited power, and who therefore wish to avoid becoming the victims of it (an idea already outlined by Callicles in *Gorgias,* 483eff.). On the general sophistic background of *nomos* and *physis*, and the social contract, see Guthrie (1969) 55–134. The idea of 'mutual fear' rather than goodwill being the cause of social cooperation has a long history: see especially the 17th century A.D. English philosopher Thomas Hobbes.

b9–c1 '**We would most effectively grasp the point…if we were to explore the following idea. Imagine…:** P. has G. reinforce his point by imagining what would happen 'if we made the following thought-experiment', Laird's translation of τοιόνδε ποιήσαμεν τῇ διανοίᾳ (Laird 20–1), which brings out the hypothetical nature of what follows. S. might subsequently have chosen to claim that G.'s scenario is flawed from the start by its very unreality, since individuals almost never have unlimited power, but he doesn't; he sets out to show that people would naturally choose justice as a good *even* in the unlikely event that they could do whatever they wished (Annas 69–70), and at the end of *Republic*, in a specific reference back to G.'s scenario, believes he has shown this to be true (10.612b2–4). The idea of people naturally gravitating towards *physis* (doing whatever they wish) when no social or physical constraints are present is found in Antiphon the Sophist (see n. on 358e4 above) and argued for by Polus and Callicles in Plato's *Gorgias* (468eff., 482eff.).

c3–5   'We should then catch the just person red-handed resorting to the same activities as the unjust, impelled by the greed which all nature naturally pursues as a good thing...: a direct contradiction of S.'s argument in Book 1 (349e1ff.) where he argued that 'greed' (*pleonexia*) will not be pursued by the person who is good and just. This, says G., is only because those who practise justice are artificially limited through lacking the capacity to do as they really wish.

d1–2   '...the power which they say was once possessed by †the ancestor of Gyges the Lydian†: this is a celebrated textual crux, the last words here obelized. Herodotus tells the story of Gyges (early 7th century), the founder of the Mermnad dynasty of Lydian kings (1. 8–13); Lydia was a powerful kingdom in West Asia Minor, having contacts with the Greeks of the 7th and 6th centuries. The latter part of Gyges' story (1.11–12) contains some details which correspond to the latter part of Plato's account here, and many scholars have supposed that Plato must be referring to Herodotus' Gyges rather than, as the text appears to indicate, his ancestor (a view strengthened by S.'s reference back to Gyges, rather than any ancestor, in *Republic* 10.612b, when recalling the story in order to claim to have refuted G.). It has also been supposed that both Plato and Herodotus are drawing on a common source with folktale elements, and possibly two versions of the story; hence the discrepancy in detail within a broadly similar framework (Smith 361–87). Many attempts have been made to emend the text here to refer to Herodotus' Gyges and so bring this passage into line with 612b, none of them particularly satisfactory (see Adam, Appendix to Book 2; Slings (1989) 381–83); against Proclus (5th century A.D.), who quotes from the unamended text, we need to note Cicero (*De Officiis,* 3.38) who, in recalling the story, clearly refers to 'Gyges' and not some ancestor.

d5   'Amazed at the sight he climbed down...: the theme of descent (*katabasis*) to see what is beyond normal human knowledge, links this story with the 'Myth of Er' at the end of the dialogue at 614bff. (Hollander). Gyges, like Er, has the privilege of return after the descent, but unlike Er, arguably fails to gain any moral insight from the experience.

d9–e1   '...wearing nothing else, but with a gold ring on its finger: it is not entirely clear if the Greek means that the corpse is naked (most translators assume this, reading ἔχειν in e1, the exceptions being Shorey and Lee). Cicero, *De Officiis, 3.38,* merely states that Gyges removed the ring which was on the corpse's finger.

360a7–b1   'As soon as he became aware of this, he immediately arranged to become one of the messengers who went to the king...: if Plato is drawing on the morality of the Herodotus story here (argued by Laird, 16–17), G.'s case against justice is perhaps strengthened by the fact that in the Herodotus story Gyges, for all his expressed misgivings (Herodotus 1.8.3–4), nevertheless chooses the expedient (over the just) path by killing the king rather than being himself killed on the orders of the queen. But in G.'s account of the palace coup here, the only part of the story which recalls Herodotus (360b1–3), the object-lesson G. intends is even clearer, since in Plato's version Gyges faces no moral dilemma of the kind dramatised by Herodotus, where he begs the queen not to force him to make such a difficult choice; on the contrary, in Plato he is the instigator of the murder of the king rather than, as in Herodotus, the unwilling co-conspirator, and the queen's role is subordinate. Moreover, while still with his fellow-shepherds, he already recognises the potential of invisibility (there is no magical ring in Herodotus), and he immediately on his own initiative puts in train a plan to use it to gain absolute power. The power conferred by invisibility and how it frees people to do as they really wish is the key point G. wishes to make in telling this version of the story; it may be significant that despite the wide provenance of the motif of the ring of invisibility in *e.g.* Germanic and Norse mythology, we know of no extant sources in Greek legend before Plato (Smith 268 n. 2). So Plato, better to support G.'s argument, may have invented a key detail, or possibly have drawn it from sources other than Herodotus and unknown to us.

b9–c3   **'...being capable of taking from the market-place whatever he wanted with impunity. He could go into houses and seduce anyone he pleased...behaving like a god among humans:** this is the licence traditionally attributed to the person with absolute power in Greek society, the tyrant (see *e.g. Gorgias* 469cff., *Republic* 576cff.). G. indicates the kind of unjust acts which would be open to both the unjust and the (seemingly) just person in the *polis*, significantly covering both public and private areas of life, outlining the social range of justice which he believes S.'s counter-argument will have to address. 'Behaving like a god' indicates the amoral power of Greek deities as traditionally conceived and may be, as Adam suggests (Adam, note *ad loc.*), an anticipation of Plato's attack on popular theology in Books 2–3.

c6–7   **'...no-one is voluntarily just...:** (*oudeis hekōn dikaios*) a direct reversal, surely deliberate, given the similar wording, of the famous Socratic paradox 'no-one does wrong voluntarily' (*oudeis hekōn hamartanei*). See *e.g. Apology* 25d, *Hippias Minor* 376b, *Protagoras* 358c.

d5–6   **'...he would be regarded as most miserable and foolish by observers, though in front of each other they would commend him...:** G. emphasises the hypocrisy of those who in public commend the just person for abstaining from wrong, but really despise him; their real opinion makes it clear that they would not hesitate to act unjustly if they were not constrained by the fear of being victims.

d8   **'So this covers that point:** note G.'s formal argumentative style. The point refers back to 359b7ff., where the argument that justice is practised unwillingly began.

360d8–362c8

G. takes his 'thought experiment' a stage further; in order to expose the real value of justice and injustice he strips from the unjust and just person all the usual consequences of their respective choices: he assumes, for the sake of argument, that the unjust person is able entirely to escape the bad consequences of his actions, and indeed on the contrary to have a perfect reputation for justice, and that the just person is exactly opposite – though just, he has a reputation for injustice. Moreover, both may be imagined to suffer the results of their popular reputations; the just person, supposed unjust, suffers great torment, whereas the unjust person reaps all the rewards of his seeming justice. G.'s argument aims therefore to demonstrate that, when both are described with the opposite consequences for each which he has outlined, injustice must deliver a better life than justice.
In this section note:–

1. Plato's emphasis on the highly formalised structure; the speech has a symmetrical 'chiastic' (ABBA) structure: unjust person's behaviour (360d8–61b5) followed by just's behaviour (361b5–d3) / just's fate (361e4) followed by unjust's fate (362a4–c6).

2. The close parallels, in G.'s reformulation, with Thrasymachus' argument for injustice at 343b1–344c9, esp. in the social consequences for the just / unjust persons.

360e1–2 '...if we distinguish the extremes of just and unjust...: G. continues in hypothetical mode (see n. above on 359b9–c1) to expand the 'Ring of Gyges' idea. In order to complete setting up the issue he wishes S. to address, he must divest justice of all its good consequences and imagine the worst possible fate for the just person and the best possible outcome for the unjust (Gyges as the happiest and most successful of kings, one might suppose). This removes the 'artificial' consequences of just and unjust conduct (i.e. social approval/disapproval), leaving justice/injustice to be judged on their own merits. S. will subsequently have to show that *even in these extreme circumstances* justice is preferable to injustice.

e6–7   'let him operate as clever skilled professionals do – for example as a first-rate navigator or a doctor...: G. is here combining two ideas from Book 1: 1. at 342c–e, S. argued against Thrasymachus that experts like the doctor and the ship's captain do not ever act in their own interest but only in the interest of those for whose benefit they exercise their skill; 2. T. had previously conceded (340d–341a) that rulers, strictly defined, do not make mistakes. G.'s perfectly unjust person is by implication an expert who has skill or art (*technē* e7); so, by combining here an implied denial of 1. (he claims, against S., that skilled professionals act in their own interest) with an acceptance of 2. (the genuinely skilled are infallible), G. turns S.'s Book 1 argument about the nature of technical expertise (and by implication, justice) on its head: the perfectly unjust person is an 'inverted Socratic' (see note on 339c1ff.), unerring in his 'expert' ability to judge the best way to do wrong for his own advantage. In the course of recasting Thrasymachus's argument against S. more effectively, G. clinches the reference back by recalling Thrasymachus's word *dēmiourgos* (340e3) for 'professional' here, and using common Socratic examples.

361a2–5 'Similarly, let the unjust person going about his wrongdoing in a faultless way escape detection...The person who is caught must be considered a bungler, for the height of injustice is to seem just when you are not: just as doctors etc. have their expertise, so concealment is part of the expert unjust person's *technē*. For the popular disapproval and punishment of boys for 'getting caught' rather than for actually committing offences at Sparta, see Xenophon, *Constitution of the Lacedaemonians* 2.8. The emphasis on concealment strongly recalls Antiphon the Sophist: 'The way to gain maximum advantage for yourself from justice, then, is to treat the laws as important when other people are present, but when there is nobody else with you to value the demands of nature...So if your transgression of regulations escapes the notice of those who have made the agreement, you avoid both shame and punishment, but incur them if it doesn't...' (*Die Fragmente der Vorsokratiker* DK87B44A; *The First Philosophers* 264–5).

a7–b1   '...but allow the greatest wrongdoer to obtain for himself the greatest reputation for justice...: 'reputation' (*doxa*) has the same root as 'seeming' (*dokein*). The completely unjust person is supremely effective at projecting (false) appearance; this is an essential part of his *technē*. G. continues to articulate the 'appearance / reality' polarity which he introduced at the beginning of the Book (see note on 357a4–b2). In articulating the 'most perfect injustice' (*tēn teleotatēn adikian*: 361a6) G. exactly recalls Thrasymachus verbally in his long *epideixis* at 344a4.

b2–4   '…and to be capable of arguing to persuade people…to use force when force is needed…**: persuasion / force is a conventional polarity in 5th century thought: in the sophists, see Gorgias *Encomium of Helen* (*Die fragmente der Vorsokratiker* DK82B11; *The First Philosophers* 228–9), and in tragedy, *e.g.* Sophocles, *Philoctetes* 102–3, and generally, see Buxton. G. emphasises that the perfectly unjust person has command of both persuasion and force, as and when necessary.

b7–8   '…a straightforward and noble man who, to quote Aeschylus, "wants not to seem, but to be" good**: from *Seven against Thebes* 592, of the hero attacking Thebes, Amphiaraus, who does not advertise his worth on his shield (591). Plato does not quote strictly, but has G. alter Aeschylus' *aristos* ('best, bravest') to *agathos* ('good'), which, with less obviously heroic overtones, better suits the context of the socially isolated just person here.

c1–2   '…for if he is going to be reputed just, he will have the honours and gifts this sort of reputation bestows on him…**: these are the 'artificial' consequences of justice, in the sense that there is no necessary link between actions and consequences; the rewards of justice in the form of what people think and how they react are equally available to the genuinely just person and the unjust dissembler. So in order to be sure that the just person is in possession of a good 'in itself' (the first half of G.'s category 2, see above 357b4ff.), in G.'s hypothetical picture these artificial consequences have to be removed by taking from the just person the appearance of justice which generates them. The difference between artificial and necessary consequences is clearly set out by Antiphon the Sophist in articulating the contrast between 'law' (*nomos*) and 'nature' (*physis*), the former approximating to G.'s 'gifts and honours' bestowed by fellow citizens. 'For the law's demands are externally imposed, but those of nature are essential, and while agreement, not nature, has produced the laws' demands, nature, not agreement, has produced those of nature.' (*Die Fragmente der Vorsokratiker* DK87B44A, *The First Philosophers* 265). G. wants S. to give an answer which demonstrates that justice and not, as he hypothesises, injustice, has an essentiality 'in nature'.

c4–5   'He must indeed be stripped of everything except his justice…**: G. pursues the extremes of the hypothesis: just as the unjust must be given the 'greatest reputation' (*megistēn doxan* (b1) for justice, so the *megistēn doxan* for the reverse must pursue the just person (c6), so that the genuineness of his justice may be thoroughly tested. The somewhat woodenly foursquare structure of G.'s polar comparison is indicated by exact verbal repetition (see immediately above) and by the frequent use in this passage of the comparatively rare impersonal gerundive: ἡγητέον (361a4), δοτέον (a6), ἀφαιρετέον, ἐατέον (a7), ἀφαιρετέον (c1) λεκτέον (e1), and, as a personal adjective describing what happens to the just person: γυμνωτέος (c4), ποιητέος (c5). This grammatical form is a characteristic of the later Platonic dialogues, and not much found in the earlier, but here Plato is clearly deliberately using it to convey an effect of formality.

d4–6   'Bless me, my dear Glaucon', I said, 'how vigorously you're scouring your two men clean as if each was a sculpture entered for a competition!: after G.'s formal speech the colloquialism effects a startling change of mood and neatly brings G. down to earth (Reeve's 'Whew!' for S.'s exclamation 'Babai' catches the mood brilliantly). S.'s mock amazement here, in its sudden informal contrast to G. in mood and style, pokes gentle fun at the 'debating society' quality of the preceding speech, as does the comparison with a sculpting competition: just as the process of scouring is designed to get rid of all extraneous matter from the stone surface of the sculpture to render it fit for an exhibition, so G. has carefully eliminated from his exposition any extraneous detail which might spoil the exactness of the polar comparison between just and unjust.

d7 **'To the best of my ability...:** G. takes over S.'s syntax here (for this characteristic of P's dialogue style, see above on 354a12–b1); a small but subtle characterisation – the young man appears to miss entirely any irony present in S.'s teasing interjection.

d8–e1 **'...the story of the sort of life that awaits each of them:** the idea of contrasted lives recalls (possibly deliberately) the Sophist Prodicus's *On Heracles,* preserved in the version of Xenophon, *Memorabilia* 2.1.21–28, where Heracles is presented with a choice between goddesses representing the life-paths of vice and virtue; in Prodicus, Vice urges her path as the way to happiness, whereas for Virtue the choice of the harder path of goodness makes those who take it '...dear to the gods, loved by their friends, and honoured by their country.' In G.'s speech, Plato exactly reverses Prodicus' polarity: the just (and so virtuous) person, because unfairly judged, meets the fate normally reserved for the unjust.

e1 **'...if my account is delivered in a somewhat vulgar manner...:** referring to the violence of the following descriptions of the tortures of the just person (the tone of which G. is obviously personally disclaiming) . The tortures (e4–362a1) appear to belong to a traditional list (see *Gorgias* 473c, Aeschylus, *Eumenides* 186–90), with the proviso that, of course, they usually happen to people who have actually committed serious crimes. However the fate of the just (apparently unjust) person imagined here is not entirely in the realm of fantasy, if we consider what befell the unjustly accused Lysias and Polemarchus at the hands of the Thirty Tyrants; and even Socrates, who, while pursuing what he believed to be justice, suffered the penalty of unjust prosecution and condemnation (see Introduction p. 8). The presence of all three to hear G.'s (hypothetical) denunciation of the just life at a dramatic date perhaps 20 years before these catastrophic events holds a certain irony.

362a2–4 **'So the saying I quoted from Aeschylus would be more correctly applied to the unjust person:** this is because the consequences of the reality of being unjust are much to be preferred to those of seeming to be so; it is the *unjust* person, therefore, who wishes be rather than to seem unjust – turning Aeschylus (quoted above at 361b7–8) on his head. The alternative of a person being just *not* for the rewards but 'for justice's sake' (361c3) *and also* (getting away from G.'s 'thought experiment' for a moment) enjoying the rewards nevertheless (the whole of G.'s category 2, see above 357c2–4), is eliminated by G., not because it cannot occur, but because in practice: 1. the rewards of *pretending* to be just are just as great or even greater than could ever arise from really being so (in G.'s assumed opinion), and so, 2. observers can never know whether the just person really is just 'for its own sake' and not merely for the consequent rewards.

a6–b1 The quotation is again from Aeschylus' *Seven Against Thebes* at 593–4, following immediately on from the previous one at 361b7–8 (see note *ad loc.*). Plato has G. attach Amphiaraus' 'heroic' power of decision and intelligence to the unjust man, perhaps deliberately exposing the ethical ambiguity of this quality in popular Greek thought – a potential either for justice or injustice (cf. Callicles on those who are 'naturally stronger' at *Gorgias* 491a–b: '...people with the intelligence to know how the cities affairs should be handled, and not only intelligence but courage; people who have the ability to carry out their ideas...').

b2–6   '...holding office in the city...marrying into any family he wishes, marrying off his children...joining up in business...engaging in lawsuits, private and public...': G. here spans all the key areas of *polis* life, private and public: political office, the *oikos* (= household), marriage, business activities and the law. G. supports his contention that the unjust person's activities are generally accepted socially by presenting him as exhibiting the standard characteristics of manly *aretē*, as defined e.g. by Meno for Socrates (*Meno* 71e) 'managing the city's affairs capably, and so that he will help his friends and harm his enemies while taking care to come to no harm himself'.

b6–7   '...he wins and gets the better of his enemies: 'get the better of' = 'outdo' *pleonektein*. S. had produced a sequence of argument in Book 1.349e1ff. in which he claimed (with Thrasymachus' reluctant agreement at 350c12) that, as an expert in that particular *technē*, the just person would show greater wisdom in not wishing to outdo (*pleonektein*) another just person. In recalling this word and attaching it to the successful and intelligent *unjust* person, G. makes it clear that he does not accept S.'s original argument (see objections made in note to 349e1–50c10 and also note on 359c3–5).

c1–6   'He will make sacrifices...so that it is reasonable to suppose that he is also more loved by the gods...: as he winds up his *epideixis,* G. makes the first mention of a key aspect of the argument, the theological. The possibility that the unjust person does not even have to fear the wrath of the gods, because they will be influenced by the size of sacrifices and offerings made possible by his wealth, raises an important theme which relates back to the Book 1 conversation with Cephalus (see esp. 331b1ff.) and forward to the 'Myth of Er' at the end of the dialogue (614bff.). Greek religion placed great importance on ritual activities towards gods (rather than attitudes expressed in other ways), which made the popular assumption plausible that even the gods could be 'bought off' by 'external' behaviour, in the form of assiduous cultivation. A major sanction against the unjust person appears to be removed. (This aspect of the argument is taken up in more detail below by Adeimantus (363e4ff.).

c7–8   '...a better life is provided by gods and men for the unjust than for the just person: 'gods and men', frequently a formulaic polar expression (= 'everybody'), here clearly has particular significance: in popular belief, not only humans but (much more significantly) gods may well be indifferent to justice, and favour the unjust person over the just (and see previous note).

362d1–363e4

After a brief exchange with S., Adeimantus takes over the argument from his brother, filling, as he sees it, a gap in G.'s case – putting the arguments which commend justice. Being just results not only in good reputation and its social consequences, but favour from the gods, and all the advantages they can give in this life and the next to the just, with corresponding punishments for the unjust – at least, according to the poets and religious pundits.

362d4   'Well yes, why not?...': S.'s emphatic affirmative; the rhetorical question (ἀλλὰ τί μήν;) 'expects no answer but gets one' (Denniston, 332). Here the answer to S. is provided by Adeimantus, who assertively intervenes. See also below e2 'You're talking nonsense...'.

d6 '**...let brother stand by brother...**: a proverb, for which the scholiast quotes Homer, *Odyssey* 16.97ff. '...a man trusts/help from these [brothers] in the fighting when a great quarrel arises'

d7–8 '**...what he has already said is quite sufficient to floor me...**: for the use of the wrestling metaphor, see *e.g. Euthydemus* 277d; here in using it, S. enters jokingly into the agonistic spirit of the speeches of the two brothers. Once again (see above 361d4–6) S. deploys his irony, but at e2 A. is not taken in by the tone, any more than Thrasymachus was at 337a4–5 (see note *ad loc.*).

e2–4 '**We should also go through the arguments contrary to what he said, those which commend justice and censure injustice...**: following the formal structure G. has laid down, G. praising the unjust life (358d5) must be followed by A. praising its opposite. G. might claim he has already disposed of the just life as clearly unprofitable in comparison with the unjust, so, as S. exclaims at d4, what can A. claim to add? Yet, there is a more serious point here; the problem with G.'s extreme hypothesis (his 'thought experiment') is precisely that it *is* extreme – he has not considered the position that in ordinary social situations the rewards for justice, albeit artificial, are nevertheless likely to be forthcoming: the just person *usually* does get *some* credit and reward for the just life, and the 'Gyges Ring' scenario is, after all, fantasy; the unjust person will not *usually* have total and unrestrained power to act as he wishes, or, even if he does, his whole position relies on at least a fair proportion of people behaving honourably, the alternative being anarchy in which nobody will gain (see *e.g.* Annas 69–70). The everyday rewards of justice are what A. initially wishes to commend, though, as we shall see, he soon alters course; in the end his object is much the same as G.'s – by being 'devil's advocate' and arguing that being just secures no real advantage, to force S. to argue that justice is a good, irrespective of any external reward.

363a1–2 '**...commending justice not as something in itself, but for the good reputation it brings:** A., ostensibly putting the case for justice, nevertheless undercuts it from the start by placing continual emphasis on 'reputation' (in his choice of words with root *dok-- =* 'seeming' 'appearance': a2, a3 (twice), a5, a6, a7)). In presenting the conventional wisdom about justice passed on to the young, A. manages to convey irony under the surface by his choice of words: 'throwing in' (a7 ἐμβάλλοντες) 'good standing' (same word as 'reputation') and 'good things without stint' (ἄφθονα...ἀγαθὰ) ('benefits galore': an apt translation by Waterfield (1993), awaiting 'the pious' (τοῖς ὁσίοις). See also below (c4) the 'still more exhilarating' (νεανικώτερα) good things to be expected in the afterlife.

a4–5 '**...all that Glaucon has just enumerated – rewards which come to the just person from being well thought-of:** what G. has just enumerated (362a5ff.) are the rewards coming to the *unjust* (seeming just) person. Some MSS. alter τῷ δικαίῳ (a5) to τῷ ἀδίκῳ; but the sense here requires 'just', understanding a clear break after 'enumerated', (a4): what G. has just enumerated as rewards coming to the unjust person are now, according to A., said by fathers etc. to be, on the contrary, rewards available to the just (see Adam, note *ad loc.*).

b1 '**...as the noble Hesiod and Homer record:** the poets are implicated in A.'s elaborately satirical review of tradition here (for the ironic overtones of 'noble' (γενναῖος), see above, note on 348c10). The Hesiod quotation (b2–4) is from *Works and Days, 232–4,* describing the natural prosperity Zeus gives to just people in the form of flourishing crops and livestock, and in Homer (b5–c3), the richly-described natural abundance stems from a single king's just rule (*Odyssey* 19.109,111–113). This 'cosmic' idea of justice – that the world, human, natural and divine is bound together in a naturally just order, though in this context thinly disguised satire, is actually a basic Platonic position, which Socrates ultimately defends in *Republic* (see also *Gorgias* 508a). The underlying purpose of A. (and G. before him), is, of course, to put the case that there is no such link (see Allen (1987) 57–60).

c4   '**...Musaeus and his son:** Musaeus and Eumolpus were legendary figures linked to Orpheus, all of whom were associated with the Mysteries and the fate of the human soul in the afterlife.

c6–d3   '**...they sit them down to a wine party of the pious...in the belief that the finest reward of virtue is to be drunk for all eternity:** the *symposium* or wine-party was a basic leisure institution of upper-class Athenians and could involve literary and musical activities, but also a lot of drunkenness (see *e.g.* Alcibiades in Plato *Symposium* 212dff.). A. is ridiculing religious traditions by removing the mystique from traditional accounts of the afterlife of the pious and introducing the more disreputable elements of everyday Athenian social activities. *Hosios* ('pious', 'holy') is a regular term for those initiated into the Mysteries. Note that A. is also poking direct fun at the poets, whose teaching this purports to be. There may possibly be a humorous alliterative jingle intended in συμπόσιον τῶν ὁσίων (*sumposion tōn hosiōn*, aptly rendered by Shorey 'symposium of the saints'.

d4–5   '**...those who are pious...leave behind children's children and an unfailing posterity:** the idea is a common one in popular Greek thought: see *e.g.* Homer, *Iliad* 20.308, Tyrtaeus 12.29ff. Gerber, both of these close enough verbally to suggest that A. is directly quoting from the poets here (as Slings assumes in his text). A. echoes 'childrens' children' below with his counter-argument (see 366a6 and note).

d7–8   '**...but the impious and unjust, on the other hand, they bury in some sort of mud in Hades and force them to carry water in a sieve...:** note the contemptuous πηλόν τινα (d7), 'something which they call mud' The punishment of pouring water into a leaky sieve is one of the eternal labours associated with the legend of the daughters of Danaus, who were thus punished in the afterlife for killing their husbands (see Plato *Gorgias* 493b). A.'s syntax is rather loose here: in c6 the subject could be either 'the gods', or 'Musaeus and his son', whereas 'they bury' etc. at d7 seems to refer to the poets (though no clear change of subject is indicated).

e3   '**they have no others to record:** i.e. the only way the poets and religious teachers can dissuade the unjust from evil deeds is through demonstrating the bad consequences of their actions: a bad reputation in this world and punishments in the next are the only sanction since the unjust have no sense of innate justice which can be appealed to in this life. Plato returns to the theme of apparent and real immorality and punishment in *Theaetetus* 176a–e.

363e4–366b3

Having set up the traditional religious view of the rewards and punishments waiting in the afterlife for people of good and bad reputation respectively, A. proceeds to undermine this through a critical examination of the poets and other pundits. Influential is the teaching which persuades those with means that the gods can be bought off with spells and incantations. Moreover, the poets and religious teachers can be quoted to support the view that the gods can be influenced by sacrifices and supplications. Naturally gifted young men, absorbing all this, will conclude that their most profitable course is to exert themselves in society to ensure that their own advantage prevails. The theological argument supports this position either way: if the gods do not exist or are not interested in human affairs, there is no need to hide from them; on the other hand, if they do, all the accumulated traditional wisdom points towards them being amenable to human persuasion.

363e5   '...another line of argument...: i.e. the argument, contrary to the previous section, that the unjust do not necessarily suffer in the afterlife. A.'s argument in the next few lines is not really new; in essence he builds on what G. has already covered concerning attitudes of ordinary people to the just and unjust at 360b4ff., but A. does add an important theological dimension: much of the criticism of traditional theology implicit in this section looks forward to Socrates' strong criticism of poetic images of the gods later in Book 2 (377eff.).

364a1–4 '...hymn moderation and justice as fine things, but hard and laborious, while licentiousness and injustice are pleasant...regarded as shameful only in opinion and by convention: the first part of the sentiment recalls the lyric poet Simonides quoted in Plato *Protagoras* 339bff., 'It is hard to be truly a good man...' (a saying of Simonides is also featured prominently earlier in S.'s argument with Polemarchus (331d5ff.)). The contrast between vice and virtue also recalls Prodicus' choice of Heracles (see note on 361d8–e1). The introduction of 'convention' (*nomos*) alongside, and as an equivalent of, the much used 'opinion' (*doxa*) is a *leitmotif* of sophistic thought.

a5–7   'They say that unjust deeds are for the most part more profitable than just, and they are quite ready and willing to call the wicked happy...: with 'for the most part', A. reverts from Glaucon's extreme 'thought experiment' to the general rule; unjust deeds are generally (but not invariably) thought to be more profitable than just. In emphasising the advantages of riches and power here, A. has in mind a position similar to that of Polus in *Gorgias* (470dff.), who claims that the Macedonian tyrant Archelaus is both wicked and happy. In articulating basic and potent but polarized Athenian value-terms, A. is establishing a clear distinction between groups of people popularly regarded as worthy of honour, and those who are (admitted to be) good but not worthy of respect because of their lack of power and wealth.

b3–4   'But strangest of all...: strange for whom, and why here particularly? A. is now effectively expounding this side of the argument (the profitability of injustice), so that what the gods are alleged to do, far from strange in the context, would seem further proof of what he has just been talking about, namely the gods' support for, or indifference towards, wrongdoing. But A. is here perhaps either commenting on the outlandishness of the sources of belief, or maybe reverting to his own sincerely held views on the perversity of divine activity. For the popular sentiment, see the 6th century poet Theognis 377–86, Sophocles, *Philoctetes* 447–452. One traditional explanation of one side of the equation (good people suffering an evil fate) is the inherited curse – later generations suffering for the deeds of their ancestors (see *e.g.* Solon 13.31 Gerber).

b6–8   'Wandering priests and prophets approaching the doors of the wealthy persuade them that there is a power from the gods conveyed through sacrifices and incantations...: Socrates'/Plato's disdain for 'prophets' (*manteis*) and divination is brought out in *e.g. Euthyphro* 6aff., *Timaeus* 71e; and, for the critical philosophical attitude generally to what are regarded as bizarre and even profane rituals and charms put up for sale by dubious vagrants relying on esoteric lore, see Heraclitus, *(Die Fragmente der Vorsokratiker,* DK22B14, vol. 1, p.154): 'night-prowlers, wizards, bacchanals, revellers, initiates...the mysteries current among men are celebrated in an unholy manner'. The type is illustrated by the oracle-monger *(chrēsmologos)* in Aristophanes, *Birds* 959–90. Note that it is in the interests of A.'s (Plato's) argument to lump all this in with conventional religion, which will be the target of Socrates' critique later in Book 2 (and 3).

c6   **'For all these stories they call on the poets as support:** the quotation in c8–d2 is from Hesiod, *Works and Days* 287–9. Characteristically quoting out of context, A. (Plato) ignores the continuation in 291–2 which goes against his argument: 'when a man reaches the top, she *[aretē]* is easy to find, though hard before.' The main thrust of Hesiod's sentiment – the ultimate advantage of following *aretē* (virtue) and the worth of persisting through hardship – is directly contrary to that of A.'s religious vagabonds. These lines of Hesiod are used elsewhere by Plato (*e.g. Protagoras* 340d, *Laws* 718e).

d3–5   **'Others bring in Homer as a witness...:** the quotation in d6–e2 is from *Iliad* 9. 497, 499–501, Phoenix speaking to the Greek hero Achilles trying to persuade him to relent in his attitude towards Agamemnon. Homer has a different word *(streptoi)* for 'moved' (d6) and A. leaves out 498: '[the gods] whose virtue, honour and strength is greater than ours', which would not help his point. Once again the poet is quoted out of context and his meaning twisted to support the present argument: the thrust of the Homeric passage is that the gods can be brought round by supplication to pardon an offending suppliant, not, as A. implies, that they can be suborned to aid human machinations.

e3   **'And they produce a babble of books by Musaeus and Orpheus..:** 'babble' (or 'hubbub', 'babel', 'uproar') implies stridency and confusion. In Athenian religion the existence of diverse doctrines produced in 'books', was a sign of unorthodoxy and marginality (cf. above on b6, the Aristophanic wandering oracle-monger and his scroll); Orphism and the other Mystery Religions were to some extent in this category. For the popular association of books with Mystery religion and a scornful attitude towards them, see *e.g.* Euripides, *Hippolytus* 953; *Alcestis* 967, and generally, Parker 55. The addition of the legendary authors with their bizarre ancestry adds to the picture of chicanery painted by A.

e4   **'...descendants...of Selene and the Muses..:** Selene was the moon goddess, particularly associated with witchcraft, see *Gorgias* 513a, Aristophanes, *Clouds* 750. The Muses were goddesses, traditionally nine in number, who inspired poets, creative artists and philosophers.

e5   **'...and persuade not only individuals but cities that they really can have remissions and purification for their wrongdoing through sacrifices...:** initiation and purification leading to a good life after death was an essential element in Mystery Religions. Epimenides the Cretan was allegedly called in to purify the city of Athens (probably late 7th century).

365a1   **'...and playful delights, while they are still alive and, equally, after death. These they actually call initiations, which free us from evils in the next world, while terrible things await those who neglect to sacrifice:** A. puns on an Orphic etymology connecting 'death' *(teleutē)* with 'initiation' *(teletē).* According to A. the book-toting prophets are attempting to persuade their audiences that their fate after death depends simply on whether or not they have performed the necessary rites, cancelling out any wrongdoing they may have done, and irrespective of their inner feelings: i.e. holiness as a commodity rather than a disposition (see Moors 87). There is here scornful emphasis on merrymaking as a key religious element in so-called atonement. However, already in the fifth century there was evidence of an element in Greek eschatology that presents good or evil conduct in life as determining an appropriate fate in the afterlife (see Pindar, *Olympians* 2.56ff, Aristophanes, *Frogs* 140ff., and recall the aged Cephalus reflecting this view of the afterlife, in Book 1.330d4ff.).

a4–b1   **'How...do we imagine the souls of young men will react on hearing all this... those young men who are naturally gifted and capable of flitting around all these sayings...and gathering from them what sort of character they should have...:** i.e. 'young men' just like G. and A. in fact, who don't believe what they are told about justice, but might be susceptible all the same. This emphasis on potential future leaders of the state 'flitting around' and imbibing popular culture (a metaphor from bees gathering honey) and shaping their characters from it, puts down a direct challenge to Socrates to outline an alternative education for those who are to govern his state, since the traditional education of the poets and thinkers is clearly inadequate.

b2   **'... in the words of Pindar:** fr. 201 Bowra, the context not known. Most editors end the quotation at 'crooked deceit', but Slings includes 'live out my life securely fenced around' (περιφράξας διαβιῶ). The words following the quotation urging the essentiality of seeming to be just, forcefully reintroduce the key 'seeming/reality' dichotomy which was a feature of Glaucon's argument: 'What began as a statement of the arguments which are opposed to those presented by Glaucon, now becomes an alternative path to the same result' (Moors 90). Like Glaucon, A. is overstating the case for 'appearance' in order to draw a response from Socrates.

c2   **'"...appearance even overmasters truth"...:** Simonides, fr. 598 (Campbell, vol. III)

c3   **'as a front and façade I must sketch out around myself a painted illusion of virtue...:** Plato's metaphor is of illusionistic painting associated with architectural façades in stage scenery designed for the backdrop to the *skēnē* (stage) in the Greek theatre. Allusion to various aspects of the theatre as an image of illusion as opposed to reality is very common in Plato (see *e.g. Republic* 583b, *Theaetetus* 208e, *Gorgias* 465d), and relates to his general critique of the theatre in Book 3 (395aff.).

c4–6   **'...that "cunning" and wily fox from the poetry of the most wise Archilochus:** the reference is to Archilochus 185 Gerber. He was an elegiac and iambic poet of the mid-7th century and uses the fox in a number of poems as an embodiment of cunning and resourcefulness. 'cunning' (*kerdalean*) is a direct quotation; in 'wily' (*poikilēn*) A. paraphrases Archilochus' epithet phrase 'having a shrewd mind' (*puknon echousa noon*).

c7–8   **'"But", someone may object, "it is not easy to be wicked and always escape detection". "Yes," we will reply, "but neither is any other major undertaking easy":** for the next few sections A. adopts the rhetorical/forensic technique of constructing objections to his position which he himself counters, and he makes sure that he has the last word (366a7–b3). The sentiment of A.'s hypothetical objector here exactly reverses the traditional proverb: here wickedness, and not virtue, is supposed to be hard to attain (for the conventional sentiment, see Hesiod, *Works and Days* 287–292, and above note on 328e3–4).

d1–2 '...if we aim to be happy we must take the path to which the steps of our argument point: again, a reversal of conventional ideas (see previous note): the path of virtue traditionally leads to happiness (*eudaimonia*) and not, as here, the path of injustice (a position actually held by Thrasymachus at 344a4–5).

d2–6 'For with a view to lying hidden we will organise conspiratorial gatherings and clubs, and there are teachers of persuasion, who, for a fee, can pass on the arts of the assembly and the court-room, where, by persuading some and forcing others, we will outdo them without having to pay a penalty: the clubs were upper-class gatherings and oligarchic in tendency; for a 5th century Athens instance, see *e.g.* Thucydides 8.54, where anti-democratic elements made use of the 'clubs' to influence political and legal decisions ('the assembly and the courtroom') with a view to getting rid of the democracy in the political coup of 411. The 'teachers of persuasion' are the sophists (*Gorgias* 452e), here firmly attached to the 'unjust' cause. For the sophistic polarity force/persuasion, see above note on 361b2–4. On 'outdoing' others (*pleonektein*), see above note on 362b7.

d8–9 'But, if the gods do not exist, or if human affairs are of no concern to them...: atheism, or at least rejection of the conventional divinities in favour of other forces, was in the air among the 5th century sophists (cf. Protagoras *Die Fragmente der Vorsokratiker,* DK80B4, *The First Philosophers* 211; Prodicus DK84B5, *The First Philosophers,* 249, and esp. 242 n.4, Critias DK88B25 (tr. in Guthrie (1969) 243–4)), and reached the comic stage *via* Aristophanes *Clouds* (Zeus being displaced by 'vortex' (380), and n.b. the charge against Socrates at his trial for impiety in 399B.C. of 'not acknowledging the gods of the city but other new divinities' (Diogenes Laertius 2.40). For the idea of the gods not caring about erring mortals, see *e.g.* Aeschylus, *Agamemnon* 370–5.

d9–e2 'But even they do exist and do care about us, our knowledge of them comes from nowhere other than what we have heard or from the laws and the poets who provide genealogies: A. thus completes the circle, as it were, harking back to the traditional stories of gods' pliability he ridiculed at 364b1ff. above. The three positions taken by humans regarding the gods: (i) outright atheism, (ii) the gods regardless of mankind (iii) the gods as beings susceptible to offerings and prayers – are all repeated by Plato as the basic causes of impiety regarding the gods in *Laws* 10.885b. For a poet who 'provided genealogies', see Hesiod in *Theogony.*

e3–4 'sacrifices, "soothing prayers"..: Homer, *Iliad* 9.499 (quoted previously above at 364d7).

e4–5 '...they should carry conviction in both aspects or neither: a rather opaque phrase, since the antecedents of 'both' and 'neither' are far from clear in the Greek. I interpret 'they' as the laws and the poets (e2) and *amphotera* ('both aspects') as referring to the ideas that a) the gods exist and b) that they are susceptible to prayer; this means, presumably, that both these aspects of divinity must be believed, the other alternative, *oudetera* ('neither'), would then imply disbelief on both counts. The poets must logically, therefore, be believed *in toto* or disbelieved *in toto.* The following sentence (365e5–366a5) gives the consequences of the first alternative, believing the poets and tradition, i.e. that the gods exist and can be bought off.

366a6 '"Not so, for we will pay in Hades...either we ourselves or our children's children.": 'children's children': the idea of inherited guilt is repeated, with verbal echo from 363d4–5 (see note). But there A.'s interlocutor envisaged well-being as a favourable inheritance from good and pious ancestors. Here, on the contrary, the idea is one of inherited culpability for crimes extending into the afterlife (although the idea of *inherited* guilt is not part of Plato's vision in *e.g.* the 'Myth of Er').

a8–b3   **"'...initiation rites and gods who give absolution are very powerful, as the greatest cities affirm and the children of gods who have become poets and prophets for the gods reveal that these things are so":** for the absolution of cities, see above 364e5 and note; poets and prophets as children of gods: one tradition (Apollodorus, 3.201ff.) makes Eumolpus, traditionally a priest of the Eleusinian Mysteries, a son of Poseidon (for a different genealogy, see above 363c4) and Orpheus a son of Apollo and a Muse (see, on these religious figures, March).

A.'s debate with himself, besides giving the winning argument to injustice, enables Plato starkly to demonstrate by implication the deep contradictions inherent in the different strands of Greek popular religion and morality which, A. maintains, have to be accepted in all their confusion or, as G. and A. clearly wish, rejected (see esp. Moors 95).

366b4–367a5

A. sums up his argument rhetorically: in the face of the weight of argument recommending injustice, what support is there for the most distinguished to want to follow justice and not ridicule its proponents? If there are any who do have the ability or acquire the knowledge to be voluntarily just, they must feel sympathy with the rest who censure injustice merely for practical reasons, *e.g.* through cowardice or old age. This takes us right back to where we started: there never has been an adequate defence of justice in itself; if there had been we would not be in a situation where we needed to guard ourselves against each other's injustice.

366b5   **'...if we possess it with a counterfeit elegance...:** the metaphor is from the adulteration of precious metals, a striking image indicating the desirability of maintaining a convincing, albeit false, outward appearance of rectitude as the most profitable course. For the metaphor as applied to individuals and their moral values, see Theognis 117.

b7–8   **'...as the argument of the majority and the acutest minds declare?:** the belief of popular opinion *and* its leaders is seen by A. as an overwhelming argument for S. to face. 'Acutest' (*akros*) is a term used by Plato above (360e7) to indicate the most skilled professional (navigator, doctor, etc) and elsewhere to designate the acknowledged authorities (*e.g. Theaetetus* 152e); in view of A.'s treatment of the poets and thinkers earlier, there must be some degree of irony intended here in 'acutest'.

c6–7   **'...who by his godlike nature disdains injustice or acquires the knowledge to refrain from it...:** this refers to an exceptional person who, either naturally or from scientific knowledge of the good, can 'internalise' a sense of justice and not have to rely entirely on external factors such as fear of the injustice of others or approaching death (see above note on 365a4–b1). A.'s assumed doubt whether such a person exists is a direct challenge to Socrates and looks forward to the 'natural' superiority of Plato's Guardians, who nevertheless are obliged to spend time acquiring the level of wisdom necessary to rule (cf. *Republic* 5.475cff.). For a denial of the possibility of such personal qualities in any individual, see the more pessimistic *Laws* (9.875a2–d5), on which see Rowe and Schofield 256.

d1   '…none of the rest are voluntarily just…: a direct reversal of a key Socratic position, echoing Glaucon at 360c6–7 (see note *ad loc.*).

e3–5   '…none has ever censured injustice or praised justice otherwise than for the reputation and honour and gifts which flow from them: the 'artificial' consequences of justice (artificial in the sense that they do not depend on the reality), as opposed to its innate value (see following note).

e5–6   '…what each of these qualities does through its own innate power when it is within the soul which possesses it…: A. has returned to the demand articulated by Glaucon at the beginning of his speech for a defence of justice in and for itself (358b5–6, and with very similar wording). A. demonstrates that none of the 'heroes of old' (Orpheus, Musaeus etc.), nor poets or prose writers (e7) has ever articulated a justification for pursuing justice/ injustice in this way, as A.'s whole speech has just amply demonstrated.

367a4–5 '"…in fear that in doing wrong he would be sharing his house with the greatest evil": for Plato's argument concerning badness of the soul as the greatest evil which exists for humans, see *Gorgias* 477cff. If Socrates were able to demonstrate the value of justice and the worthlessness of injustice for the health of the soul, then there would in Plato's eyes no longer be any need to advance prudential motives for being just.

367a6–e5

In the concluding section of his speech A. rearticulates his challenge to Socrates to demonstrate, against the most forceful opposing arguments, what the effect of justice and injustice are on the person who possesses them. This can only be done by removing their popular reputations. If Socrates does not succeed in doing this he can be seen as tacitly agreeing with Thrasymachus that justice is the interest of the stronger. Socrates therefore has to justify putting justice in the category of goods which are inherently worth possessing for themselves rather than for their consequences, justifying something which he has been examining for his whole life.

367a8–9 '…inverting their true potential, crudely, in my view: 'crudely' (*phortikōs:* literally 'of those who carry burdens', i.e. like the masses), referring to the popularity of the arguments A. and G. have articulated; A. is here returning to his real *persona* – someone who does not actually believe the views he has been advancing.

b3   '…having exerted myself as much as I can…: as G. also promised at 358d5. Both young men have made an exceptional effort to produce closely-argued speeches (*epideixeis*), which Socrates in his turn will have to exert himself to refute.

b3–4   '…don't merely demonstrate by your argument to us that justice is superior to injustice…: to do this would simply be reversing Thrasymachus' position (Book 1.343b1ff.), and be giving justice the superior desirability in terms of its consequences.

b7–8   'For if you don't remove from each of them their true reputation and add on the false…: this would be G.'s 'thought experiment' (above 360d8ff.) in which the just and unjust are saddled with entirely false reputations. But why should A. think that Socrates will have to be concerned with adding on *false* reputation if (as the subsequent argument of *Republic* shows) he is not to be concerned with opinion at all, but with truth? This looks very like overkill on A.'s part. Moors makes the suggestion (106–7) that A. is concerned that Socrates should be compelled to separate a life based on truth from one based on opinion, and the best way, he feels at this point, of bringing this dichotomy into sharp relief is to require Socrates to argue for the just/unjust life which appears entirely as its opposite. 'Adeimantus desires a radical separation between the nature of either justice or injustice and its appearance or "seeming to be". Since the concern with the condition of the soul is likewise a concern with the condition of that which does not admit of sensual appearance, the most direct path to a radical separation between nature and appearance, Adeimantus seems to believe, is to replace true appearance with false appearance' (*ibid.*). In other words, A. expects S. to argue within the structure which he and G. have laid down, which, of course, S. has no intention of doing. Another possibility behind A.'s insistence here, Moors also suggests, is the key part played by 'false appearance' as a positive element in the *aporetic* dialectic of the early dialogues; mistaken reliance on appearances in the definition of concepts acts as a stage in the progression towards truth: '…to purge progressively the participants' reliance on appearance and the opinions occasioned by it, while at the same time indicating by the very presence of false appearance or opinion that something more certain is required' (107–8). This S. of course does, but in a manner far different from that which G. and A. appear to expect.

c2–3   '**…and that you agree with Thrasymachus that justice is the good of someone else…**: see Book 1. 343b1ff.

c6–8   '**Now, you have admitted that justice is among the greatest goods, those which are worth possessing for their consequences, but far more for their own sake, for example, sight, hearing, intelligence, and health too of course…**: S. made this choice at 358a1. However, in articulating category 2. right at the beginning of Book 2 (357c1ff.), neither G. nor S. placed the value of justice in and for itself *above* that of its consequential value, but alongside it. Surely not simply an 'exaggeration' on A's part (so Adam, note *ad loc.*), because A. also alters the order of the examples from this category as enumerated by G. at 357c3, adding 'hearing' to the list. It seems clear that A. has altered his perception of the categories and their contents to relate more closely to his concerns as expressed in his own speech – clearly what he is urging S. to do (and what S. does subsequently concentrate on) is justice as a good 'for its own sake'. A.'s revised list and order of 'goods', Moors again suggests (110), might well be *both* reflecting the order of A.'s own presentation *and* looking forward to the basic direction of *Republic* as a whole, in an ascending order of importance: from apprehending appearance to what is said about it, to understanding its deficiencies and the philosophic mission, right up to a focus on the most important concern of all – the health of the soul.

c9–10   '**…all other good things which are inherently so by their very nature…**:: the imagery of the words 'inherently…by their very nature' (*gonima tēi hautōn phusei*) suggests something which is biologically natural like, it is implied, justice in the human being, since A. puts it in the same category as sight etc.

d1   '**…praise that very aspect of justice:** there is perhaps a lurking irony in A.'s beguilingly naïve assumption that Socrates' reply will take the form of 'praise', i.e. a four-square *epideixis* like his and Glaucon's – especially in the light of the strikingly original and far-reaching answer Socrates actually comes up with.

d7   '**…because you have passed your whole life considering nothing else but this**

subject: i.e. justice in general; a brief allusion to the fact that a sub-text of *Republic* is Socrates' justification for his life, his '...true apology to the accusations made against him before the Athenian court' (Moors 112).

e3–4 '...**whether observed or not by gods and humans...**: as on a previous occasion (see 362c7–8 above, and note) this polar expression is far from conventional; in his speech A. has clearly demonstrated from traditional wisdom the different ways in which not only mortals, but also the gods can be deceived.

367e5–368c4

A bridge-passage to the start of Socrates' great exposition, which takes up the remainder of *Republic*. Socrates praises the two speech-makers and doubts his ability to find any new arguments to counter theirs other than those which he had used against Thrasymachus in Book 1. But he must nevertheless try to come to the aid of Justice.

e5–6 '...**much as I had always admired the inborn abilities of Glaucon and Adeimantus, on this particular occasion I was especially pleased...**: *physis* ('inborn abilities', 'natural character') recalls the person with 'his godlike nature' (*theiai physei*) of 366c6, who is naturally able to resist injustice in the face of popular opinion. If G. and A., despite so cogent a case against justice, are still able to say that they don't believe their own logic, must it not be, S. semi-jokingly suggests (368a5 below), because of some similar innate quality in them?

368a1 '**Sons of that man...**: Adam (note *ad loc.*) ingeniously suggests here that by 'that man' the still present Thrasymachus is jokingly meant, and that G. and A., as inheritors of his argument, are his 'sons' (citing an exact parallel in *Philebus* 36d, where Protarchus, 'son of that man', has inherited an argument from his friend Philebus). Just as Polemarchus was the son and heir to Cephalus' conversation at 331d8, so G. and A. are 'sons' of Thrasymachus. But 'Sons of Ariston' in the line of verse quoted at a4 clearly echoes 'Sons of that man...' here, which makes it most likely that an honorific reference is intended to the literal father of G. and A., Ariston 'best of men' (pun on *aristos* = 'best) who, we must not forget, is also Plato's father; Plato and G. and A. are actually brothers, so there is possibly also a covert authorial self-reference here, with Plato pulling his brothers' legs; see also below a4).

a2 '...**Glaucon's lover...**: G's (male) lover, and supposed author of the elegiac line a4, is unknown. (Critias, S.'s associate, sophist and oligarchic sympathiser, has been conjectured). Homosexual relations between younger and older men were acceptable in Athenian society, especially among the upper classes (see Dover (1978).

a3 '...**when you had distinguished yourselves in the battle of Megara:** there is more than one possible battle of Megara; to fit the ages of G. and A. we must assume S.'s reference is to the one which took place in 409, which, if we assume a basic dramatic date for *Republic* of c. 420, represents an anachronism not untypical of Plato (on the complications of the dramatic date of *Republic,* see further Introduction, pp. 5–6).

a4 '**Sons of Ariston, divine race, sprung from a famous man:** the 'compliment overkill' here (and elsewhere in this short passage) suggests a degree of Socratic irony, but only partly; the 'divine race' (*theion genos*) might recall the 'divine nature' of 366c6 (and see note above on 367e5–6), strengthening the likelihood of a deliberate allusion to G. and A. there, especially in view of the explicit allusion by Socrates to 'something godlike in your disposition' subsequently in a5.

b1–2   '...this I infer from your general character...**: 'character' (*tropos*) was emphasised by Cephalus as being a key factor in securing the good life; the fact that Socrates is here coupling it with G. and A.'s 'inherent' qualities suggests that, despite its apparent limitations at the time, Cephalus' contribution is resurfacing, albeit transforming itself, as an essential element in S.'s plan. G. and A.'s *tropos* belies their words, and must be what prevents them from being persuaded by their own rhetoric.

b3   '...the more I trust you, the more I am at a loss as to what I should do**: the striking parallelism of S.'s words here with a similar passage at the end of Book 1 marks this out as the end of the corresponding section of Book 2 (the restatement of the case against justice). S. is here 'at a loss', i.e. in *aporia,* just as he was at the conclusion of the argument with Thrasymachus (see note on the end of Book 1); moreover, he doubts his ability to reply (see Book 1.354b9–10). Many translators, *e.g.* Lee, Waterfield, make a section break round about here.

b5–7   '...you did not accept from me the arguments I used...**: A. has just explained why for him these arguments were not acceptable; Socrates had not demonstrated why justice was a good in and for itself in the soul (see above 367b5–6). S.'s arguments in Book 1, especially the final argument against Thrasymachus concerning the particular excellence of the soul (353d3ff.), might be thought to answer G. and A. adequately since they claimed to provide the proof that G. and A. want – that justice is a good in itself. But there is a dramatic point here; it is clearly important for S. not to go back over old, and disputed, ground, since Plato plans very shortly to send him in another direction entirely.

b7   'Nor...do I know how I can refuse to come to your aid...**: S. emphasises the images of help and cooperation (*boēthein* b7, c1; *epikourein* c3) throughout the latter half of this section; this is the alleged basis of the whole Socratic *elenchus*, and here, particularly, marks the transition from the adversarial part of the *Republic* to the wholly cooperative, from disputation to dialectic.

     With his vow to 'support justice to the best of my ability', markedly more positive and resolute than his *aporia* at the end of Book 1 (the 'First Introduction'), S. embarks on the development of his Ideal State.

INDEX

General Index (Introduction and Commentary)

Index of ancient sources

Printed and bound by CPI Group (UK) Ltd, Croydon, CR0 4YY

09/06/2025

14685941-0001